Günter Grass Revisited

Twayne's World Authors Series

German Literature

David O'Connell, Editor

Georgia State University

TWAS 879

GÜNTER GRASS
Courtesy of the German Information Center and IN Press

Günter Grass Revisited

Patrick O'Neill

Queen's University, Canada

Twayne Publishers
New York

Twayne's World Authors Series No. 879

Günter Grass Revisited
Patrick O'Neill

Twayne Publishers
1633 Broadway
New York, NY 10019

Library of Congress Cataloging-in-Publication Data

O'Neill, Patrick, 1945 –
   Günter Grass revisited / Patrick O'Neill.
        p.   cm. — (Twayne's world authors series ; no. 879)
   Includes bibliographical references and index.
   ISBN 0-8057-4571-8 (alk. paper)
   1. Grass, Günter, 1927 –   —Criticism and interpretation.
   I. Title.   II. Series: Twayne's world authors series ; TWAS 879.
   PT2613,R338Z772   1999
   838'.91409—dc21   98-33278
                                                                  CIP

This paper meets the requirements of ANSI/NISO Z3948-1992 (Permanence of Paper).

10 9 8 7 6 5 4 3 2 1

Printed in the United States of America

For Trudi, as always

Contents

Preface

Günter Grass, then in his early 30s, burst upon the German literary scene in 1959 with an astonishing first novel, *Die Blechtrommel,* which quickly went on to conquer the English-speaking world in Ralph Manheim's translation as *The Tin Drum.* Within the next four years Grass produced two further narrative works, *Katz und Maus* and *Hundejahre,* translated as *Cat and Mouse* and *Dog Years,* respectively, that caused almost as much furor both in Germany and abroad. All three, quickly dubbed the Danzig Trilogy, were instant bestsellers both in German and in translation; all three were immediately greeted as literary masterpieces by some readers; all three were violently condemned by other readers (and nonreaders) as sacrilegious, blasphemous, obscene, pornographic, treasonous, corruptive of youth, and an offense to the morals of all right-thinking people. Over the succeeding four decades Grass's steady stream of extraordinary narratives has continued to evoke a substantially similar reaction from his readers, especially from his German readers. His works regularly sell by the hundreds of thousands, regularly arouse the fervid admiration of literary specialists, and are regularly condemned, frequently with amazing venom, by readers (many of them professional literary critics) no longer appalled on religious or moral grounds but all the more bitterly and enduringly offended on the grounds of Grass's outspoken political opinions.

And Grass has outspoken political opinions on a panoramic range of topics, from the details of local, regional, and national German elections to the geopolitical maneuverings of superpowers, the threat of nuclear winter, the destruction of the environment, third-world poverty, and the rights of oppressed groups everywhere. He has been a vocal and indefatigable advocate of the policies of the German Social Democratic Party since the early 1960s. He has delivered thousands of political speeches and is the author of a good 20 volumes of political commentaries. In addition to all this, however, Grass is a highly respected poet with a dozen volumes of remarkably original poetry to his credit; he has written stage plays, radio plays, and ballet scripts; his collected literary essays fill several volumes; and he is a very highly regarded graphic artist whose work has been exhibited internationally for the past four decades. Very few people, indeed, can hope to achieve in one career what Grass has succeeded in accomplishing separately in (at least) three.

Most important, however, Grass is a narrative artist of great virtuosity, imagination, and originality. As long ago as 1970, *Time* magazine featured him in a cover story as probably Germany's, and possibly the world's, greatest living novelist.[1] Twelve years later the writer John Irving felt justified in declaring *The Tin Drum* to be still unsurpassed as the greatest novel by a living author: "Günter Grass is simply the most original and versatile writer alive."[2] Celebrating Grass's 70th birthday in October 1997, Salman Rushdie echoed Irving's praise of *The Tin Drum*, and Nadine Gordimer declared that only Thomas Mann among all the authors of the century rivaled Grass's accomplishments in taking up the challenge of addressing the world around him in his work.[3] Following the deaths within a few years of each other of Heinrich Böll and Uwe Johnson as well as of Max Frisch, Friedrich Dürrenmatt, and Thomas Bernhard, Grass is now clearly the grand old man of German letters, widely agreed to be the greatest living German author.

This is a book for an English-speaking and primarily North American audience rather than a German audience, and therefore Grass's political activities, which are understandably a matter of considerable interest to German readers, will play a much lesser role than they would if the book were written with a German audience primarily in mind. In one sense, this decision results in a loss, since Grass's continued and very vocal involvement in all levels of German and international politics throughout much of the past four decades is very much a part of what makes him the man (and therefore the writer) he is. It also results in a clear gain, however, for by paying less attention to his politics we can pay more to his skills specifically as a literary artist—and it is these skills that are the centrally important factor in his writing.

This is by no means to deny the importance of politics in the consideration of literary works or to deny other readers the freedom to read and discuss Grass's work primarily as political discourse if they so desire. The specifically literary quality of any literary work, however, is before and above all else a matter of technique, which is to say, of choosing individual words and combining them one by one in particular patterns and constellations. Good writers are made neither by good politics nor by good intentions; good writers—and Günter Grass is a very good writer indeed—are made by good writing. In this context it is worth noting that, because of the complexity of his language on the one hand and its highly characteristic texture on the other, the demands made by

Grass's work on his translator are always immense and sometimes little short of insuperable. The English-speaking reader is fortunate in being able to benefit from the heroic efforts of Ralph Manheim to meet those challenges over more than 30 years. Finally, Grass's most important work is clearly the body of his narrative writings, on which the discussion here is closely focused. His numerous activities in other fields are discussed only for their relevance to the particular texts under consideration, relatively little space is devoted to specific analysis of his dramatic work, and even less attention is paid to his poetry.

Attempts to divide a particular author's works into periods, even if only early, middle, and late, in most cases approach an act of violence on the work of the author concerned. For readers new to Grass, however, it may be helpful to observe that his work to date can conveniently (if provisionally) be divided into five stages. The Danzig trilogy is an obvious first group; a second, whose thematic focus is the tension between action and impotence in the political arena, is centered on *Local Anaesthetic*. A third group, focused on the relationship of the writer of fiction and the fiction of history, is centered on *The Flounder*, while a fourth, whose focus is on the apocalyptic potential of modern industrial and technological development, is centered on *The Rat*. A fifth, focused on the perennial German question, is centered on *Ein weites Feld* (scheduled to appear in translation as *Too Far Afield*). Other groupings are possible, and any grouping is likely to tell us more about the critic who proposes it than the texts it ostensibly orders.

Several chapters or parts of chapters in this book are based in varying degrees on previous papers, articles, and book chapters that I have written over the past two decades and more on Günter Grass, whose work has been one of my enduring professional interests. Where the debt seems substantial enough to be worth noting, it is appropriately acknowledged; otherwise I silently incorporate my previous work. In both cases, my thanks are due to the relevant editors and publishers for the reuse of this material as indicated. Thanks are likewise due to several colleagues in various parts of the world for their assistance over the years in locating materials and answering queries, including Friedhelm Bertulies, Helga Dunn, Marketa Goetz-Stankiewicz, Monika Holzschuh-Sator, Brigitte McConnell, Andrea MacTeigue, Volker Neuhaus, Anthony Riley, Julia Stevenhaagen, Florentine Strzelczyk, Leslie Willson, and Krishna Winston. Thanks are also due to the German Information Center in New York and the Steidl Verlag in Göttingen; to several academic generations of graduate and undergraduate students at the University of

British Columbia and at Queen's University for enduring and enriching my classes and seminars on Grass; to both Queen's University and the Social Sciences and Humanities Research Council of Canada for generous research assistance at various stages of this project; to the staff of the Douglas Library and the Stauffer Library at Queen's University and the Deutsches Literaturarchiv in Marbach am Neckar; and as always to my wife, Trudi O'Neill, for her continued encouragement, support, and patience over the past 30 years.

Chronology

1927	Günter Grass born 16 October in Danzig, the first child of Willy and Helene Grass.
1933–1944	Schooldays in Danzig disrupted by war. Becomes member of Hitler Youth.
1944–1945	Serves on active duty in the military. Visits Dachau concentration camp.
1948–1951	Studies sculpture at Düsseldorf Academy of the Arts.
1953	Moves to Berlin to study sculpture at Berlin Academy of the Arts.
1954	Marries Anna Schwarz.
1955	First reads from his work at a meeting of Group 47.
1956	Publishes first book of poems, *Die Vorzüge der Windhühner* (The Merits of Windfowl). Has first exhibition of drawings. Moves to Paris.
1957	The play *Hochwasser* (*Flood*, 1967) and the ballet *Stoffreste* (Remnants) premiere.
1958	The play *Onkel, Onkel* (*Mister, Mister*, 1967) premieres. Receives Group 47 prize.
1959	Publishes *Die Blechtrommel* (*The Tin Drum*, 1961). The ballet *Fünf Köche* (Five Cooks), the farce *Beritten hin und zurück* (*Rocking Back and Forth*), and the play *Noch zehn Minuten bis Buffalo* (*Only Ten Minutes to Buffalo*, 1967) all premiere. The radio play *Zweiunddreißig Zähne* (Thirty-Two Teeth) is broadcast.
1960	Publishes *Gleisdreieck* (Triangle of Tracks). Returns to Berlin. Receives Berlin Critics' Prize.
1961	Publishes *Katz und Maus* (*Cat and Mouse*, 1963). The play *Die bösen Köche* (*The Wicked Cooks*, 1967) premieres. Meets Willy Brandt and begins political activity in support of the Social Democratic Party (SPD).
1962	Receives French *Prix pour le meilleur livre étranger*.

1963   Publishes *Hundejahre* (*Dog Years*, 1965). The radio play *Eine öffentliche Diskussion* (A Public Discussion) is broadcast. The play *Mystisch, barbarisch, gelangweilt* (Mystical, Barbaric, Bored) premieres. Elected to Berlin Academy of the Arts.

1964   The play *Goldmäulchen* (Goldmouth) premieres.

1965   Participates in his first major campaign for the SPD. Publishes *Dich singe ich, Demokratie* (Of Thee I Sing, Democracy), a collection of political pieces. Receives Georg Büchner Prize of Darmstadt Academy. Receives honorary doctorate from Kenyon College in Gambier, Ohio.

1966   Publishes *Die Plebejer proben den Aufstand* (*The Plebeians Rehearse the Uprising*, 1966). Campaigns for the SPD in Bavarian state elections.

1967   Publishes *Ausgefragt* (Interrogated), a collection of poems and drawings, and *Der Fall Axel C. Springer* (The Case of Axel C. Springer), a collection of political pieces. Campaigns for the SPD. Film version of *Katz und Maus* by Hansjürgen Pohland premieres.

1968   Publishes *Über meinen Lehrer Döblin* (On Döblin, My Teacher), a collection of literary essays. Publishes *Über das Selbstverständliche* (On the Self-Evident) and *Briefe über die Grenze* (Letters across the Border), collections of political pieces. Receives Berlin Fontane Prize. Campaigns for the SPD.

1969   Publishes *Örtlich betäubt* (*Local Anaesthetic*, 1969). *Davor* (*Max: A Play*, 1972) premieres. Receives Theodor Heuss Prize. Campaigns for the SPD.

1970   The ballet *Die Vogelscheuchen* (The Scarecrows) premieres. Publishes *Theaterspiele* (Collected Plays). Campaigns for the SPD. Elected to American Academy of Arts and Sciences.

1971   Publishes *Gesammelte Gedichte* (Collected Poems). Campaigns for the SPD.

1972   Publishes *Aus dem Tagebuch einer Schnecke* (*From the Diary of a Snail*, 1973). Campaigns for the SPD.

1973   Publishes *Mariazuehren* (*Inmarypraise,* 1974), a poem with drawings and photographs.

1974   Publishes *Liebe geprüft* (*Love Tested,* 1975), a collection of poems and etchings, and *Der Bürger und seine Stimme* (A Citizen and His Voice), a collection of political pieces.

1976   Receives honorary doctorate from Harvard. Campaigns for the SPD.

1977   Publishes *Der Butt* (*The Flounder,* 1978) and *Als vom Butt nur die Gräte geblieben war* (When Only the Bones of the Flounder Were Left), a collection of etchings and poems. Receives Italian Premio Internationale Mondello.

1978   Publishes *Denkzettel* (Reminders), a collection of political pieces. Establishes Alfred Döblin Prize for young writers. Receives Italian Premio Letterario Viareggio. Divorced from Anna Grass.

1979   Publishes *Das Treffen in Telgte* (*The Meeting at Telgte,* 1981). Marries Ute Grunert. Film version of *The Tin Drum* by Volker Schlöndorff premieres.

1980   Publishes *Kopfgeburten* (*Headbirths,* 1982) and *Aufsätze zur Literatur* (Essays on Literature). Campaigns for the SPD.

1982   Publishes *Zeichnungen und Texte 1954–1977* (*Drawings and Words 1954–1977,* 1983) and *Vatertag* (Father's Day), a collection of lithographs. Receives Italian Feltrinelli Prize.

1983   Publishes *Ach Butt, dein Märchen geht böse aus* (Alas, Flounder, Your Tale Will Have a Bad Ending), a collection of etchings and poems. Elected president of Berlin Academy of the Arts. Officially joins the SPD.

1984   Publishes *Radierungen und Texte 1972–1982* (*Etchings and Words 1972–1982,* 1985) and *Widerstand lernen* (Learning to Resist), a collection of political pieces. Cofounds a national association to support foreigners in Germany.

1985   Donates house in Wewelsfleth as a center for writers, in memory of Alfred Döblin.

1986   Publishes *Die Rättin* (*The Rat,* 1987) and *In Kupfer, auf Stein* (In Copper, on Stone), a photographic record of his graphic work.

1987   Publishes *Werkausgabe* (Collected Works), in 10 volumes, and *Mit Sophie in die Pilze gegangen* (Gathering Mushrooms with Sophie), a collection of poems and lithographs.

1988   Publishes *Zunge zeigen* (*Show Your Tongue,* 1989), a collection of texts and drawings, and *Die Gedichte 1955–86,* the complete poems. Resigns from Berlin Academy of the Arts.

1989   Publishes *Skizzenbuch* (Sketchbook), drawings and sketches from Calcutta, and *Wenn wir von Europa sprechen* (Speaking of Europe), a political discussion.

1990   Publishes *Totes Holz* (Dead Wood), a collection of lithographs and texts, and *Kahlschlag in unseren Köpfen* (The Clearcut Mind), a collection of lithographs. Publishes *Deutscher Lastenausgleich* (Sharing the German Burden), *Ein Schnäppchen namens DDR* (East Germany at Bargain Prices), and *Deutschland, einig Vaterland?* (Germany, A Single Fatherland?), collections of political pieces. Delivers *Schreiben nach Auschwitz* (Writing after Auschwitz), the Frankfurt Poetics Prize lecture. Receives honorary doctorate from University of Poznań.

1991   Publishes *Gegen die verstreichende Zeit* (Writing against Time), a collection of political pieces, *Vier Jahrzehnte* (Four Decades), an autobiographical account, and *Brief aus Altdöbern* (A Letter from Altdöbern), drawings and text.

1992   Publishes *Unkenrufe* (*The Call of the Toad,* 1992), *Meine grüne Wiese* (My Green Field), a collection of early short prose, and *Rede vom Verlust* (On Loss), a political piece. Resigns from the SPD. Receives Italian Premio Grinzano Cavour. Receives Hamburg Academy of the Arts award. Establishes Chodowiecki Foundation in support of Polish writers and artists.

1993   Publishes *Novemberland* (Novemberland), a collection of sonnets and drawings, and *Schaden begrenzen* (Damage Control), a political discussion. Receives fifth honorary doctorate, from University of Gdańsk. Granted honorary citizenship of Gdańsk. Receives Spanish Hidalgo Prize and Italian Comites Prize. Steidl Verlag begins a 12-volume *Studienausgabe* (Study Edition) of his collected works. Deutscher Taschenbuch Verlag begins a paperback edition of his collected works.

1994 Publishes *Angestiftet, Partei zu ergreifen* (Forced to Take Sides), a collection of political pieces. An expanded edition of *In Kupfer, auf Stein* (In Copper, on Stone) is issued. Receives Literature Prize of Bavarian Academy of Fine Arts and the Czech Karel Čapek Prize. Campaigns again for the SPD.

1995 Publishes *Ein weites Feld* (*Too Far Afield,* scheduled to appear in 2000), *Die Deutschen und ihre Dichter* (The Germans and Their Writers), a collection of literary essays, and *Gestern, vor 50 Jahren* (Yesterday, 50 Years Ago), political correspondence with Kenzaburo Oe. Receives Hans Fallada Prize. Moves to Lübeck.

1996 Receives Danish Sonning Prize and Lübeck Thomas Mann Prize.

1997 Publishes *Rede über den Standort* (A Place to Stand), a collection of political pieces, and *Fundsachen für Nichtleser* (Found Objects for Nonreaders), a collection of poems and watercolors. Steidl Verlag publishes the 16-volume *Werkausgabe* (Collected Works). Television version of *Die Rättin* (*The Rat*) by Martin Buchhorn premieres.

Chapter One
The Role of the Writer

Günter Grass was born on 16 October 1927 in the family apartment over his father's small grocery store at what was then Labesweg 13 in Langfuhr, a suburb of the Free City of Danzig, and is now Ulica Lelewela 13 in Wrzeszcz, a suburb of the Polish city of Gdańsk. His father was of local, lower-middle-class, German Protestant origins, while his mother came from working-class, Kashubian Catholic stock from the nearby rural community of Bissau (now Bysewo). His only sibling, a sister, was born three years after him. Grass's boyhood in Danzig, where he entered the Conradinum High School in 1937, two years before the outbreak of the Second World War, was typical of his generation in Nazi Germany: "At fourteen I was a Hitler Youth; at sixteen a soldier; and at seventeen an American prisoner of war. These dates mean a great deal in an era that purposefully slaughtered one year's crop of young men, branded the next year's crop with guilt, and spared another. You can tell by my date of birth that I was too young to have been a Nazi, but old enough to have been moulded by a system, that, from 1933 to 1945, at first surprised, then horrified the world."[1]

After an initial stint in a Danzig anti-aircraft battery, the 17-year-old left home in 1944 as a German soldier, saw action in the field as a tank gunner, was slightly wounded near Cottbus in eastern Germany, and was eventually hospitalized in Marienbad in Czechoslovakia during the Russian advance. During his brief internment by the American forces in Bavaria at the end of the war, he experienced an event that fundamentally altered his subsequent life: as part of the American reeducation program he was taken on a tour of the concentration camp at Dachau, just outside Munich.

Released from prison camp in 1946, he briefly attempted, as a 19-year-old, to complete his interrupted high school program; he then abandoned that attempt and worked temporarily, first as a farm laborer in the Rhineland, then in a potash mine near Hannover, and later as apprentice to a stonemason in Düsseldorf. Grass's original artistic aspiration was to be a sculptor, and in 1948 he enrolled in the newly opened Düsseldorf Academy of the Arts to study sculpture and drawing. During this time he also began to write poetry, played the washboard in a jazz skiffle group, and developed what would be a lifelong interest in political socialism.

In 1951, like thousands of other young Germans immediately after the war, Grass undertook a cultural pilgrimage to Italy, the traditional mecca of generations of German poets and painters, hitchhiking south to the cultural treasures of Florence and Rome and returning home through France and Switzerland. During this time he began to work on the earliest version of what would become *Die Blechtrommel* (*The Tin Drum*), initially conceived of as a long poem but then temporarily abandoned. In Switzerland he met Anna Schwarz, a Swiss student of ballet, whom he married two years later, after having moved from Düsseldorf to Berlin in order to continue his study of sculpture at the Berlin Academy of the Arts. During the early Berlin years he began to write his first plays.

In 1955 Grass commenced his public career by winning third prize in a poetry competition sponsored by South German Radio. During that same year he published several poems in the influential journal *Akzente,* and he traveled to Spain for the first time. Most important, he received an invitation from the established writer Hans Werner Richter to read at the annual meeting of what was by then the dominant literary circle of the country, the powerful Group 47, named for the year of its foundation. From 1956 to 1959 he lived in Paris, working on several further drafts of *Die Blechtrommel* (*The Tin Drum*), and established a friendship with the poet Paul Celan. He also fathered twins; traveled to Poland; saw the publication of his first book, a slim collection of poems entitled *Die Vorzüge der Windhühner* (The Merits of Windfowl); held the first exhibitions of his sculpture and drawings; and saw the first performances of his first play, *Hochwasser* (*Flood*), his first ballet, *Stoffreste* (Remnants), and a second play, *Onkel, Onkel* (*Mister, Mister*). In 1958 he won the prestigious Group 47 prize for a reading from the still unfinished manuscript of *The Tin Drum,* an irreverent and highly colored digest of twentieth-century German history as seen through the very selective eyes of a drum-obsessed midget, Oskar Matzerath, from the safety of his bed in a mental hospital.

The year 1959 was an astonishing one for the 32-year-old Grass. Not only did *The Tin Drum* appear, turning him into an instant celebrity, but three separate premieres of his work took place, namely, a second ballet, *Fünf Köche* (Five Cooks), the one-act farce *Beritten hin und zurück* (*Rocking Back and Forth*), and the one-act play *Noch zehn Minuten bis Buffalo* (*Only*

Ten Minutes to Buffalo). His first radio play *Zweiunddreißig Zähne* (Thirty-Two Teeth) was also broadcast, and another exhibition of his drawings was mounted.

In 1960 Grass moved back to Berlin and published a second collection of poetry, *Gleisdreieck* (Triangle of Tracks). The following year saw the appearance of a fifth play, *Die bösen Köche* (*The Wicked Cooks*), but this was completely overshadowed when *Katz und Maus* (*Cat and Mouse*), the story of a highly dubious wartime friendship, turned into another runaway bestseller. Two years later, he repeated that success by completing what has since come to be known as the Danzig Trilogy, one of the most impressive achievements of modern German literature, with the final novel of the series, the long and intricate *Hundejahre* (*Dog Years*), which expands at enormous length on the same theme of friendship and betrayal before, during, and after the Second World War. Barely 35, Grass, "the drummer of Danzig," as the critics were now happily dubbing him, had established himself without any doubt as one of the most important voices on the German—and international—literary scene.

Reactions to the trilogy differed widely. Grass's prepublication literary prize from Group 47 was followed in 1959 by another prize, awarded by a panel of critics in the northern German city of Bremen but immediately vetoed by the Bremen city government. He received the Berlin Critics' Prize in 1960 and the French *Prix pour le meilleur livre étranger* in 1962, was elected a member of the German Academy of the Arts in 1963, and received the prestigious Georg Büchner Prize in 1965—the same year that *The Tin Drum* was publicly burned in Düsseldorf by a religious youth organization. By that time he was also the defendant in some 40 legal actions—none of which was successful—that had been launched against *The Tin Drum* and *Cat and Mouse* on grounds of sacrilege, blasphemy, and obscenity. Yet sales in Germany were in the hundreds of thousands, and sales in translation were booming. *The Tin Drum* alone was translated into 15 different languages over the next 10 years.

The trilogy reached North American readers in Ralph Manheim's translations over a more concentrated period of time than they had appeared in Germany: *The Tin Drum* was published in the United States in February 1963 (though it carried a 1961 copyright date), *Cat and Mouse* only six months later, in August 1963, and *Dog Years* in May 1965. They arrived preceded by their European reputation, and *The Tin Drum,* in particular, unleashed a flood of reviews. Though opinions were by no means undivided, North American readers were obviously less likely to be upset by the pointed historical and political implications of the three books than their German counterparts had been. Furthermore, the general reaction of North American reviewers was that a German author at long last forcing German readers to come to grips, however uncomfortably, with the still unresolved national past was a very good thing. As to its style, *The Tin Drum* was variously declared to be fantastic, romantic, expressionist, surreal, grotesque, absurd, realistic, and/or naturalistic, and to have more or less marked affinities with the work of Dante, Rabelais, Grimmelshausen, Bunyan, Swift, Sterne, Voltaire, Goethe, Melville, Proust, Thomas Mann, Joyce, Beckett, Faulkner, Camus, Dos Passos, Kafka, Döblin, Brecht, Böll, Johnson, Ionesco, Nabokov, and/or Heller.[2] *The Tin Drum* was on the *New York Times* list of bestsellers for three months and sold some 400,000 copies in its first year, thus largely guaranteeing the instant success of *Cat and Mouse* and *Dog Years* as well. There was some disappointment expressed that *Cat and Mouse* was such a slim volume; this deficiency was more than made up for by the imposing bulk of *Dog Years,* which was praised as taking up the Danzig saga again along the lines laid down in *The Tin Drum.* This reaction was to become a recurrent one in both Germany and North America over the next decade or so. For all the praise (and censure) that might also be lavished on it, each novel was in turn greeted with some degree of disappointment that Grass had not chosen to write *The Tin Drum* all over again.

The enormous success of the Danzig trilogy (and the attendant mixture of fame and notoriety) turned Grass's name into one of the best known in Germany. Over the following decade he turned his public renown to practical use by entering vigorously into German national politics. As early as 1961 he had already spoken out on behalf of the Social Democratic Party of Germany (SPD), then led by his friend Willy Brandt, whose chief political adversary was the combined Christian Democratic Union and Christian Social Union (CDU/CSU) of Konrad Adenauer, who had served as federal chancellor since 1949. Brandt's 1961 campaign was unsuccessful, as the small Free Democratic Party (FDP) swung the balance of power toward the CDU/CSU. Two years later Adenauer resigned and was succeeded as chancellor by Ludwig Erhard. Under Adenauer's 14-year chancellorship the country had made an astonishing economic recovery from the devastation of German cities and industries during the war. The so-called *Wirtschaftswunder* or "economic miracle," however, had gone hand in hand with a cold war policy of confrontation toward the Warsaw Pact bloc and a determined refusal to recognize the legitimacy of the East German regime. Brandt's SPD, a party of moderate reform, advocated the recognition of the de facto existence of East Germany as a separate state, the abandoning of the notion of German reunification, the improvement of relations with communist countries, and the strengthening of the recently formed European Economic Community.

Grass campaigned on behalf of Brandt and the SPD during the next electoral campaign, in 1965, traveling throughout the country and holding speeches on more than 50 separate occasions. The campaign was again unsuccessful, but the following year brought the withdrawal of the FDP from their coalition with the CDU/CSU, the resignation of Ludwig Erhard, and the formation of the so-called Great Coalition between the CDU/CSU and the SPD, with Kurt Kiesinger as chancellor. Three years later another electoral campaign saw Grass on the road again, driving thousands of miles through West Germany in a Volkswagen bus over the seven months of his campaign activity and giving campaign speeches on more than 90 separate occasions. This time the SPD was successful, taking power in coalition with the FDP, and Willy Brandt succeeded Kiesinger as chancellor. One of Brandt's earliest symbolic gestures of reconciliation toward Eastern Europe was his historic trip to Poland in 1970, in the course of which he laid a commemorative wreath on the site of the Warsaw ghetto. Grass, appropriately, accompanied Brandt on this journey of reconciliation.

Grass kept up an impressive literary output during these hectic years. *Mystisch, barbarisch, gelangweilt* (Mystical, Barbaric, Bored), which had already appeared as a chapter in *The Tin Drum,* premiered as a stage production in Düsseldorf in 1963. The radio play *Eine öffentliche Diskussion* (A Public Discussion), based on an episode in *Dog Years,* was broadcast in 1963 and was first performed as a stage play, under the title *Goldmäulchen* (Goldmouth), in Munich in 1964. A brief one-act play espousing the cause of the SPD, *POUM oder Die Vergangenheit fliegt mit* (POUM or The Past is Also a Passenger), appeared in 1965, as did a revised version of the play *Onkel, Onkel (Mister, Mister).* Grass's fifth and most ambitious play, *Die Plebejer proben den Aufstand (The Plebeians Rehearse the Uprising)* was produced at the Schillertheater in Berlin in 1966 and appeared in book form the same year. A third volume of poems, *Ausgefragt* (Interrogated), much more openly political than either of its predecessors, followed in 1967, as did two volumes of political speeches and writings and a volume of literary essays in 1968. The play *Davor (Max: A Play)* appeared on stage and in print in 1969, the year that also saw the publication of his fourth novel, *Örtlich betäubt* (*Local Anaesthetic*). Another ballet, *Die Vogelscheuchen* (The Scarecrows), based on an episode in *Dog Years*, was first performed in 1970. The year 1970 also saw the publication of his collected plays (*Theaterspiele*), and the following year that of his collected poems (*Gesammelte Gedichte*).

The Plebeians and *Local Anaesthetic* (as well as the thematically related *Max: A Play*), the major products of the later sixties, reflect Grass's political activism of these years. Unlike the Danzig trilogy, they move away from both the Nazi past and the Danzig locale that had served as Grass's trademark; they are centered firmly on the here and now of contemporary West German reality. *The Plebeians* is set in East Berlin, on 17 June 1953, in Bertolt Brecht's theater. While outside the theater the East German workers rise in revolt against oppressive government labor norms (as, in historical fact, they did on that day), inside the theater the famous dramatist contents himself with rehearsing his adaptation of Shakespeare's *Coriolanus*. *Local Anaesthetic* and *Max* both focus on the threatened burning of a dachshund by an idealistic West Berlin student protesting the American napalming of Vietnam—and on the efforts of his middle-aged teacher to persuade him that radical action is never as useful in the long run as reasoned, legal, democratic action.

The Grass of the later sixties is a very different writer from the Grass of the early sixties. There is little of the old Rabelaisian gusto, the grotesque characters, the absurd detail, the expansive delight in language. Rather, in both *The Plebeians* and *Local Anaesthetic,* each of which is concerned with the central problem of how one should behave responsibly in a world filled with pain, there is an overall discipline and restraint that is something quite new in Grass's work. *The Plebeians,* composed largely in dignified, restrained, quasi-Shakespearean verse, was promptly declared a complete failure by German audiences. It also met with a lukewarm response in North America—with many reviewers flattening it into a personal attack on Brecht by his ungrateful pupil Grass. *Local Anaesthetic,* on the other hand, though similarly greeted in Germany with general disappointment, fared very well indeed in the United States and, in a sense, set the capstone on Grass's North American reputation. Its appearance in early 1970 was greeted enthusiastically in the major reviewing organs, the final seal of approval being publicly confirmed when *Time* magazine ran a cover story on Grass, saluting the now 42-year-old author as possibly the world's greatest living novelist. Grass's final narrative experiment of these years, *Aus dem Tagebuch einer Schnecke* (*From the Diary of a Snail*) appeared in 1972. This sophisticated blend of fiction and nonfiction was received with no great enthusiasm either in Germany or abroad, but it nonetheless occupies a key position in Grass's technical development as a writer.

Grass continued his political involvement with dogged determination throughout the seventies, campaigning for Brandt and the SPD again in 1972, making 129 appearances in all. After this campaign (Brandt's last), however, Grass's involvement in frontline politics was considerably less visible and less time-consuming than it had been in the sixties. (He did speak out for the Social Democrats long after Brandt's resignation over a spy scandal in 1974, however, and took up the cudgels yet again in the electoral campaigns of 1976 and 1980 on behalf of Helmut Schmidt, who succeeded Brandt as federal chancellor.) In 1972 he bought a secluded house in Wewelsfleth, near Itzehoe, in Schleswig-Holstein, where he began work on his next major project. The years between 1972 and 1977 constitute a reflective, preparatory period for Grass, issuing in the major novel *Der Butt* (*The Flounder*), much as his first, experimental phase in the fifties had resulted in *The Tin Drum*. That first period had produced a number of minor works in the course of writing *The Tin Drum;* similarly, after *From the Diary of a Snail,* a number of minor works prepare the way for *The Flounder.* In 1973 a volume combining drawings, photographs, and a poem, *Mariazuehren* (*Inmarypraise*), appeared, followed in 1974 by a collection of political commentaries, *Der Bürger und seine Stimme* (A Citizen and his Voice). A luxurious bibliophile edition of seven etchings with poems, *Liebe geprüft* (*Love Tested*), appeared in the same year. In 1976 Grass received an honorary doctorate from Harvard.

Heralded by a lavish advance publicity campaign, *Der Butt* (*The Flounder*), a narrative exploration of the war of the sexes throughout history, appeared in 1977. It sold 450,000 copies within two years and realized a profit on its first edition alone of some 3 million marks—with part of which Grass established a literary prize to celebrate the centenary of the writer whom he had long claimed as his literary model, Alfred Döblin (1878–1957). *The Flounder,* set in Danzig once again and far closer to the style of *The Tin Drum* and *Dog Years* than to that of the more recent novels, met with generally highly enthusiastic critical and popular reaction in Germany and North America alike, though there were occasional condemnations of Grass's political opinions. In 1978 another collection of political essays, *Denkzettel* (Reminders), appeared, and Grass's marriage to Anna Grass ended in divorce. He also traveled widely in the Far East and collaborated with the director Volker

Schlöndorff on a film version of *The Tin Drum,* which was released in 1979 to both popular and critical acclaim, culminating in an Oscar for the best foreign film of the year.

The year 1979 saw Grass's second marriage, to Ute Grunert, an organist from Berlin, as well as the publication of *Das Treffen in Telgte* (*The Meeting at Telgte*), a fictionalized meeting of Group 47, the literary circle in which Grass had first made his name, transported three hundred years back in time to the chaotic Germany of the Thirty Years' War. *Telgte,* riding on the coattails of *The Flounder,* was very well received both in Germany and in North America. *Aufsätze zur Literatur* (Essays on Literature), a collection of his major literary essays over the preceding 20 years, appeared in 1980, as did the narrative *Kopfgeburten oder Die Deutschen sterben aus* (*Headbirths or The Germans Are Dying Out*), based on the imaginative transformation of his impressions and experiences in the Far East. Pushing further still the narrative techniques first employed in *From the Diary of a Snail* and then in *The Flounder,* Grass weaves fact and fiction, East and West, comedy and melancholy, past, present, and future into a complex literary web. *Headbirths* aroused the almost invariable reaction to Grass's books in Germany during the eighties and nineties: outraged (and highly publicized) indignation on the one hand, from those who saw only SPD electioneering in the thin disguise of narrative fiction; enthusiastic (but far less newsworthy) praise on the other, from those who saw one more demonstration of Grass's mastery of the art of narrative.

The seventies also witnessed a major expansion of Grass's nonliterary artistic activities. Grass has remained active as a graphic artist throughout his career—especially, since 1972, which marks a watershed in his artistic development, as a producer of etchings that (like his narratives) evocatively blend a meticulous naturalism with overtly fantastic elements. Grass began to experiment seriously with etching only as a 45-year-old—at which point, however, he threw himself into the medium with tremendous vigor, producing more than two hundred works over the next decade. From *The Flounder* on, Grass's major literary works have been paralleled by series of etchings, in some cases very extensive, on the same theme or combination of themes. In the early eighties, after *Headbirths,* Grass wrote little or nothing for four years. During this time he rediscovered sculpture, working in clay (including terra-cotta) and bronze, and also began to experiment in greater depth with lithography. In 1982 *Zeichnungen und Texte 1954–1977* (*Drawings and Words 1954–1977*) appeared, a selection of his drawings in various media with poems and extracts mostly from the earlier narrative texts, followed two years later by *Radierungen und Texte 1972–1982* (*Etchings and Words 1972–1982*), a selection of 116 etchings and dry points with poems and extracts mostly from the later narratives. In 1986 the coffee-table retrospective volume *In Kupfer, auf Stein* (In Copper, on Stone) appeared, a photographic record of Grass's complete graphic work since 1972, consisting of 228 etchings and 52 lithographs.[3]

In 1982 Grass received the Feltrinelli Prize in Rome. The collection of etchings and poems *Ach Butt, dein Märchen geht böse aus* (Alas, Flounder, Your Tale Will Have a Bad Ending) appeared the following year. In 1983 he was also elected president of Berlin Academy of the Arts for a three-year term, and he officially joined the SPD, the party on whose behalf he had already been active for more than 20 years. *Widerstand lernen* (Learning to Resist), a collection of political essays protesting the placement of American Pershing missiles on German soil, appeared in 1984; in that year, together with Heinrich Böll and others, he also founded a national support network for foreign workers and their families in Germany. In 1985, in memory once again of Alfred Döblin, he donated his house in Wewelsfleth as a center for creative writers.

The major novel *Die Rättin* (*The Rat*), set in a Germany devastated by nuclear holocaust, with mutant rats as the new masters (and mistresses) of the radioactive earth, appeared in 1986. In the same year Grass bought a house in Behlendorf, near Lübeck in northern Germany, and paid a five-month visit to Calcutta (at least partly in flight from the massive hostility that had greeted *The Rat* in the German press). To mark his sixtieth birthday in 1987, his long-term publisher Luchterhand issued a 10-volume *Werkausgabe,* an edition of his collected works, while *Mit Sophie in die Pilze gegangen* (Gathering Mushrooms with Sophie), a new collection of poems and lithographs, also appeared. An edition of his complete poems, *Die Gedichte 1955–86,* was published in 1988. The visit to Calcutta provided the material for *Zunge zeigen* (*Show Your Tongue*), a mixed-media experiment combining sketches, drawings, poetry, narrative, and diary that focused on poverty in the third world. Appearing in 1988, *Zunge zeigen* met with almost universal critical disparagement in Germany.

During the late eighties and early nineties, with German reunification in the air, Grass kept up a blistering pace in terms of artistic, literary, and political activity alike. In 1988 he formally resigned from the Berlin Academy of the Arts in protest against its lack of public support for his friend Salman Rushdie, who had been condemned in absentia by fundamentalist Islamic religious leaders to a heretic's death. In 1989 he produced a *Skizzenbuch* (Sketchbook), containing drawings and sketches of Calcutta; delivered an impassioned address on conditions in Calcutta to the Club of Rome; published a political discussion with Françoise Giroud entitled *Wenn wir von Europa sprechen* (Speaking of Europe), a dialogue about the concept of Europe in general and about the role and relationship of Germany and France in particular; and performed an exhausting one-man public reading of *The Tin Drum* in Göttingen on 12 successive evenings. The following year he produced *Totes Holz* (Dead Wood), a collection of lithographs and texts protesting the environmental devastation of central Europe; *Deutscher Lastenausgleich* (Sharing the German Burden), *Ein Schnäppchen namens DDR* (East Germany at Bargain Prices), and *Deutschland, einig Vaterland?* (Germany, A Single Fatherland?), a political dispute with Rudolf Augstein, all three protesting the reunification of Germany; *Kahlschlag in unseren Köpfen* (The Clearcut Mind), another collection of lithographs protesting environmental damage; and *Schreiben nach Auschwitz* (Writing after Auschwitz), the Poetics Prize lecture at the University of Frankfurt, in which he argued that the national disgrace of Auschwitz made the reunification of Germany a moral impossibility. In 1991 he published *Gegen die verstreichende Zeit* (Writing against Time), a further collection of political pieces, and *Brief aus Altdöbern* (A Letter from Altdöbern), a combination of drawings and text once again protesting environmental devastation in eastern Germany. He also received an honorary doctorate from the University of Poznań for his role in introducing a heightened consciousness of German-Polish relations into German literature.

A striking feature of Grass's work of these years is the degree to which it is increasingly informed by an apocalyptic tone. *Headbirths* (1980), written at the very beginning of what it called the "Orwell decade," initiates a series of visions of catastrophe whose highpoint is *The Rat* (1986) and that continue in a minor key with *Show Your Tongue* (1988) and the volumes of environmental protest. As Grass's first three major works have come to be known as the Danzig Trilogy, one might see the texts of these years as forming a Cassandra Complex, embodying the voice of a prophet crying doom and being largely ignored and even ridiculed for his pains. Grass's writing career began with the catastrophe of the German past; with the group of apocalyptic texts centered on *The Rat* he turns to the perhaps no longer avertable catastrophe that may constitute the future of humankind. Once again it would be incautious to oversimplify the ostensible message of these texts. Grass himself has repeatedly drawn attention to the distinction between his necessarily univocal political work and his consciously polyvocal artistic work. The apocalyptic mode has always been at least a background presence in Grass's work—but that work has also consistently advertised its continued ironic questioning of its own positions.

In 1991 the Steidl Verlag (Grass's new publisher, following a controversial parting of the ways with the Luchterhand Verlag after more than 30 years) published the autobiographical *Vier Jahrzehnte: Ein Werkstattbericht* (Four Decades: An Account of Work in Progress), an expensively produced, large-format volume sumptuously illustrated by Grass's own graphic work and photographic reproductions from his various manuscripts. It presents Grass's unsentimental retrospective account of his own artistic development, from his boyhood in Danzig to his most recent work. For the Grass enthusiast it is a treasury of biographical detail, ironic self-commentary, and previously unpublished lyric and graphic work, especially from the very early years. *Vier Jahrzehnte* provides a striking demonstration of the extraordinary range of Grass's interlinked and interactive artistic skills in various media.

The fall of the Berlin Wall in November 1989 and the wave of popular euphoria it unleashed in both Germanys culminated in a proclamation of reunification of the two existing German states less than a year later, on 3 October 1990, now a German national holiday. Since the sixties, Grass had been publicly speaking out against the possibility of German unification and in favor of a confederation of the two German states. His opinions, which he staunchly continued to proclaim, now exposed him to an extraordinary degree of hostility in the public press. Grass persisted in portraying reunification as a hostile invasion of a struggling neighboring state by the mighty Deutschmark, as the old eastern dictatorship of ideology gave way to a new western dictatorship of money. Grass argued at every conceivable opportunity that what was necessary, instead of a single state, was a much slower process of gradual rapprochement between the two German states, leading to a federation of the two in a single "cultural nation" held together by its language, literature, and culture as well as by a new and democratically established joint constitution. Though not entirely alone in his opinions, Grass was one of a very small minority, and his incessantly reiterated views earned him a large number of new and very vocal enemies.[4]

In 1992, inaugurating a new group of texts focused on the German Question rather than on the wider issues of global ecological concern, Grass published *Unkenrufe* (*The Call of the Toad*), a surprisingly mild satire on the expansionist tendencies of the new Germany whose reunification he had so vehemently opposed. *Rede vom Verlust* (On Loss), a political statement characterizing the rise of right-wing extremism as a predictable sign of the times in the new Germany, also appeared in 1992. During that same year, after 30 years of vigorous and very public involvement, Grass renounced his membership in the Social Democratic Party, in protest against both its refusal to sponsor a rally in support of Salman Rushdie and its support for more restrictive asylum policies—though we find him less than two years later campaigning once again for the SPD, this time in the former East Berlin. In 1993 Grass published *Novemberland* (Novemberland), a slim volume of 13 sonnets excoriating neo-Nazi atrocities, and *Schaden begrenzen* (Damage Control), a political discussion concerning the long-term future of the united Germany. He was also awarded his fourth honorary doctorate by the University of Gdańsk, honorary citizenship of the city of Gdańsk, and the Spanish Hidalgo Prize. The Steidl Verlag began publication of a 12-volume *Studienausgabe* (Study Edition) of his collected works, sold rights for a paperback edition in individual volumes, and announced a new and complete critical edition for 1997 to mark his seventieth birthday.

In 1994 *Angestiftet, Partei zu ergreifen* (Forced to Take Sides) appeared, a collection of political pieces from 1961 to 1993, and Grass was awarded both the major Literature Prize of the Bavarian Academy of Fine Arts for his cumulative literary work and the Czech Karel Čapek Prize. In early 1995 a collection of his literary essays appeared under the title *Die Deutschen und ihre Dichter* (The Germans and Their Writers). A major new novel, *Ein weites Feld* (*Too Far Afield*) centered on a great German writer, Theodor Fontane, caused the eruption of the so-called Grass Affair of late 1995, when Grass's complex and intricately structured narrative was torn to pieces with triumphant relish by critics who chose to ignore the novel's obvious literary merit and concentrate instead on condemning its author's political stance on reunification. In 1996 he was awarded the Sonning Prize of the University of Copenhagen and the Thomas Mann Prize of the city of Lübeck, where he had moved the previous year. In 1997 he published *Fundsachen für Nichtleser* (Found Objects for Nonreaders), a collection of poems and watercolors, and the Steidl Verlag published a new 16-volume *Werkausgabe* (Collected Works). A television version of *Die Rättin* (*The Rat*) by Martin Buchhorn was broadcast on the evening before Grass's seventieth birthday in October 1997, which was publicly celebrated before an audience of 1,200 in a theater in Hamburg. On that occasion his contributions to literature and political culture alike were honored by an international panel of literary luminaries, including Salman Rushdie and Nadine Gordimer as well as the German writers Siegfried Lenz and Christa Wolf.

"A writer," Grass wrote in *From the Diary of a Snail,* "is someone who writes against the passage of time."[5] In Grass's case that also means someone who consistently has the courage to write against the grain, against the pieties of received opinion. Grass has done exactly that, in a wide variety of contexts, ever since his first monumental success with *The Tin Drum* almost 40 years ago. There is a high price to pay for such courage, and Grass has admitted in interviews of the early nineties to feeling both increasingly isolated in the brave new Germany and bitterly disappointed at having his artistic work so often mercilessly pilloried because of his political opinions. Outside of Germany the 70-year-old Grass is universally regarded as the most important German-language writer of the later twentieth century. In Germany itself his literary works sell by the hundreds of thousands and are regularly judged by readers whose primary interest is in literature and its possibilities to be among the most impressive products of modern German writing. What more often seizes the headlines, however, is that they are equally regularly condemned, frequently with extraordinary virulence, by ostensibly literary critics whose overriding interests are openly political rather than literary. That these critics' reaction has a great deal more to do with the culture of popular German literary criticism than with the strengths of Grass's writings is a central contention of the present book.

Chapter Two
Aspects of the Absurd

The years before Grass's sudden leap to fame with the appearance of *The Tin Drum* in 1959 were apprenticeship years, filled with formal experimentation in an impressive variety of media. The earliest products of his prodigious talent are intricately detailed pieces of work, miniatures poised on a single stylistic or thematic point or on a cluster of points. The central impulse is lyric, even in pieces that present themselves as narrative or, as was more often the case in these early years, dramatic. Our central emphasis in this chapter will be on these early plays, all of which were written between 1954 and 1957.

Grass's theatrical ambitions reach back almost as far as his earliest lyric experiments. His first poems and his first brief narrative study, "Meine grüne Wiese" (My Green Field), appeared in print in 1955; his first play, *Hochwasser* (*Flood*), premiered only two years later. None of Grass's early plays was a critical success; none of them enjoyed a run of any length; only one, *Die bösen Köche* (*The Wicked Cooks*), premiered in Berlin (and that rode on the coattails of *The Tin Drum*'s phenomenal success). For the student of Grass's work, however, these plays have considerable importance. Grass himself (duly followed by other critics) has employed the term "poetic theater" to describe them as a group, acknowledging that most of the plays were in fact dramatic elaborations of poems. He has also called them "absurd theater," as does Martin Esslin in his classic study *The Theatre of the Absurd*.[1] That label should give some pause to those who might insist on reading "deeper meanings" into these texts. The essence of the absurd theater, which reached one of its early high points with the appearance of Samuel Beckett's *Waiting for Godot* in 1953, is to reject interpretation while at the same time offering all too inviting footholds for interpretive endeavors.

Grass published two major theoretical essays in these years, "Die Ballerina" (The Ballerina) in 1956 (republished as a slim volume in 1963) and "Der Inhalt als Widerstand" (Content as Resistance) in 1957.[2] "The Ballerina," as Ann Mason observes, already makes quite clear Grass's conception of the way modern art relates to tradition—namely, as "critical reappraisal through parody."[3] In "Content as Resistance," Grass posits form and content not as allies but as enemies. Literary form, that is to say, is not just a transparent pane allowing the reader untroubled and immediate access to the content of the literary work. Instead, form and content are natural antagonists, and art is produced by virtue of the tension between them. It is the artist's task, the essay argues, to maintain that tension at all times. Almost everything Grass has written since these two essays—whether poem, play, narrative, or essay—is a renewed demonstration of their fundamental maxims. Grass's first poems and "Meine grüne Wiese" (My Green Field) appeared in the journal *Akzente* in 1955. In 1956, the essay "Die Ballerina" appeared in *Akzente* and his first book, the collection of poems *Die Vorzüge der Windhühner* (The Merits of Windfowl) was published. The combination represented a considerable triumph for the young author, who had not yet reached his thirtieth birthday. *Akzente,* edited by Walter Höllerer, was the official organ of Group 47 and, as such, the leading literary journal in the country. The doctrines espoused in both "The Ballerina" and "Content as Resistance" are much in evidence in *Die Vorzüge der Windhühner* (a second edition of which, partially repaginated and with some new graphics, appeared in 1963). Many of the poems both parody traditional literary forms and values and defy interpretation in any traditional sense. Also emerging clearly in this work is Grass's predilection for concrete objects rather than abstract ideas: images usually involving tangible objects and frequently deployed in startlingly unexpected conjunctions play a far more important role in these poems than does formal control or logical coherence. As Keith Miles puts it, "they are explorations rather than statements, purveyors of mood rather than of meaning."[4] These early poems also illustrate Grass's lifelong tendency to recycle concepts and images, altering and developing them in the process. Many of them contain ideas and motifs that will recur in Grass's narratives and plays for years, even decades, to come.

Flood

Grass's first play to be produced, the two-act *Hochwasser,* written in 1955, premiered in January 1957 in Frankfurt. It first appeared in print in 1960 in *Akzente* (498–539), with a revised version appearing in 1963. An English translation by Ralph Manheim, *Flood,* appeared in *Four Plays* in 1967.[5] Like others of the early plays, *Flood* is a theatrical elaboration of a poem, in this case the poem "Hochwasser" ("Flood") from *Die Vorzüge der Windhühner.* The play operates on three physical levels. As rains pour and flood waters inexorably rise outside and in, the protagonist, Noah, busily labors in the basement to rescue his collection of historic inkwells and candelabras.

One floor up, Noah's sister-in-law, Betty, worries about saving her photographs, while his bored teenage daughter, Yetta, and her bored teenage boyfriend, Henry, are too fatigued by their boredom either to consider helping Noah or to worry unduly about the possibility of impending disaster or anything else. On the roof, meanwhile, two large rats, Pearl and Point, theorize in desultory fashion on the nature of disaster and how to cope with it. Noah's son Leo arrives from distant parts accompanied by a highly virile friend, with whom Yetta soon takes to bed, banishing Henry to the roof. Aunt Betty has meanwhile taken to sewing parasols, on the grounds that the sun will surely shine again some day and it's better to be prepared. Pearl and Point, as Greek chorus, provide ongoing commentary. When the rain eventually does stop, and the floods abate, everybody is surprised to feel so let down. Leo and his friend depart for further foreign climes; Yetta and Henry, since anything else would involve too much effort, are reconciled; and Pearl and Point, suspecting that normality will signal a return of rattraps, decide to set out for Hamelin, where there seem to be opportunities for enterprising rodents. Disaster and how society chooses to cope with it will become one of Grass's most central themes throughout his work. It informs the entire Danzig trilogy and reappears in intensified form (together with the rats, who notoriously leave sinking ships) almost 30 years later in *Die Rättin (The Rat)* and a whole series of other texts of the 1980s, what Grass would call "Orwell's decade."

Mister, Mister

Grass's most substantial play of this period, the four-act *Onkel, Onkel,* was written in 1956 and premiered in Cologne in 1958. Published in revised form in Berlin in 1965, it was translated two years later by Ralph Manheim (in *Four Plays*) as *Mister, Mister.*[6] The play centers thematically on violence and what society in general is prepared to do to prevent it. The four acts, each preceded by a prologue, chronicle the rise and fall of Bollin, a mass-murderer-in-training whose homicidal plans are continually thwarted—but more by his own comic ineptitude than by any efforts of others to stop him.

After a prologue in which Bollin unsuccessfully offers candy to two worldly-wise children, Sprat and Slick (who would rather see the "thingamajig" he has in his pocket), the first act shows him equally unsuccessful in attempting to rape and murder 16-year-old Sophie, who is sick in bed with the flu. Glad of the distraction, Sophie has him help her with her crossword puzzle, until he is frightened off (almost leaving behind his revolver or, as Sophie calls it, his "thingamajig") when her widowed mother displays amorous intentions. In the second act, after a prologue in which he vents his frustration by first stabbing and then shooting a doll he has stolen from Sophie, Bollin lures a forester into a mantrap. The forester escapes, however, when Sprat and Slick (whom the forester later rewards with an interminable lecture on trees) arrive on the scene to harass Bollin with further inquiries about his "thingamajig." Following a prologue in which Bollin savagely chops down a Christmas tree, the third act finds him in the bathroom of his next putative victim, an opera singer who persuades him from her bath to join her in a duet from *The Barber of Seville* and then frightens him off with improper suggestions.

The fourth act finds Bollin, who by dint of conscientious effort appears by now to have succeeded in killing several people after all, exhausted and dejected by the rigors of his chosen career. He is himself about to become the victim of the two inquisitive children, Sprat and Slick, whose insistent "Mister, mister" gives the play its title. They trick him into letting them steal first his watch, then his pen, and finally the "thingamajig," his revolver, with which Sprat more or less accidentally kills him. The play ends with the 13-year-old Sprat explaining to her companion, the 14-year-old Slick, that since he will now be able to rape her at gunpoint just like in the newspapers (though they will have to work out the exact mechanism), they can have a baby, get married, and live happily ever after. More dangerous than the bumbling Bollin ever was, Sprat and Slick skip innocently away to the nearest barn to practice, singing a childish little song about the "thingamajigs" people carry in their pockets.

Reminiscent of Brecht's *The Resistible Rise of Arturo Ui* (1941) and Max Frisch's *Firebugs* (1958) in its satiric treatment of the resistible rise of violence and demagoguery, *Mister, Mister* anticipates the extended treatment of this same theme throughout the Danzig trilogy. Slick will reappear as the juvenile delinquent Störtebeker in *The Tin Drum;* Sprat is the first of a whole series of bored and dangerous young women, including Lucy Rennwand in *The Tin Drum,* Tulla Pokriefke in both *Cat and Mouse* and *Dog Years,* and Vero Lewand in *Local Anaesthetic.*

Only Ten Minutes to Buffalo

Written in 1957, the one-act play *Noch zehn Minuten bis Buffalo* first appeared in print in the journal *Akzente* in 1958 (5-17) and was first staged in Bochum in 1959. It was translated by Ralph Manheim in 1967 (in *Four Plays*) as *Only Ten Minutes to Buffalo*. The title borrows the refrain of a well-known German ballad, "John Maynard," written by the nineteenth-century novelist Theodor Fontane. This ballad tells the dramatic story of a steersman on a Lake Erie steamer who dies after refusing heroically to abandon his burning ship just ten minutes short of Buffalo, New York. In Grass's play, it need hardly be said, there is neither drama nor heroism. The action takes place in a flowery Bavarian meadow, where the engineer Krudewil and his fireman Pempelfort sit in an abandoned and long-immobilized locomotive and fantasize a train journey to "Buffalo." Their imagined journey runs through the pleasant countryside, past grazing cows in the background and the painter Kotschenreuth in the foreground, who, in turn, is busily at work on a seascape while extolling to a local cowherd the power of the creative imagination. The cowherd, Axel, is moved to reflect on the creative tension between form and content, and the curtain falls as the locomotive, now driven by Axel, slowly steams off stage, a triumph of the artistic imagination that feeds on such paradoxes.

Krudewil and Pempelfort, by their own account, are onetime sailors, thus motivating, at least to some extent, both their belief that they are heading for Buffalo and Kotschenreuth's ability to paint a seascape. These characters are borrowed from the theoretical essay "Content as Resistance," published in *Akzente* in 1956, in which they are portrayed as poets, walking through meadow filled with flowers while discussing the nature of the creative process. The play also contains a bizarre and parodically overdetermined female character, Frigate, who is both Krudewil and Pempelfort's former sea captain, now an admiral, *and* a frigate under full sail. Frigate has been read by critics as a personification of the spirit of violence and war, but she need not necessarily be read as such, however, nor need the play be read as a transposition into theatrical form of the theoretical essay, as other critics have suggested.

Slight as it is, this one-act play is distinctly interesting for a variety of reasons. In particular, the play overtly rejects interpretation while simultaneously (and duplicitously) inviting it. Although it is clear that the play, like the essay "Content as Resistance," centers on the interaction of form and content, that is all that is clear. The process of interaction between the two is a necessary part of every creative act—including the reader's. *Only Ten Minutes to Buffalo* is a play about its own functioning, not a play about something else; it is a reflexive parable that is not improved by attempts to thrust allegorical readings upon it. In "Content as Resistance," as we have seen, Grass argued that form and content are not allies but enemies and that it is the artist's task to maintain and exploit that tension at all times. *Only Ten Minutes to Buffalo* is a practical demonstration of how one might set about doing exactly that.

Written as early as 1954, the one-act farce *Beritten hin und zurück: Ein Vorspiel auf dem Theater (Rocking Back and Forth)* first appeared in print in 1958 in *Akzente* (399–409); it premiered in Frankfurt and Hamburg in 1959.[7] The central character, Conelli, a circus clown, rocks back and forth on a child's rocking horse, while a Director, an Actor, and a Playwright discourse learnedly on the role of the clown in contemporary drama. Conelli resists all attempts, whether theoretical or practical, to involve him, and the play ends as it began with Conelli still rocking back and forth. For the German-speaking reader, the subtitle parodically evokes Goethe's prologue to *Faust,* which is subtitled "Vorspiel auf dem Theater" (A Theatrical Prologue) and involves a Director, a Poet, and a Comedian discussing the nature and aims of dramatic production. In Goethe's drama the *Vorspiel* is indeed a prologue to the dramatic action that ensues; in Grass's play, like Beckett's *Godot* of five years earlier, the point (however "absurd") is that, once again, there *is* no action.

Grass's second collection of poetry, *Gleisdreieck* (Triangle of Tracks), appeared in 1960. Many of the themes, motifs, and techniques from the first collection are carried over into these new poems. However, unlike the earlier work that had tended to rely predominantly on startling imagery, *Gleisdreieck,* just as *The Tin Drum* and *Cat and Mouse* had done, introduces clearly audible political notes. These notes begin with the collection's title—the name of a railway station near the border dividing Berlin, the onetime (and future) capital of Germany.

The Wicked Cooks

At some point before 1957, Grass wrote a ballet, *Fünf Köche* (Five Cooks), which premiered in Aix-les-Bains and Bonn in 1959. This ballet served as a preliminary study for the most ambitious of the early theatrical attempts, namely, the five-act play *Die bösen Köche,* which was written in 1957, premiered in Berlin in 1961, and first appeared in print in a collection of modern dramas the same year.[8] *Die bösen Köche* was translated by A. Leslie Willson in 1967, in *Four Plays,* as *The Wicked Cooks.*

Cooks and cooking had already played a significant role in Grass's imaginative writing up to that point—most notably in the *schwarze Köchin,* literally the "black cook" (Ralph Manheim's "black witch") of *The Tin Drum.* In *The Wicked Cooks,* five cooks attempt, with increasing urgency, to obtain the recipe for a particularly successful cabbage soup (which tastes of ashes) from its inventor, "the Count," who calls it his "November soup." Various stratagems—accompanied by much singing, dancing, and pantomime-like stage business—are all to no avail. As a last resort, one of the cooks persuades his own fiancée, Martha, to marry the Count, on condition that he divulge the secret. The Count agrees, the marriage takes place, and the cooks believe their ambition is finally about to be realized, only to have their hopes dashed when the Count discovers that his love for Martha has caused him to forget the recipe, for which he now has no further need. Unable to keep their part of the bargain, the Count and Martha commit suicide, and the wicked cooks scatter in all directions.

The play was not a popular success, in spite of the fame Grass had by now achieved as author of *The Tin Drum.* It is characterized by long stretches of inactivity interrupted by frenetic interludes, and, in the end, the lengthy quest for enlightenment, for a final answer that will satisfy all questions, comes to nothing. This ending reminds the reader once again of *Waiting for Godot,* where a similarly long wait leads to similarly little result, likewise portrayed by means of a theatrical (or antitheatrical) exploitation of inactivity. Critics of *Die bösen Köche* have once again striven mightily to find allegorical meaning in the play, which all too invitingly offers itself as a latter-day version of a quest for the Holy Grail. The Count has consequently, and entirely predictably, been seen as a figure of the artist and/or as a Christ figure, the wicked cooks as representative of the rise of philistinism and/or that of totalitarianism, and so on. Such interpretations are in the end unsatisfying because they are reductionist, insisting on a would-be bottom-line solution. As in the case of *Only Ten Minutes to Buffalo, The Wicked Cooks* is an obdurately enigmatic text—and it is preferable by far to accept it on those terms rather than to force allegorical meanings upon it.

The poetry of these early years was politely received; the plays were received with a distinct lack of popular enthusiasm. As has variously been pointed out, however, there is much to be thankful for that this was so. For if the poetry and plays had earned more lavish applause, Grass might never have turned to writing novels, and we might never have had *The Tin Drum*—and that would have been an incalculable loss.

Chapter Three
The Tin Drum

Oskar Matzerath, the first-person narrator and central character of *The Tin Drum,* is a 30-year-old inmate of a mental hospital at the time of writing his autobiography (as he informs us in his opening sentence).[1] As a three-year-old aficionado of the tin drum of the book's title, Oskar (by his own account born clairvoyant and clairaudient) decides to have nothing more to do with the world of grown-ups, especially those who threaten to take his drum away. To achieve this end, he flings himself headlong down the cellar stairs, suffering no ill effects other than the desired one of curtailing his growth. For the next 18 years, until his son (who is probably his brother) knocks him (or perhaps doesn't) into the open grave of his recently deceased father (who may, in fact, not be his father at all), Oskar retains the stature of a three-year-old. A midget who refuses adamantly ever to be parted from his drum, Oskar has the supplementary gift of a miraculous voice that enables him to smash glass at will with a well-directed scream.

One reason that *The Tin Drum* has emerged so decisively as "one of the monumental reference points of post-war writing" in Germany, as John Reddick has phrased it, is very clearly the relationship of Oskar's eccentric narrative style and the half century of modern German history over which his highly unlikely story unfolds.[2] The ambiguity of the German term *Geschichte,* encompassing both "story" and "history," permeates Oskar's account of his life and times. His personal story (to the extent that it is possible to speak of one in any realistic sense in the first place) is told against and intimately implicated in the constant backdrop of the course of German history in the twentieth century. Born in 1924, Oskar completes his narrative in 1954, the intervening 30 years having seen the incubation, the triumph, and the publicly acknowledged defeat of Nazism in Germany. His account begins in 1899, for "no one ought to tell the story of his life who hasn't the patience to say a word or two about at least half of his grandparents before plunging into his own existence."[3] Not all his readers, Oskar clearly implies, would have either the patience or the desire, in the Germany of 1954, to put their memory to such a test—or if they did, it is very possible that the resulting account

would be just as strange a blend of fact and fiction as Oskar's own determinedly garbled and ostentatiously unbelievable version of how things
really were in the Central Europe of his time. Indeed, Oskar's account of
life in Danzig and Germany before, during, and after the Second World
War achieves its satirical thrust precisely because of its relentless and
often highly comic obliquity, because of the elaborate care with which
fact is disguised as fiction and fiction presented as unassailable fact.

Grass's novel, Oskar's narrative, is divided into three books, their
satirical thrust focused, respectively, on the period before, during, and
after the war. Oskar, like Grass, grows up in the Free City of Danzig, the
focus of German-Polish tensions over many years. These tensions are
presented both in Oskar's claim to have two fathers (the German
Matzerath, the Polish Bronski) and, typically obliquely, in the account of
his grandfather Joseph Koljaiczek's brief involvement as an advocate for
the Polish cause. Koljaiczek is dismissed from his job as a sawmill
worker for painting a fence red and white, the Polish national colors,
and he reiterates this chromatic theme (reflected in the colors of Oskar's
drum) by sending the whitewashed mill up in red flames (*TD*, 27). The
entire First World War merits only a reference to the changing design of
postage stamps; the depression of 1923 passes by in a subordinate
clause. Oskar's first day at school, where he listens to the "barbaric
voices" of his classmates, is described in rather more detail. Presented in
greater detail still is the apparently innocuous beating of carpets in the
communal courtyard, which, "as the house regulations decreed" (*TD*,
96–97), took place twice a week: "With a great display of bare arms a
hundred housewives, their hair tied up in kerchiefs, emerged from the
houses carrying carpet corpses, threw the victims over the rack, seized
their plaited carpet beaters and filled the air with thunder" (*TD*, 97). In
this idyllic scene of domestic industry, cleanliness, communal spirit, and
order, only the phrase "carpet corpses" suggests an element of subli-
mated aggression. This is sharply though again obliquely highlighted
when, in the same courtyard, a group of children, under the leadership
of one Susi Kater, trap Oskar and force him to swallow a nauseating
brew whose recipe includes live frogs and assorted flavors of urine. It is
1932, and every Thursday Oskar's mother conscientiously betrays her
German husband, Matzerath, with her Polish lover, Jan Bronski.

In the wake of drinking Susi Kater's brew, Oskar utilizes the destructive powers of his miraculous voice to smash every window in the facade
of the Municipal Theatre. The rise to power of the Nazi party is relegated to the inconsequential background in Oskar's account: Oskar

prefers to talk about his suddenly increased contact, around 1933, with the theater as an institution. After his encounter with the Municipal Theater come a public performance of the story of Tom Thumb; an open-air Wagner recital, as a result of which Oskar's mother takes to "domesticating" Wagner on the living-room piano (*TD*, 113); a visit to the circus; and a visit to a Nazi rally. The picture of Beethoven over the piano is quietly joined by that of "Hitler's equally gloomy countenance" (*TD*, 115). Meanwhile, little by little, Matzerath the greengrocer is piecing together his new uniform. "If I remember right," as Oskar offhandedly phrases it, "he began with the cap, which he liked to wear even in fine weather with the 'storm strap' in place, scraping his chin. For a time he wore a white shirt and black tie with the cap, or else a leather jacket with black armband. Then he bought his first brown shirt and only a week later he wanted the shit-brown riding breeches and high boots. Mama was opposed to these acquisitions and several weeks passed before Matzerath's uniform was complete" (*TD*, 116).

Grass brilliantly choreographs the way in which the lower-middle-class society, of which Oskar is part, pieces together its acceptance of Nazism, just as Matzerath puts together his uniform, starting with the cap signifying allegiance to a political ideal and ending with the "shit-brown" boots that soon will be kicking in the windows of Jewish storefronts. The heroic ideals are domesticated, in easy arrangements, just as Oskar's mother domesticates Wagner between her furtive and increasingly obsessive visits to Jan Bronski. German Idealism, canonized and revered and represented by the heroics of Wagnerian tenors, by the demonic eyebrows of Beethoven, by the Olympian serenity of the adulated poet-prince Goethe, is ground down and churned out nightly in the "coffee mill" (*TD*, 104) of the culture industry, to form a fertile humus for that same idealism's latest and perverted offshoot—which also comfortably accommodates the latent atavistic savagery of an apparently well-ordered bourgeois society. The difference between the heroic facade and the grimy underpinnings is evoked especially in the episode of the Nazi rally, which takes place in front of an immaculate and imposing rostrum with its serried ranks of swastika banners, flags, pennants, standards, and assorted uniforms. Distrustful of this highly polished symmetry, Oskar, as he tells us, prefers to examine the backside of the rostrum, for "everyone who has ever taken a good look at a rostrum from behind will be immunized ipso facto against any magic practised in any form whatsoever on rostrums" (*TD*, 119). A Jonah in the whale's belly (*TD*, 122), a Tom Thumb, a tiny resistance fighter, Oskar

disrupts the gleaming symmetry of the martial platform from under-
neath by undermining the military rhythms above with the rhythms of
the Charleston and Viennese waltzes from below, and the political rally,
to the fury of its organizers, degenerates into a *gemütlich* open-air dance.
Oskar's autobiography—written from his hospital bed over the two-
year period from September 1952 to September 1954—maintains a
constant but entirely oblique relationship with the course of modern
German history. The events of those years, events of world-shattering
importance, serve merely as an offhandedly reported temporal grid
against which the daily life of Oskar and his family is carefully (if
entirely idiosyncratically) plotted. Throughout the first book of the
novel, covering the period from 1899 to 1938, Oskar's distorted refrac-
tion of German society strips away the facade of respectability and reti-
cence veiling the rise of Nazism in Germany. Grass's satirical thrust, for
all the obliqueness of its application via Oskar, is quite clear. Nazism
was not at all some kind of demonic hero-frenzy of the German psyche,
some kind of almost supernatural eruption of evil incarnate (such as
Thomas Mann had evoked in his *Doctor Faustus* a decade before), horrifying indeed, but in its excess fascinating and even grandiose. Rather, it
was the coordinated channeling, on a huge scale, of the petty viciousness, the petty hypocrisies, the petty greed and frustration and spite and
boredom of very ordinary people, people leading painfully ordinary lives
until presented with a clearly defined and universally agreed-upon focus
for their concerted discontent and resentment. The holocaust came
about not in spite of but because of the ordinary man in the street, and
when it came about, it involved little or no disruption of the existing
system of values. Storm trooper Meyn, for example, is unable to be present when his comrades, during the *Kristallnacht* (Crystal Night) of
November 1938, kick in the windows of Jewish storefronts, burn down
the synagogue, and terrorize Jewish citizens. Very properly, Meyn has
been expelled in disgrace from the storm troopers for cruelty to animals.
    Oskar the resistance fighter, however, quickly acquires other and
more disturbing traits as well. It emerges that his disruption of the Nazi
rally may have had less heroic motives after all, for Oskar goes on to
relate that he was so pleased with the success of this little trick that he
repeated it frequently over the next few weeks, breaking up further ral-
lies not only of the Nazis but also of the Socialists, the Conservatives,
the boy scouts, the vegetarians, and the Young Polish Fresh Air Movement (*TD,* 124). From being apparently a pint-sized freedom fighter
and defender of humanity's cause, Oskar (always according to his own

account) becomes an aimless destroyer, a rejecter not just of Nazism but, apparently, of all causes. Never reluctant to supply the gullible reader with possible interpretive parallels, Oskar mentions at various points his dual intellectual heritage. After rejecting the public school system, Oskar undertakes his own education through a close reading of two books, Goethe's *Elective Affinities* and a volume promisingly entitled *Rasputin and Women,* whose pages, for simplicity's sake, he has torn out and shuffled together at random to make a single new volume. He notes at several points his (carefully orchestrated) similarity to the Christ child; uses the name Jesus during his days as leader of a gang of juvenile delinquents; much later informs a nurse, whom he is unsuccessfully attempting to rape, that his name is Satan. He claims two fathers, one German and one Polish, and, finally, suggests in Nietzschean vein that he subsumes not only Apollo but Dionysus as well.

Grass originally intended to call the novel "Der Trommler" (The Drummer). Critics have pointed to the fact that Hitler, who shared with Oskar his lower-middle-class origins, his blue eyes, and his status as "artist," was also known to his intimates as "the drummer" and, like Oskar, referred to himself as the savior of his people. Certain of Oskar's exploits can even be read as constituting a self-parodic allegory of the rise and fall of Nazism. His involvement in the death of his Polish father, Bronski, coincides with the German invasion of Poland in 1939, and his self-reported sexual conquest of his cousin Maria coincides with the invasion of France in 1940. His again self-reported campaign on the shaky virtue of Lina Greff coincides with the Russian campaign of 1941. His amorous conquest of the Italian midget Roswitha Raguna begins under the sign of the *Anschluss* with Italy in 1938, and his involvement in her death very literally coincides with the invasion of Normandy in 1944, as Roswitha reaches the coffee urn simultaneously with a Canadian shell. Finally, his involvement in the death of his German father, Matzerath, coincides with the fall of Germany in 1945.

From being predominantly an (apparently) uninvolved observer before the outbreak of war, in other words, Oskar apparently becomes a participant, and as such implicated in guilt, during the war. His participation, however, is impossible to categorize in realistic terms. There are, first of all, the grotesque "facts" of his continued three-year-old's stature and his glass-demolishing scream (which he eventually redeploys as a nightclub act for the amusement of the troops.) There is, secondly, the continued obliqueness and indirection of the account offered by the narrating Oskar, which repeatedly makes clear that it should not be taken at face value but still exploits the reader's natural impulse to believe a first-person narrator. The focus of the second book of the novel, indeed, is less the specific details of guilt than the fact of guilt itself, as Lester Caltvedt has argued. Oskar's account of his own involvement, though more flamboyantly unreliable, may well be no more fictional than many an answer to the question "What did you do in the war, Dad?"[4] What really happened, if it ever happened, is perhaps best forgotten, in other words. This is exactly what West German society sets about doing in the third book of the novel, covering the immediate postwar years. Oskar, who has moved from his initial role of clear-eyed observer to one involving pseudomythological implication in guilt, now acquires a third role. In a grotesque normalization, he attempts to become a part of that grown-up society he had vowed as a clairvoyant infant never to join. At Matzerath's funeral Oskar throws his drum into the open grave and begins to grow. At the same moment he is struck on the head by a stone flung by his four-year-old son (who may not be his son) and pitches headlong into the grave of his father (who may not be his father). However, like the West Germany of the *Wirtschaftswunder,* the economic miracle of the immediate postwar years, Oskar arises from the grave and grows rapidly. The expensive suits he is soon able to afford elegantly conceal the misshapen hump he has now also acquired during his socially inspired growth.

Oskar's new wealth is honestly come by, for in postwar Germany Oskar has become a practitioner of the arts, a constructor of alternative worlds, a reshaper of reality—an activity that in the new Germany finds numerous enthusiastic adherents. His first artistic endeavors are on the more functional side: he apprentices himself to a gravestone carver. Later he takes up modeling for a painter named Raskolnikoff. He is persuaded to take up his drum again and becomes a recording star. He performs in a nightclub, drumming up memories for clients who are thoughtfully provided with presliced onions to facilitate weeping. The proprietor of this establishment for properly regulated remorse is one Schmuh, and "Schmuh's smile was like the smile on a copy of a copy of the supposedly authentic Mona Lisa" (*TD,* 524). Not only do guilt and tears find their proper and authorized outlet; anger and aggression do too. There is Oskar's landlord, Zeidler, who gives vent to his feelings by regularly smashing liqueur glasses with great violence—before carefully sweeping up the remains. There is Schmuh, who enjoys nothing as much as shooting sparrows, but never shoots more than his self-imposed quota of a dozen a day and sheds bitter and therapeutic tears over those he has just allowed himself to shoot. The odd similarity of postwar Germany to prewar Germany and its carpet-thrashing squadrons of housewives is not lost on Oskar. Victor Weluhn is one who experiences this meticulous regard for order and tidy-mindedness. Having escaped a Nazi execution squad in Danzig in 1939, he is pursued conscientiously by his would-be executioners, who attempt to complete their interrupted duties in 1954. An order is an order, as one of them explains, duty is duty, and he's just doing his job like everyone else.

Meanwhile, for all his professional success, Oskar fails in his postwar efforts to assert himself as his "son" Kurt's father; his marriage proposal to Kurt's mother (and his own stepmother) Maria is likewise rejected; and he becomes involved in a series of abortive sexual liaisons, always with nurses, one of whom he is eventually suspected of having murdered. Oskar flees the country, but only gets as far as Paris before he is arrested, eventually convicted of murder, and found to be criminally insane. As he finishes his 500-page account, it is two years later, it is his thirtieth birthday, and he is still, as he volunteered in his first sentence, the inmate of a mental hospital.

The satirical thrust of the third book is anticipated in Oskar's earlier musing on the ambiguity of the German title of the Polish national anthem, "Poland Is Not Yet Lost." The ambiguity resides in the question, "Lost to whom?" "Some carry Chopin in their hearts, others thoughts of revenge. Condemning the first four partitions of Poland, they are busily planning a fifth; in the meantime flying to Warsaw via Air France in order to deposit, with appropriate remorse, a wreath on the spot that was once the ghetto. One of these days they will go searching for Poland with rockets. I, meanwhile, conjure up Poland on my drum. And this is what I drum: Poland's lost, but not forever, all's lost, but not forever, Poland's not lost forever" (*TD*, 107–8). This lament for Poland is expressed in a tone that immediately strikes the reader as more overtly sincere than many of Oskar's pronouncements mentioned so far. It is one of a number of places in the text, in fact, that point to Oskar's view of history and of human existence as totally random, arbitrary, undirected, indifferent—and unchangeable, whether by satire or otherwise. In this perspective, the disturbances over the first half of the twentieth century, for all the impressiveness of their immediate scope, constitute just one more episode in the interminable and uninterrupted war we call history.

Critics—especially John Reddick—have drawn attention to a number of such passages, all in one way or another illustrating the bleakness and hopelessness of Oskar's existential vision. Oskar dreams at one stage that he is riding on a giant merry-go-round with 4,000 children whose death he has just heard of. All of them, including Oskar, want to get off, but the merry-go-round is operated by a smiling God the Father, who merely inserts another coin in the slot for his own amusement. Life is no Hegelian spiral toward some ultimate meaning that will retrospectively put everything else in its proper focus; life is simply an eternal and eternally meaningless round. The same inescapable and pointless circularity recurs in the image of the eels caught after the battle of the Skagerrak, eels grown fat on sailors grown fat on eating eels. We find the same bleakness of vision in the episode of the fisherman using a horse's head on a clothesline as bait for eels, a head so completely covered by scavenging gulls that it seems white rather than black and seems to scream rather than neigh (*TD*, 152). We find it in the account of Matzerath's death, which fails to disturb the endeavors of the ants carrying off the sugar from a split sack, "for the sugar that trickled out of the burst sack had lost none of its sweetness" (*TD*, 395). We find it in the fragile house of cards Bronski builds with infinite care during the shelling of the Polish Post Office, a metaphor for all human endeavor—including the bombardment that destroys the Post Office and the house of cards alike and the account that describes the bombardment—its very inception acknowledging the inevitability of its own disintegration. We find it most consistently of all in the figure of the "Black Witch," the wicked witch of a children's rhyme who appears continually to Oskar in an ever-growing variety of disguises and who comes to dominate the closing pages of the novel. The Black Witch, for Oskar, represents everything we have to fear; in the closing pages of his narrative what we have to fear is precisely everything. "She had always been there . . . . Don't ask Oscar who she is! Words fail him. . . . Black, she was always behind me. / Now she is facing me too, black" (*TD*, 588–89). Thus ends Oscar's story. Words fail him.

Oskar's final confession (or profession) of terror is impressive and highly effective. It is also—if only partly—fake, for it is quite clear that Oskar is at least in part playing at being terror stricken, casting himself in the hero's role in a melodrama of his own devising. The most immediately striking characteristic of *The Tin Drum,* as we have seen, is the flaunted unreliability of its narrator and central character, who begins his lengthy and complex autobiographical narrative with the provocative concession: "Granted: I am an inmate of a mental hospital" (*TD*, 15). This initial concession potentially undermines every subsequent

statement over the next 500 pages and invites the reader to weigh every
single subsequent statement against that crucial opening admission that
the entire account must be considered suspect. We cannot, however,
assume him to be consistently unreliable either, for, as John Reddick
puts it, "the question as to whether Oskar is truly mad, or only pretend-
ing to be mad, remains one of the ultimate ambiguities of the fiction"
(Reddick, 50).

By his own account, in order to provide a "plausible ground for my
failure to grow" (*TD*, 61), Oskar thus carefully flings himself headfirst
down the cellar stairs. After the fall and four weeks of convalescence,
Oskar develops not only a lifelong passion for prolonged bouts of drumming but also a glass-shattering scream. But does "after" the fall mean
"because" of it or not? That, indeed, is exactly the sort of interpretive
decision *The Tin Drum* continually and consistently demands of its
reader. In this particular case, for example, there are several possible
conclusions we may reach as to what really happened. First, we may
take Oskar completely at his word: according to Oskar's account, it
wasn't a fall at all but a carefully orchestrated jump, designed to provide
an apparent explanation for a previous and calculated decision on his
part. Second, however, even if that was indeed Oskar's original plan,
there is the obvious possibility that the plan went wrong and he sustained at least some degree of mental as well as physical injury. To take
Oskar's account at its word again, his original plan was simply to stage a
fall that would explain why he wasn't growing any taller; there is no
mention of the glass-shattering voice as part of any plan. A third possibility is that there never was a plan in the first place, and Oskar simply
fell down the stairs as a three-year-old, sustaining permanent mental
and physical injury, including the extraordinary vocal side effects.
Fourth, while Oskar's mental and physical growth were both affected by
the fall as a three-year-old, there never was any glass-shattering voice in
the first place: Oskar himself admits that at the time of writing his
memoirs he has no such voice (*TD*, 72). Fifth, there was never any plan,
there was never any fall, there was never any glass-shattering voice, and
Oskar, possibly as the result of horrors experienced during the war years,
suppressed or disguised in the account we read, simply lost his mind at
some point and invents everything as a lunatic rationalization of how
things "must" (or might) have been. The one exception to this view is
the fact of his diminutive stature, which is independently reported by
Oskar's keeper, Bruno (*TD*, 428). Sixth, even his midget stature is simply an invention, for Oskar invents Bruno's narrative too, just as he

invents everything else we read. In this case, Oskar is either indeed completely insane, as his unbelievable narrative makes abundantly clear—or he is quite simply an author, whose job it is to invent things, including unbelievable things, just like his creator, Günter Grass, who after all does invent everything we read, including Oskar himself. One could, indeed, make a plausible case for any one of these options—and for other possibilities as well. The crucial question for the reader is how to decide which reading is more appropriate than any other.

Traditionally, the status of the narrator in a work of narrative fiction has been regarded as entirely above any suspicion of unreliability. From Homer to the late 1700s, whether the narrator was a so-called third-person narrator endowed with narrative omniscience and total recall or a first-person narrator who related his own story or someone else's, the reader was essentially in a position to take whatever he (or occasionally she) said completely at face value. The odd rogue elephant like *Tristram Shandy*, where the ostensible reliability of the narrator was shown to be purely a literary convention, was very much the tolerated and well-marked exception that proved the "natural" rule that the narrator, by definition, spoke the truth. While a central discursive function of most traditional narratives, fictional or otherwise, is thus to assist us in our readerly endeavors to reconstruct the story, *The Tin Drum* gains much of its distinctive fascination precisely from the way in which the discourse pervasively hinders us in determining exactly what the story told really is. Grass's text is by no means unique in this among modern and postmodern narratives, but it is a particularly brilliant example of the genre.

The problem with Oskar's story is that it is precisely Oskar's story, not only the story *of* Oskar but also and very emphatically the story *by* Oskar. At an early stage, Oskar himself obligingly draws our attention to the most essential characteristic of any story: its capacity for arrangement. "How shall I begin?" Oskar, as narrator, asks himself and the reader with ostensible ingenuousness. He proceeds to develop one or two of the available options: "You can begin a story in the middle and create confusion by striking out boldly, backward and forward. You can be modern, put aside all mention of time and distance and, when the whole thing is done, proclaim, or have someone else proclaim, that you have finally, at the last moment, solved the space-time problem. Or you can declare at the very start that it's impossible to write a novel nowadays, but then, behind your own back so to speak, give birth to a whopper, a novel to end all novels" (*TD*, 17). There are, indeed, any number of ways in which one can begin a story—and develop and conclude a story as well. In fact, by the time Oskar is assailed by such narratological considerations, his own narrative is already well underway. He has drawn attention to his status as a psychiatric patient; discussed the artistic tendencies of his keeper Bruno; and described his white-painted hospital bed with the bars, the embarrassment of visiting days, the commissioned purchase of a sufficient quantity of paper by Bruno, and Bruno's account of the furious blushes of the salesgirl who filled Oskar's order for 500 sheets of "virgin paper" (TD, 16).

Oskar's reflections on how one *might* begin a narrative might very well distract the reader's attention not only from their overt spuriousness (in that he has already begun) but also from the fact that both the single most important thematic concern of The Tin Drum, on the one hand, and its central narrative strategy, on the other, have also already been clearly marked in the ostensibly peripheral reference to the salesgirl's blushes. The very buying of the paper for Oskar's narrative is already implicated in the dialectic of guilt and innocence that is the central theme of Grass's quasi-historical novel of all too successful *Vergangenheitsbewältigung* (mastery of the past), as the German phrase has it— but the weightiness of such a theme finds expression by narrative means that are flauntedly inappropriate. Here the incipient theme of a nation's guilt, rather than being presented as the cataclysmic result of some national pact of mythic dimensions with the forces of evil, is reduced to its trivialized lowest common denominator, namely, the entirely everyday guilty conscience of entirely everyday people who are no better than they should be. In the process it is demonstrated that what society defines as guilt, or the lack of it, is a constructed and freely assignable quality: we witness neither the salesgirl's implied lack of innocence nor even her blushes; neither, moreover, does Oskar, who simply reports Bruno's report. Of course, he may even more simply have invented it, for we notice the suspiciously appropriate introduction at precisely this point of a color symbolism that will pervade his entire account: the salesgirl's red blushes concerning white paper foreshadow the red flames with which Koljaiczek burns down white sawmills and the red and white of the Polish flag, of nurse's uniforms, and of Oskar's tin drum that produces such artistic rearrangements of old favorites.[5]

The cumulative guilt of the nightmare years of German history is refracted and rearranged most overtly in Oskar's grotesquely distorted narrative of his own personal guilt or lack of it. Oskar's account, after all, is that of an insane killer, at least as far as the courts are concerned. Those courts found that he did indeed, though insane, kill one Sister

Dorothea Köngetter—whom Oskar freely admits to having also unsuc-cessfully attempted to rape on an earlier occasion. In the closing pages of his narrative, however, Oskar's thirtieth birthday brings what his lawyer calls "a happy coincidence" (TD, 578), with the discovery that the murder was "in fact" the handiwork of a jealous fellow nurse instead. The case is to be reopened, Oskar will be set free, as Oskar claims—and Oskar, again as Oskar claims, is terrified at the prospect, much prefer-ring the safety of his hospital bed to any freedom the outside world can offer him. The text offers considerable (though not conclusive) support for the case that Oskar did indeed kill Sister Dorothea (TD, 569); what is of more compelling interest to us here, however, is the suspiciously theatrical discovery, as the curtain falls, of his innocence all along. For Dorothea's death is by no means the first death in which Oskar, by his own account, is involved. Indeed, Oskar achieves the unique distinction, always according to his own account, of being no less than a triple parri-cide, for he claims at various points to be responsible for the death of all "three" of his parents. But "involved" is a very slippery word, and the details invite—indeed demand—considerable further scrutiny.

The first of the three deaths to occur is that of Oskar's mother. We note that though Oskar makes much of his own grief on that occasion, his initial account of Agnes's grotesque death—she gorges herself to death on fish—makes no mention of any feelings of guilt on his part (TD, 132). He first accuses himself—or rather reports that others accuse him—of having been responsible for his mother's death only consider-ably later, in an impassioned speech to the exotic Roswitha, when he claims that "everybody" says that "the gnome drummed her into her grave. Because of Oskar she didn't want to live any more; he killed her" (TD, 171). Immediately afterwards Oskar admits that he "was exagger-ating quite a bit, probably to impress Signora Roswitha" (TD, 171), since in fact most people blamed Matzerath and Bronski for her death. Only two or three pages later, however, Oskar abruptly reverses his story and informs the reader that he did indeed hear his grandmother saying that Agnes died "because she couldn't stand the drumming any more" (TD, 174). He immediately begins his next paragraph with the admission, "Even though guilty of my poor mama's death . . ." (TD, 174).

Oskar, in other words, apparently expects the reader to take at face value the admission of guilt he himself has just conceded was simply a ruse to make himself more interesting in Roswitha's Mediterranean eyes the last time he admitted (or claimed) it. Has Oskar had a change of heart in between, been granted the major insight that he was not, after all, exaggerating when he spun what he thought was a fancy tale for Roswitha's benefit? At any rate, Oskar seems to think so (or wants to make us think so): some 60 pages later he talks of his involvement in Jan Bronski's death as definitely "my second great burden of guilt," for "even when I feel most sorry for myself, I cannot deny it: it was my drum, no, it was I myself, Oskar the drummer, who dispatched first my poor mama, then Jan Bronski, my uncle and father, to their graves" (TD, 247).

The occasion of Bronski's death was the quixotically futile defense of the Polish Post Office in September 1939. As Oskar presents it, however, Bronski is no hero prepared to die for his beliefs, defending his homeland against the German oppressor. In fact, Jan had already fled the Post Office once and finds himself there again only because Oskar persuades him to take him there to ask the janitor Kobyella to repair one of his broken tin drums. Far from fighting for his country, Bronski is discovered after the battle in a back room, half dead with fear, dazedly attempting to play a three-handed card game with Kobyella, who is quietly bleeding to death, and Oskar, who reveals himself as an expert card player and has little patience with the sloppy play of the other two. Jan is duly taken away to be shot by the quickly victorious Germans, the Queen of Hearts still pathetically clutched in his hand as the condemned man waves a last good-bye to a grieving Oskar.

Or something like that, at any rate, for Oskar begins his next chapter by observing that he has just reread the account of Bronski's arrest and is not entirely satisfied. Moreover, "even though I am not too well pleased, Oskar's pen ought to be, for writing tersely and succinctly, it has managed, as terse, succinct accounts so often do, to exaggerate and mislead, if not to lie" (TD, 246). There are three separate points that need correction, in fact, for Oskar "wishes to stick to the truth, to go behind Oskar's pen's back and make a few corrections" (TD, 246). First, Jan's final hand had been incorrectly described, for it was "not a grand hand but a diamond hand without twos." Second, Oskar left not just with a new drum he had accidentally found, as previously reported, but with his old one as well, just in case. And third, "a little omission that needs filling in," when the soldiers led the defenders out of the Post Office, "Oskar made up to two Home Guards who looked like good-natured uncles, pretended he was looking for protection, put on an imitation of pathetic sniveling, and pointed to Jan, his father, with accusing gestures that transformed the poor man into a villain who had dragged off an innocent child into the Polish Post Office to use him, with typically Polish inhumanity, as a buffer for enemy bullets" (*TD*, 246). Oskar's ruse, he reports, saves his two drums from any possible damage, as he had planned it would, while Jan is conscientiously kicked and beaten by the properly scandalized German soldiers before being led off to be shot. Oskar's guilt still haunts him: "But like everyone else I make allowances for my ignorance, the ignorance that came into style in those years and that even today is worn by so many like such a becoming little hat" (*TD*, 248).

As the Second World War, in Oskar's telling of it, opens with the Polish Bronski's death, so it closes symmetrically with the death of the German Matzerath, Oskar's "other" father, who is cowering in a cellar with his family when Russian troops burst in, just as German troops had once burst into the storage room where Jan was hiding. Matzerath hurriedly attempts to hide the damning evidence of his political colors by kicking his Nazi party pin into a dark corner of the cellar, where Oskar retrieves it. Under the eyes of the Russians, Oskar obligingly passes the pin back to Matzerath, who, in desperation, foolishly tries to swallow it. "If only he had first . . . closed the pin" (*TD*, 394), Oskar philosophically observes in retrospect. As it is, the frantically gagging Matzerath is saved from choking to death only because one of the Russians equally obligingly "emptied a whole magazine into him before Matzerath could suffocate" (*TD*, 394).

As in the case of Bronski's death, Oskar's complicity is again evident, but the form of its presentation makes it read, at worst, like a childish lack of understanding. Oskar admittedly claims he had in fact first fought his "son" Kurt for the discarded pin, on the grounds that it would be far too dangerous for Kurt to have if the Russians found it, yet he casually passes it (pin thoughtfully opened) to his presumptive father, allegedly because he needs free hands to pick a louse off the collar of one of the Russians. He then promptly loses interest in the lice and goes back to watching a column of marching ants. Perhaps it was not the right thing to do, Oskar admits in retrospect: "You may say I shouldn't have done that. But one could also say that Matzerath didn't have to take it" (*TD*, 393). One can, in fact, once again, say anything one wants, and this is a freedom Oskar exercises to the full.

Perhaps the most revealing self-narrated example of Oskar's "guilt," however, is his account of his grandfather's death. Joseph Koljaiczek is first said by Oskar to have drowned while on the run from the police, attempting to make good his escape by swimming out to a raft in the mouth of the Mottlau river. Apparently there are those who do not accept this story, however. "My grandfather's body was never found. Though I have no doubt whatever that he met his death under the raft, I suppose if I am to retain my credibility I have to put down all of the variants in which he was miraculously rescued" (*TD*, 36). In order to remain thus "credible," Oskar goes on to give these competing versions—ostensibly other people's, not his own—of how Koljaiczek met his end. One of these is that Koljaiczek simply hid under the raft until it was dark, then escaped unscathed on a Greek tanker. Another is that Koljaiczek swam underwater clear across the river, emerged undetected on the other side, and eventually left the country on a Greek tanker— "here the first two versions converge" (*TD*, 37). Only "for the sake of completeness" does Oskar mention "the third preposterous fable" that his grandfather is washed out to sea, picked up by Swedish sailors, escapes to Sweden, "and so on and so on" (*TD*, 27). Even more nonsensical than all this "nonsense and fishermen's fish stories" is the further fairy tale that his grandfather was seen five years or so later in Buffalo, New York, by then a highly successful businessman living under the name of Joe Colchic (*TD*, 37). Within three pages it is precisely this last version that Oskar, without further comment, adopts as historical fact (*TD*, 40).

We are at liberty, as psychologically acute readers, to interpret Oskar's evasiveness when it comes to matters of personal guilt as symptomatic of an obsessively guilty conscience. His conscious or unconscious desire to direct attention away from his real guilt in the death of Sister Dorothea, we might thus reason, leads to extravagantly exaggerated self-accusation in cases where he is either obviously innocent (Koljaiczek), very likely innocent (Agnes), or in all likelihood only very peripherally involved as a possible minor contributing factor (Bronski would have been shot anyway, Matzerath might well have survived if he had not panicked so disastrously). But to indulge in such an eminently reasonable interpretation is to fall spectacularly into the hermeneutic mantrap that is the central characteristic of *The Tin Drum* as a whole: namely, that we take seriously stories that are quite literally entirely impossible to believe.

Critics have indulged in vigorous debate as to which sides of Oskar's narrated personality represent the "real" Oskar, which of his narrated actions are real and which only fantasized. But in the end, the only thing we can be sure of about Oskar is that he does indeed narrate. Oskar is less the literary simulacrum of a human being than a disembodied narrative voice; a "dressmaker's dummy" (*TD*, 95), who is less a character than a literary device; a "realized contrivance," in Ann Mason's phrase (Mason, 28), for generating possible narratives inviting possible responses—including extratextual narratives that are implied rather than narrated, possible narratives implied by impossible narratives.

The narrative art of *The Tin Drum* is an art of indirection, allowing us to glimpse things not by making us stare straight at them but by directing our attention to something beside them or beyond them or where they should be but are missing or to something else entirely that might remind us of them, whether because of the existence of some more or less logical connection or, more often, because of an implied connection that is outrageously inappropriate. Grass's brilliant use of disturbingly astigmatic objective correlatives—typical of the narrative strategy of the text throughout—has been noted by almost all critics. Agnes's long-drawn-out dying is introduced by a meticulous description of her vomited breakfast (*TD*, 150); the greengrocer Greff's suicide is counterpointed by a "washbasin with the grey soapsuds from the previous day" in a dingy room that needed Greff's death "to achieve a new, terrifyingly cold radiance" (*TD*, 313); Matzerath's death fails to disturb a column of marching ants, for the sugar they are salvaging from a burst sack "had lost none of its sweetness while Marshal Rokossovski was occupying the city of Danzig" (*TD*, 395).

Gaudily painted "symbols" whose flaunted symbolicity invites skepticism likewise abound, the most relevant of them in our present context being that "Black Witch"—"Don't ask Oskar who she is! Words fail him" (*TD*, 589)—whose (alleged) omnipresence allows Oskar to conclude his account with a gratifying portrayal of abject existential terror. So overwhelming is this terror that the reader might well forget Oskar's previous claim that his fright was initially self-induced in order to lend some realistic motivation to his flight—"No fright, no flight" (*TD*, 580). The flight, in turn, was allegedly undertaken merely out of consideration for his friend Vittlar, who has just turned him in to the police. Vittlar's denunciation, for its part, had "in fact" been at Oskar's generous suggestion, since Vittlar had always wanted to see his name in the papers (*TD*, 576).

The reflexivity and unreliability of Oskar's account are underscored, paradoxically, by the fact that he allows parts of it to be narrated by two other narrators, whose independent testimony might perhaps be expected to serve as yardsticks against which Oskar's own account might be measured. The two narrators in question, however, are Vittlar and Bruno, and each of their narratives, while in some degree corrective of Oskar's own account, very quickly reveals itself as equally untrustworthy—if not entirely Oskar's own invention. Vittlar, a window dresser by trade, is first discovered lying in the fork of an apple tree and takes the opportunity himself of drawing attention to inviting Biblical parallels (*TD*, 470). "Vittlar always liked to confuse me" (*TD*, 578). His account (*TD*, 563–76), which largely concerns Oskar's fantastic rescue of Viktor Weluhn, a onetime defender of the Polish Post Office, from the hands of the West German police in 1952, hardly inspires confidence in Vittlar as an independent witness. Bruno Münsterberg, "him on his side of the peephole, me on mine" (*TD*, 17), provides an account of Oskar's flight from Danzig (*TD*, 419–28) that is in a considerably more sober style, but, to say the least, is also rendered somewhat suspect by Bruno's own artistic leanings. For Bruno, like Oskar, is an artist, too, who "knots ordinary pieces of string . . . into elaborate contorted spooks, dips them in plaster, lets them harden" (*TD*, 15). He discusses with Oskar whether they would be more effective if he added color. Listening to Oskar's stories, Bruno reshapes them in string and plaster, but like Oskar, he is frequently dissatisfied with the end result: "what I knot with my right hand, I undo with my left; what my left hand creates, my right fist shatters" (*TD*, 424).

Bruno and Vittlar are members of a whole series of quasi-artist figures that ghost through the pages of *The Tin Drum*. These figures include Oskar's friend Klepp, who assists Oskar in cutting up and reassembling passport photos of themselves, creating, they hope, new and happier combinations (*TD*, 52); Bebra, leader of a troupe of midget circus acrobats, whose most successful trick is knowing how always to be on the winning side; Roswitha Raguna, *femme fatale* and most famous somnambulist of all Italy; Schugger Leo, who is gloriously mad and conjures up glowing visions of redemption before he dies riddled with bullets; Meyn, the storm trooper who plays the trumpet so beautifully when not otherwise engaged; and Corporal Lankes, who has a thing about nuns, casually machine-gunning a group of them during the war, equally casually raping another after the war, and subsequently establishing an artistic reputation as a painter of accomplished studies of nuns. Grass himself notes, in an interview, the extent to which all of these (quasi-)artist figures are hypothetical extensions of Oskar himself, "marginal figures as footnotes to the marginal figure Oskar,"[6] developing further possibilities of his character, synecdochic projections and reflections alike of the artist/historian's ability both to shape and to distort the reality on which he draws, and, in any event, either to accept or to reject as he chooses any given degree of responsibility for the results of his labors.

In the end, *The Tin Drum,* by relentlessly urging the reader throughout to recognize the total unreliability of its narrator, invites the reader to confront the question of narrative unreliability itself, the question as to how reliable any discourse can ever be, since discourse is always a matter not just of presentation but of context-appropriate presentation, putting things in a particular perspective, a particular context—and your context is not necessarily mine, nor mine yours. What is true of literary narrative is equally true of historical narrative, even if one of the most enduring generic conventions of the latter has been its concealment of its own fictionality. The readiness with which Oskar admits to, or even eagerly claims, guilt for events that are clearly not his responsibility very overtly implies the possible existence of other events for which certain readers in the Germany of 1959 were perhaps equally unwilling to accept responsibility. The narrative draws the reader's attention to what is omitted by allowing Oskar to exaggerate grotesquely what is not omitted. By unsettling the reader's reaction to Oskar, who is allowed to present himself now as an innocent and defenseless child, now as a complete monster, now as a freedom fighter, now as the very face of Nazism itself, *The Tin Drum* pervasively implies the degree to which the line between such comfortingly black and white positions can be a shifting one. It also implies the degree to which the determination of that line is not just the author's but also the reader's responsibility.

Chapter Four
Cat and Mouse

While Oskar's story in *The Tin Drum* is played out against the backdrop of half a century of German history, the narrated time of *Cat and Mouse* is just five years. The story is related several years later by a narrator whose subsequent life seems to have been indelibly stamped by those few years. The narrator is a now 32-year-old social worker named Pilenz, and the story he tells is of the rise and fall of his best friend, Joachim Mahlke, during the troubled years between 1939 and 1944, when they were both adolescents, growing up in wartime Danzig. The resulting narrative—in which what is not told is at least as important as what is told—is one of the richest and most fascinating of modern German literature.

The story of Mahlke, in its broad outline, is a simple and a poignant one, an account of the psychological problems of a troubled teenager and their fatal outcome. As a sickly 14-year-old, Mahlke is an only child who lives with his mother and an aunt, having lost his father in a railway accident. He can neither swim nor ride a bicycle and is excused from school gymnastics classes on health grounds. The following summer, however, suddenly spurred on by his friends' tall tales of heroic exploits on the partly submerged wreck of a minesweeper sunk in the mouth of Danzig harbor, Mahlke quickly learns both to swim and to dive. Although his style is reportedly atrocious, he soon completely outstrips all comers in both areas, especially in diving, where he performs feats of great daring and endurance.

There is clearly a considerable element of overcompensation in these impressive achievements, for that same summer he also begins to wear a screwdriver around his neck, the first of several such accoutrements—multicolored woolen pompoms, a large can opener, huge safety pins, heavy scarves—with which he attempts to distract attention from the bane of his life in those years, a "gigantic" Adam's apple that attracts much juvenile ridicule from his fellows. A silver medal portraying the Madonna also gyrates wildly around his neck as he now performs similarly unbeatable and equally awkward feats in gym class, for Mahlke is of both Roman Catholic and (as the name suggests) Polish origins.

Among the various schoolboy treasures he salvages from areas of the wreck that no one else can reach are a bronze medallion of the Polish hero Marshal Pilsudski and a silver medal showing another Polish icon, the Black Madonna of Czestochowa. Mahlke is unable to display either of these unpatriotic articles on school premises, however, since Dr. Klohse, the principal of the Conradinum High School—"a high party official, though he seldom wore his uniform at school"—expressly forbids it.[1]

Mahlke rapidly becomes the uncontested center of attention among his peers, partly because of his now unrivaled athletic prowess, partly because of an equally unrivaled ability to make them laugh. He even plans, for a while, to become a clown when he grows up, so that he can keep everybody laughing. His exploits become increasingly impressive—and increasingly outlandish. He outdoes all challengers in memorizing detailed schoolboy lists of military statistics; salvages from the wreck a phonograph that he is even able to make work; salvages a long-submerged can of frogs' legs that he calmly eats on the spot before a gagging audience; develops a fanatic and ostentatious devotion to the Virgin Mary; and performs heroic feats of public masturbation that beggar all competition.

By the summer of 1942 Mahlke is 17, and his apparently almost pathological need to impress suddenly takes a new and quite different turn as the result of separate surprise visits to the Conradinum by two recent graduates who are now officers and war heroes. Each of these heroes proudly wears Germany's highest military honor, the Knight's Cross. The particular decoration is significant: the Knight's Cross is not only the highest of the three grades of the prestigious and historical Iron Cross instituted in 1813; while the Iron Cross first and second class are both worn on the chest, the Knight's Cross, as if expressly designed to conceal Mahlke's overgrown Adam's apple, is worn on a band around the neck.

The first of the two visitors is a young Luftwaffe lieutenant who has shot down 44 enemy planes in winning his Iron Cross. He delivers an inspirational address to the assembled schoolboys on life in the air force at war, a life demanding personal qualities that he portrays as not very different from those demanded of any member of the school sports teams (*CM*, 46). Mahlke listens to his presentation with a mixture of tense excitement and obvious anxiety, as the watching Pilenz relates. The air force lieutenant is followed by a second celebrity, a submarine commander, who paints equally glowing pictures of the wonders of the deep and the poetry of war. This commander's Knight's Cross mysteriously goes missing during the course of his visit. At about this time the nickname "The Great Mahlke" achieves currency, for it soon becomes clear that the thief is none other than Mahlke. Pilenz discovers him on the minesweeper, sitting stark naked except for the purloined Knight's Cross around his neck. What never emerges, even for the reader, is why Mahlke almost immediately decides to return the stolen decoration to Principal Klohse—and, not surprisingly, is immediately expelled for his pains.

Mahlke is transferred to another school and is seen no more on the minesweeper. He becomes an ostentatiously pious churchgoer, develops a new self-confidence that allows him to laugh about his onetime obsession with the size of his Adam's apple, and eventually volunteers for active service in the submarines. He is accepted instead into the infantry, where he distinguishes himself in action before being transferred to a panzer regiment and duly promoted to sergeant. His conscientiously regular letters home to his mother and aunt are now often embellished with tallies of the number of enemy tanks he has knocked out. Just two years after his expulsion in disgrace from the Conradinum for the theft of the U-boat commander's Knight's Cross he triumphantly wins his own, presented by the hand of the Führer himself.

This moment of glory, the pinnacle of his career, is all too fleeting, however. Sergeant Mahlke takes advantage of his eagerly awaited next leave to return in full regalia to the Conradinum in expectation of a hero's welcome. He has in his pocket the lecture he has meticulously prepared and that he expects to be invited to deliver to the assembled school, but he is peremptorily refused permission by Dr. Klohse, for disciplinary reasons, to address the institution he has so recently dishonored. Pilenz, Mahlke's friend through thick and thin, arranges for several alternative invitations to speak, but Mahlke refuses all such attempted consolation. Instead of returning to his regiment once his leave is over, Mahlke abruptly goes absent without leave—though not before having stiffly and formally slapped Klohse twice across the face. At Pilenz's urging, he agrees to hide out, at least temporarily, on the half-submerged wreck that had been the scene of his boyhood triumphs. A favorite refuge of his there had been the onetime radio shack, situated above the waterline though accessible only after the sort of prolonged and difficult dive that Mahlke alone could perform and had performed many times. Carrying enough provisions to see him through the next few days, Mahlke dives once more—and (at least according to Pilenz) never again resurfaces.

The qualification in the previous sentence is very necessary, however, for the more we examine Pilenz's role in Mahlke's story, as related by Pilenz himself, the more complex and the more suspect it becomes. When Mahlke dives for the last time he is carrying two two-pound cans of pork that Pilenz, a friend in need, has managed to find for him. What he is *not* carrying, however, is the can opener that Pilenz has indeed remembered to bring—but has carefully kept hidden under his boot until after Mahlke dives. Only after Mahlke has already been underwater for some time does Pilenz begin to pound long and hard on the deck to remind him of the can opener. When there is no response, he eventually rows back to shore—but only after flinging the can opener as far out to sea as he can throw. The psychological complexity of Pilenz's motivation in this climactic scene of the narrative has, in fact, been in evidence throughout, if never so pointedly.

Pilenz's first-person narrative begins with the group of schoolboys lying between games in the grass of the school sports field, "one day, after Mahlke had learned to swim" (*CM*, 7). Pilenz, lying beside Mahlke, has a throbbing toothache that he manages to forget only in a sudden moment of excitement when the caretaker's cat, attracted by the jerky swallowing motion of Mahlke's newly developed Adam's apple, abruptly leaps at Mahlke's throat, causing Mahlke to yell out in momentary fright, though he suffers only superficial scratches. No sooner has Pilenz related the incident, however, than he doubly qualifies it—in the space of a single sentence—in a manner strongly reminiscent of Oskar's account of Jan Bronski's death. Perhaps the cat did not exactly leap, perhaps "one of us caught the cat and held it up to Mahlke's neck; or I, with or without my toothache, seized the cat and showed it Mahlke's mouse" (*CM*, 8). The incident gives the narrative its title and is entirely emblematic of the cat-and-mouse relationship that develops between Mahlke and the group—and most particularly between Mahlke and Pilenz.

The incident is also emblematic of Pilenz's procedure as narrator, for, again and again, the reader will encounter episodes characterized by a similar narrative ambivalence. Pilenz, it emerges later in the narrative, is writing his account in 1960, 16 years after Mahlke's disappearance and 20 years after the incident just related, so allowances certainly need to be made on the reader's part for possible lapses of memory. The ostentatious uncertainty of Pilenz's formulation, however, seems to make a point of inviting an equally uncertain reading. Perhaps Pilenz really cannot remember the exact details of the cat-and-"mouse" incident, insignificant in itself; perhaps, guilt-ridden still by his own part in Mahlke's apparent self-destruction, he assigns himself a greater role in the incident than was actually the case; perhaps, on the other hand, since even a dead hero is still a hero (and in many ways easier to deal with than a live hero), he actually wishes to magnify his own role in the entire affair, as, indeed, in Mahlke's life and accomplishments in general. Pilenz's presentational style ensures that the reader's response will also be characterized by a systemic uncertainty.

Pilenz's relationship to Mahlke, in short, is characterized from the beginning by an intense ambivalence, examples of which may be found on almost every page of the narrative. Admiration, even hero-worship, is certainly a major factor, for Mahlke succeeds in doing almost everything he attempts better than anybody else, and certainly better than Pilenz. Pilenz's interest in Mahlke, as he occasionally admits, does not seem to be reciprocated to any significant degree: "I admired you, even though you were not trying to arouse my admiration" (CM, 25). A tentative suggestion that they were, in fact, close friends who sat at the same desk in school is casually advanced, then immediately retracted, but only partially (CM, 26). And again, much later, Pilenz relates that "I alone could be termed his friend, if it was possible to be friends with Mahlke" (CM, 73).

Certainly Pilenz sees himself as an insider, one of the gang, while Mahlke was always an outsider: "We racked our brains and we couldn't understand you" (CM, 26). "Of course we admired Mahlke," Pilenz writes of himself and his friends, but sometimes "we thought him so repulsive we couldn't look at him"; sometimes "we felt moderately sorry for him. We were also afraid of Mahlke; he bullied us. And I was ashamed to be seen on the street with him. And I was proud . . ." (CM, 57). When a talented classmate, to great general glee, draws a strikingly successful caricature on the school blackboard of a Mahlke with piously sorrowful features, halo, and "monstrous Adam's apple" (CM, 35), it is Pilenz who wipes his "Redeemer's countenance" (CM, 35) off the board. While, on a first reading, readers are likely to see this as the tactfully supportive act of a friend, Pilenz's motivation becomes considerably more questionable in retrospect. When some years later he finds Mahlke's name carved into one of the boards of an army latrine, he takes an ax and likewise obliterates it (CM, 99).

All of this, of course, we know only from Pilenz's own narrative, and that narrative is once again, like Oskar's, not merely unreliable but frankly advertises and even flaunts its own unreliability and ambivalence. Pilenz's account demonstrates an extreme self-consciousness, an extreme awareness of the artistically constructed (and thus retractable) nature of his own apparent confession and of his own advanced ability to situate remembered events in one context or another, as appropriate (*CM*, 8). The apparent compulsion to confess is balanced by an at least equally powerful compulsion to manipulate. It is reasonable, for example, that Pilenz may well have forgotten in which particular summer something or other happened (*CM*, 17), but the reader will find it less reasonable, to take just one example, that he should have forgotten that Mahlke lived not on Osterzeile but on Westerzeile when he remembers quite clearly that his own house was on Westerzeile (*CM*, 19). Such lapses of memory are accompanied by evidence of real or ostensible lack of insight: "we couldn't understand you" (*CM*, 26), Pilenz admits (or claims), and "as for his soul, it was never introduced to me" (*CM*, 29). Lapses of memory and lack of insight alike are complemented by artistic license. Pilenz refers in passing, for example, to Mahlke's hands being sticky from running them over his hair, which he kept in place with sugar water, but he then observes that perhaps they were not sticky at all, perhaps he had just inferred their stickiness from the remembered sugar water. The admission of artistic license in this insignificant instance may well cause the reader to wonder how many other—and more significant—instances of it there might be.

What we never unambiguously discover, however, is the degree to which such lapses are conscious or unconscious—or the degree to which their primary purpose is to deceive the reader or to deceive Pilenz himself. For more than half of the entire narrative, the narrating Pilenz remains nameless, concealing an identity he suddenly (but, typically, only partially) reveals—"I, Pilenz—what has my first name got to do with it?" (*CM*, 73). This revelation comes only in the middle of the eighth of 13 chapters, as he recounts how he swam out alone to the wreck where he knew he would find Mahlke with the stolen Knight's Cross.

Guilt is ambiguously central to Pilenz's narrative—as it was to Oskar's. Pilenz's account has to do not only with the destruction of Joachim Mahlke but also with his own need (for whatever reason) to reconstruct and recontextualize the degree of his personal involvement and responsibility. Pilenz, who, like Mahlke, is a Catholic (*CM*, 54), and who spends his free hours after his daily duties as a social worker reading "the *Confessions* of good old St. Augustine" (*CM*, 73), as he tells us, is writing on the pastoral advice of his priest, in order to finally come to grips with a half-buried past that is tormenting him: "I can't help writing, for you can't keep such things to yourself" (*CM*, 76). His attempt at self-therapy and self-absolution, however, is clearly less than wholly successful. "Who will supply me with a good ending?" (*CM*, 126), he asks, even in the third-to-last paragraph of his confession, any hoped-for catharsis far less in evidence than the continuing attempt to reshape the tormenting past.

Cat and Mouse is centered on the eponymous cat-and-mouse relationship of Mahlke and Pilenz, a relationship portrayed as indelibly stamped by the corrupt society of the Third Reich that fosters it. That society is crucially marked, as it was in *The Tin Drum*, by a latent savagery just barely concealed under a facade of fatal boredom and deadening sameness. Those conditions emerge repeatedly from the text in a variety of examples, some peripheral and some monstrously central: the bored teenagers lounging idly on the wreck waiting for anything at all to happen; the skinny preteen nymphet, Tulla, ready to do just about anything for a little excitement; each little front garden just like every other, each boasting its individuality with green ceramic frogs that all look exactly the same (*CM*, 20); the popular but politically embarrassing teacher "Papa" Brunies who is discreetly spirited off to a concentration camp; a pervasive remembered smell of stewed onions in those years that, for the narrating Pilenz, "contaminated all Germany, West Prussia and Langfuhr, Osterzeile as well as Westerzeile, preventing the smell of corpses from taking over completely" (*CM*, 87).

The Conradinum High School becomes the central emblem of this perverted society and its need for scapegoats and victims: "it was the school that drove you, later on, to your supreme effort" (*CM*, 34), as Pilenz ambiguously puts it. Before Mahlke admits to having stolen the Knight's Cross, teachers and students alike pick an immediate scapegoat in the unfortunate Buschmann, who must obviously be guilty since a facial tic gives him a permanent uneasy grin, even under rigorous interrogation (*CM*, 66). Pilenz "hopes" he wasn't one of the many students who ensured Papa Brunies's removal to the concentration camp by testifying against him (*CM*, 37). Just before Mahlke's existence is finally undermined by Klohse's refusal to allow him to deliver his speech, Pilenz finds him waiting in front of a glass display case containing a stuffed cat that only needs a mouse to pounce on to make it entirely realistic (*CM*, 104). Pilenz himself is deeply, if ambiguously, implicated in this cycle of viciousness and exploitation: it was he after all (or was it?) who symbolically initiates Mahlke's destruction by the act of setting the cat onto his "mouse," the overgrown Adam's apple that fatally marks him as perennial outsider and victim.

The peculiar motivational ambiguity that marks Mahlke's behavior may be read as a function of his inability to escape this role of sacrificial victim, as John Reddick has suggested (Reddick, 132). The medals, pompoms, can openers, screwdrivers, and other assorted paraphernalia he affects as a boy are all ostensibly intended to divert attention from his fatal flaw, but they also and obviously attract attention to it and to him. Mahlke, a victim of his own enforced overcompensation, moves from underachievement to overachievement, from the relative safety of initial anonymity to the fatal exposure of unmatchable prowess—"from the very first day he was tops" (CM, 11)—and thus makes himself ripe for destruction. Indeed, he connives in his own destruction from the moment he decides not only to steal the Knight's Cross but to return it. His motivation here is entirely obscure: scruples, misjudgment, simple overconfidence, contempt for the school or the system as a whole, or even a desperate desire for recognition at all costs—all are possibilities, but none offers a complete explanation.

Grass's original working title for what became *Cat and Mouse* was "Der Ritterkreuzträger" (The Holder of the Knight's Cross). The change of title appropriately reflects the double focus of the narrative and the complexity of the relationship between its two chief actors. For while Mahlke's Adam's apple is most obviously at once mouse (in attracting ridicule and persecution) and cat (in chasing Mahlke through life, forcing him to deeds of exaggerated compensation), Pilenz is likewise both cat and mouse with regard to Mahlke. As cat, Pilenz is the most obvious representative of the diseased society that finally destroys Mahlke; as mouse, he is obsessed with Mahlke, whose presence, however ambivalently Pilenz reports himself as reacting to it, gave his life form and meaning then, just as his absence does now.

The fall of Mahlke is clearly paralleled in the narrative by the rise of Pilenz, who takes complete control of the demoralized Mahlke during the final pages of the story. Pilenz bullies Mahlke into taking refuge on the wreck, lies to him that the military police have already been asking his mother questions, first provides and then throws away the vital can opener, and finally fails to return to the wreck, even though he has specifically promised to do so. Mahlke's final disappearance, however, paradoxically gives him the upper hand over Pilenz once again.

For Pilenz, the reshapable past is employed to fill an empty present, the psychological need to repress a possibly incriminating past balanced by a need to emphasize, even to exaggerate, his own role in it. His compulsion to confess is balanced by an equally powerful compulsion to manipulate the story told, a balancing of exposure and flight that strikingly parallels Mahlke's pendulation between similar extremes. The essential ambivalence of Pilenz's account and its continual search for the most retrospectively appropriate narrative distance are most obviously signaled in the text by his constant shifting between "you" and "he" to refer to Mahlke, much as Oskar's (narrated) ambivalence toward his own (narrated) past is signaled in *The Tin Drum* by his constant shifting between "I" and "Oskar" to refer to himself.

What makes *Cat and Mouse* a particularly fascinating text is that Pilenz, as Ann Mason observes, is well aware of all this, consciously portraying both his own ambivalence and his portrayal of that ambivalence. Echoing Oskar, he is a "kind of post-Freudian character, simultaneously neurotic and aware of the mechanism of his neurosis" (Mason, 65). In *The Tin Drum,* Grass clearly demonstrated his skepticism toward the redemptive power of literature. In *Cat and Mouse,* the satiric edge is equally evident in the parodically self-reflective use of the confessional mode "to point up its own inadequacy: it is just one more literary convention that Pilenz can utilize and manipulate, without being able to get beyond himself to either truth or catharsis" (Mason, 66).

"If only I knew who made up the story, he or I, or who is writing this in the first place" (*CM,* 89), Pilenz somewhat theatrically muses at one point, referring to an offhand account by Mahlke himself of the emblematic cat-and-mouse incident and indicatively stylizing his own writing as potentially Mahlke's. In fact, Pilenz's account contains a number of highly suggestive points of contact between Mahlke and himself, points whose psychological relevance or lack of relevance is left up to the reader to gauge. Mahlke, an only child, lost his father at an early age. His father, a locomotive engineer, was killed in a train crash, but he died a hero by managing to prevent the whole train from being wrecked and was awarded a medal posthumously. His father's heroism is clearly important to Mahlke, who relates the story to Pilenz casually but with obvious pride (*CM,* 89). His mother seems to play only a minor role in his life, at least according to Pilenz, who emphasizes instead Mahlke's fanatic devotion to the Virgin, who, again according to Pilenz, is the only woman in his life: "Apart from the Virgin he didn't have much truck with girls. . . . His relations with Tulla Pokriefke don't count, they were an anomaly" (*CM,* 29). At another point, however, Pilenz recounts without further comment a report that Mahlke got into

trouble in the army by having a very vigorous affair with his command-
ing officer's wife (*CM*, 100).

Pilenz's father, on the other hand, seems to have little importance for
Pilenz. He is mentioned only in the context of his mother's flaunted infi-
delity, for while his father "was sending APO letters from Greece, my
mother was indulging in intimate relations, mostly with noncoms" (*CM*,
88). Moreover, while Mahlke is justifiably proud of his hero father,
Pilenz has a hero brother whom he resents bitterly. His mother, who
pays little attention to Pilenz himself, idolizes this dead elder brother,
Klaus (whose first name Pilenz does mention, we may notice, though he
omits mentioning his own), who fell in battle as a sergeant and wearer
of the Iron Cross, both first and second class (*CM*, 97). The degree to
which Pilenz's role in the destruction of the decorated war hero Mahlke
may be read as a displaced fratricidal impulse is left to the reader to
decide—as is the significance of one of Pilenz's last acts. After deposit-
ing Mahlke on the wreck and before complying with his own draft
papers, Pilenz purloins Mahlke's prized photograph of his father, only to
lose it later in action (*CM*, 126).

Pilenz's ambivalent account of Mahlke's sexual prowess is coupled
with the self-ironizing admission of his own sexual failure and its importance to him: while his friends "rollicked to the best of [their] ability in
the beach thistles, always with the same girls or their sisters, I alone
accomplished nothing at all. Hesitation was my trouble; I haven't got
over it yet, and this weakness of mine still inspires me with the same
ironical reflections" (*CM*, 93). The specific focus of his attention is the
same Tulla with whom Mahlke's alleged relations allegedly "don't
count" (*CM*, 29)—and whom Pilenz remembers (or at any rate presents)
as at once a link and an obstacle between him and Mahlke. Perhaps
indicatively, Pilenz claims to be unable to remember either one of them
precisely as far as their physical features are concerned, even with the
help of his friends, whom he consults several years later: "in the end we
weren't sure whether we hadn't mixed up Mahlke and Tulla" (*CM*, 34).
The inadequately remembered Tulla becomes one more component of
the ambivalently manipulative process of writing toward a remembered
or constructed intimacy with Mahlke: "As I swam and as I write, I tried
and I try to think of Tulla Pokriefke, for I didn't and still don't want to
think of Mahlke" (*CM*, 72).

The centerpiece of the Danzig trilogy, *Cat and Mouse* is marked by a
formal restraint and economy of expression that is strikingly different
from the baroque luxuriance of either its immediate predecessor, *The Tin*

Drum, or its immediate successor, *Dog Years.* While *The Tin Drum* tells a sprawling story set against the backdrop of the entire sweep of twentieth-century German history, *Cat and Mouse* limits itself to a closely focused vignette framed by the years of the Second World War in Danzig. Its characters are entirely realistically portrayed, with little of the grotesquerie and none of the magic realism of either *The Tin Drum* or *Dog Years.* It is the story of a double failure: Mahlke's to adjust, Pilenz's to forget. It is also the story of a highly dubious friendship, an emblematic tale of betrayal and victimization, told from the perspective of an appropriately (but not always entirely convincingly) rueful aggressor. Grass returns to this productive constellation in *Dog Years,* the final volume of the Danzig trilogy, in the equally dubious friendship of Walter Matern for Eduard Amsel, another variation on betrayal and victimization, related this time, however, from the perspective of the victim.

Chapter Five
Dog Years

The long and complicated story of *Hundejahre* (1963; translated by Ralph Manheim as *Dog Years*), is presented in three books. The first is divided into 33 chapters or "Morning Shifts," as Manheim accurately translates, although the German also implies "early layers." These comprise an account by one Brauxel (or Brauksel or Brauchsel, as he also variously spells it, the variation in spelling an early indication of the indeterminacy of his character) of the boyhood years in Danzig of Eddi Amsel (which turns out, much later, to have been Brauxel's original name) and Walter Matern. Amsel, a natural victim as a schoolboy because of his excessive fatness, is the son of a prosperous Jewish merchant cautiously turned Protestant; Matern, whose most striking characteristic is a frequent and furious grinding of his teeth, is the son of a Catholic flour miller. Matern's initial relentless bullying of Amsel eventually changes to an equally obsessive (but by no means always reliable) friendship, and he duly becomes Amsel's devoted (but uncertain) henchman and protector. Amsel, for his part, begins at an early age to demonstrate a marked artistic talent, though his abilities manifest themselves somewhat unusually (reminiscent of Oskar's early artistic prowess as a drummer) in the construction of highly imaginative and highly effective scarecrows.

The second book, "Love Letters," takes up the story where the first leaves off, and does so in a quite different stylistic vein. It consists of a lengthy series of "letters" ostensibly written by Harry Liebenau, son of a Langfuhr cabinetmaker, to his cousin Ursula Pokriefke. Ursula's nickname is Tulla, and we are already familiar with her from *Cat and Mouse*. Harry is as infatuated with her as Pilenz was, and the continuing story of Matern's obsession with Amsel is now strongly colored by Harry's own continuing obsession with Tulla, who, for her part, has only limited time for him and enjoys nothing so much as getting other people into as much trouble as possible. The second book (like the second book of *The Tin Drum*) covers the fatal years of National Socialism and the war. Matern (reminiscent of Klepp in *The Tin Drum*) first becomes a committed Communist, then an equally fervent member of the storm troopers.

His activities culminate in a brutal attack on Amsel by a Nazi gang under his leadership. Amsel, though badly beaten, survives and flees Danzig, emerging much later as a successful West German ballet impresario known as Haseloff, alias "Goldmouth," because of his ostentatiously false teeth. Matern's attack on Amsel is paralleled by an almost equally savage attack by Tulla on Jenny Brunies, a Gypsy foundling, who is almost as fat as Amsel and whose enduring ambition is to become a ballet star. After Jenny's adoptive father, a woolly-minded local high-school teacher who is not careful enough about keeping his political opinions to himself, is transported (with Tulla's eager assistance) to a concentration camp, Jenny, too, flees Danzig and becomes a ballet star in West Germany under Amsel-Haseloff's tutelage.

It is only in the second book that the title theme is introduced in the figure of the black Alsatian dog Harras, who belongs to Harry's father. After the accidental death by drowning of Tulla's brother Konrad, the only person she ever seems to have any affection for, she shares Harras's kennel and food for a week, refusing any contact with others. When Harras is given poisoned meat by an embittered and drunken Matern as a "political protest," however, after his expulsion from the storm troopers (reminiscent of Meyn in *The Tin Drum*), it is a fascinated Tulla who, far from attempting to save the dog, ensures that he eats the poisoned meat. Harras, meanwhile, has sired a black police dog named Prinz, who is presented to Hitler on an official visit to Danzig and becomes the Führer's favorite dog.

The third book, which carries the story from 1945 to 1957, is again in a quite different stylistic register. It consists of 12 chapters in which Walter Matern ostensibly relates an again lengthy series of so-called Materniads. Matern, who shares a birthday with Hitler but has now (conveniently) seen the error of his former ways, embarks on a private mission of "denazification," accompanied by the dog Prinz, who also abandoned Hitler during the fall of Berlin in 1945 and is now similarly reborn as Pluto. In the course of this mission, using the public washroom of Cologne railway station as a base, Matern travels through postwar West Germany as an avenging fury, conscientiously punishing ex-Nazis by killing their budgerigars, burning their stamp collections, and, most particularly, sleeping with their wives, girlfriends, and daughters. His own Nazi past eventually comes to light again in a radio discussion conducted by Harry Liebenau, however, and Matern abandons the ungrateful West for pastures new in the recently created East Germany. In Berlin he again meets Amsel (now the successful businessman

Brauxel), who takes him on a guided tour of his thriving business, an underground scarecrow factory, which occupies an abandoned potash mine in the Harz Mountains. The scarecrows turn out to be a caricatural presentation of recent German history (reminiscent perhaps of *Dog Years*) and, as such, constitute an underground realm finally character-ized by an overwhelmed Matern as "a hell," although Amsel/Brauxel assures him that the real hell is above ground rather than below.[1] The narrative concludes indeterminately with each of the two onetime friends taking a cleansing bath after their subterranean exertions.

The most immediately accessible level of *Dog Years*—as is the case for both *The Tin Drum* and *Cat and Mouse*—is that of overt, if highly obliquely expressed, social criticism. Where *The Tin Drum* focuses firmly on the construction (and deconstruction) of guilt, *Cat and Mouse,* as we have seen, expands the range by combining the theme of guilt with that of betrayal and symbolic violence. Betrayal is also a central theme (indeed *the* central theme) of *Dog Years,* whose opening scene has a teeth-grinding nine-year-old Matern furiously hurling into the river Vistula a pocketknife presented to him by Amsel with which the two boys had scored their arms in token of everlasting blood brotherhood only a few months before. Violence and aggression are at the heart of the narrative. Ten years later, the still teeth-grinding Matern, still Amsel's "best friend," is the masked leader of the gang of nine Nazi thugs who beat the "sheeny" Amsel senseless and leave him for dead in the snow. Matern's treachery is paralleled by Tulla's, who masquerades as Jenny's friend before likewise viciously attacking her and leaving her in the snow.

Matern and Tulla are linked by the fundamental violence of their natures. Matern, as a boy, spends hours practicing fly shots using live frogs instead of a ball; as a young man he and his friends, for want of anything better to do, indulge in endless barroom brawls when not planning an assault on some Jewish or otherwise politically incorrect neighbor. Tulla, for no particular reason, casually sets the dog Harras on the inoffensive (if pretentious) music teacher Felsner-Imbs, casually ensures that the equally inoffensive teacher Brunies (whom we have already met in *Cat and Mouse*) is condemned to almost certain death in Stutthof concentration camp, casually orders the faithful Harras to eat the poisoned meat. The degree to which that violence is endemic to soci-ety itself is portrayed in Brauxel's expansive accounts in book one of the endless ebb and flow of murder and mayhem that constitute what we call Central European history—or European history, or just history. Matern comes by his violent nature honestly. His grandmother, the direct descendant of a medieval bandit, becomes so enraged during a trivial domestic squabble that she is felled by a stroke that reduces her to sitting completely motionless for the next nine years in her oak chair; only her unbounded rage at a second and equally trivial domestic incident enables her to flout the dictates of medical science and celebrate an avenging resurrection (*DY*, 29). The central role of the (achronological) earliest "morning shifts" or "layers" of the story of Matern and Amsel, focusing emblematically on betrayal and barely suppressed violence is likewise to underline the importance of history: everything has a pedigree, nothing is new, nothing is pure—including, by heavy implication, the newly created postwar Federal Republic. Once Matern metamorphoses into a member of that state, as John Reddick observes, the emphasis shifts from the innate violence of his nature to his falseness and facile role-playing, as a parodic representative of all those who would wish to draw a convenient veil of forgetfulness over an all too inconvenient past (Reddick, 213).

The dogs of the title—associated primarily with the treacherous Matern, the vicious Tulla, the colluding Harry Liebenau, and, of course, the megalomaniac Hitler—are also clearly associated with violence and its pedigree. The first named member of the line, Perkun, who is Harras's grandfather and the grandson of a Lithuanian wolf, bears the name of a Lithuanian god of fire and war. His daughter, Senta, Harras's mother, mates with Pluto, who bears the name of the god of the underworld, and Harras's son, Prinz, who becomes Hitler's dog, is renamed Pluto by Matern. It is typical of the polyvalence of *Dog Years*, however, that its dogs are characterized not only by savagery but also by the proverbial loyalty of "man's best friend," echoing the conflict in Matern's relationship with Amsel (which itself echoes that of Pilenz and Mahlke).

The purest incarnation of violence and malevolence for their own sake, however, is neither the vacillating Matern nor his ostentatiously symbolic dog, but rather the schoolgirl Tulla, the object, then and later, of Harry Liebenau's undying if ambivalent devotion. Tulla, who played a relatively minor role in *Cat and Mouse*, reveals herself unambiguously in *Dog Years* as another manifestation of Oskar's Black Witch. She, too, is provided with a pseudohistorical, pseudomythological pedigree in an earlier manifestation as "Duke Swantopolk's little daughter" (*DY*, 63). She is also entirely localizable to the petit bourgeois milieu of working-class Langfuhr as Harry's cousin, whose father is an employee in Harry's father's carpenter's shop. The uncontrollable violence of her nature is graphically suggested by her habit—paralleling Matern's teeth-grinding—of rolling her eyes in rage until only the whites remain visible, a phenomenon Harry and the other children indicatively refer to as Tulla "bashing in her windows" (*DY*, 131). The frightening animalism of her nature is graphically portrayed in the "dog days"—paralleling the "dog years" of the novel's title—she spends in Harras's kennel when her beloved brother is drowned. During those days she completely abandons her human characteristics for those of her canine companion, eating, sleeping, and relieving her bowels in the dirt. Harry, again indicatively, remembers her most vividly for her oversized and usually crusted nostrils, her pronounced incisors, and her pervasive smell of carpenter's glue—a glue from which Harry, as he puts it himself, nonetheless finds it almost impossible to escape.

Tulla practices viciousness not as an incidental means but as an entirely self-sufficient end. She is no more than six years old when, for no immediately apparent reason, she launches her first attacks on the doll-like Jenny, who is coddled and pampered by her doting adoptive father, the teacher Brunies. The significance of the date—1933—is unlikely to escape the reader. Tulla takes a similarly unreasoning dislike to the artist Amsel, whom she triumphantly victimizes as soon as she discovers his Jewish origins; to the foppish pianist Felsner-Imbs, on whom she repeatedly sets the dog Harras; and to the unfortunate Brunies, whose sweet tooth, leading him to steal vitamin pills intended for his charges, delivers him fatally into Tulla's unforgiving hands. Harry, in retrospect, sees her as the very incarnation of violence, her mere presence in a barroom being enough to unleash a deadly brawl. Her final feat before disappearing out of Harry's life—if certainly not his memory—is to destroy her own unborn child through a spontaneous abortion caused by recklessly (and childishly) insisting on jumping from the platform of a moving streetcar.

Matern's violence is more complexly motivated and more complexly unstable: where Tulla's violence is instinctive and unreflected, Matern's is self-conscious and provides no therapeutic relief, only an increasingly guilty conscience. Matern, as the son of a miller, an expert in adroitly changing direction to catch any favoring wind, is the most immediate object of the novel's satire. Changing direction, indeed, seems to be almost as central to his character as is his natural tendency to violence. Initially Amsel's unrelenting tormentor, in the days when both were schoolboys, he abruptly, and without explanation, metamorphoses into his most aggressive protector, though his protection, as we have seen, is far from dependable. For years he refuses to admit to his role as leader of the gang that beats Amsel almost to death, though he suffers (intermittent) agonies of remorse. An enthusiastic member of the Party during the war, he is an equally enthusiastic wreaker of vengeance on all Nazis (other than himself) after the war.

In both *The Tin Drum* and *Cat and Mouse* the unadmitted complicity of ordinary people in a system of almost unimaginable evil during the years of the Third Reich is adumbrated; in *Dog Years* it is central. Matern's pronounced ability to close his eyes to what he has decided not to see emerges most clearly in his unrelenting unwillingness to admit that a mound of human bones piled by the side of Stutthof concentration camp is anything of the sort. Instead, Matern employs a quasi-Heideggerean gobbledygook to persuade himself and others that the mound has no relevance whatsoever to the world of human practice, only to that of philosophical theory. When Tulla, for her own amusement, proves him wrong by producing incontrovertible evidence in the shape of a human skull, his instinctively violent solution to this new problem is to slap her hard across the face, to her typically malevolent glee.

Matern is, of course, not the only target of the novel's political satire, which is also and simultaneously—as in *The Tin Drum*—massively directed against what Grass presents as the complacent and convenient amnesia of the new West Germany, an amnesia constructed on fields of corpses and caught up in the self-indulgent throes of a fatally tainted Economic Miracle. This is the true home of the fascist antifascist, a world in which rape can be considered a morally appropriate vengeance for murder, a world in which "miracle glasses" that would reveal what successful financiers and lawyers really did in the war qualify only as children's playthings, without any acknowledged relevance to the world of grown-ups. Matern's protracted series of quasi-heroic avenging "Materniads" concludes with his being publicly unmasked himself as a onetime Nazi, but he nonetheless stubbornly persists in seeing himself in the more attractive and politically opportune role of the antifascist crusader. Rather than acknowledge his onetime involvement, he undertakes a second major change of ideologies. Having abandoned Nazism for capitalism, the miller's son, in search as always of a favorable wind, now abandons capitalism for socialism and flees, a hollow man, stuffed with superficially adopted ideologies, from the Federal to the Democratic Republic. In Berlin, however, before his intended new career, doubtless as a trafficker in new evasions, can get under way, he reencounters his onetime victim Amsel. Their final surrealistic confrontation provides Grass's narrative with its pyrotechnic and quasi-apocalyptic conclusion.

Matern is the primary object of satire in *Dog Years,* but his guilty complicity in disaster is interestingly paralleled in the role of Harry Liebenau, whose "love letters" to and about his cousin Tulla make up the central book of the narrative, covering the fateful years from 1927 to 1945. Very much like Pilenz in *Cat and Mouse,* Harry (as presented by himself) strikes us as a basically decent but also fundamentally weak person, pendulating indecisively between victim and aggressor, whether Amsel and Matern (whose relationship is viewed by Harry from a distance), on the one hand, or Jenny and Tulla (a relationship viewed from much nearer at hand), on the other. His defining characteristic, indeed, as both character and narrator, is this all too "reasonable" unwillingness to adopt and adhere to a firm position. Harry, like Pilenz, is a watcher, an observer rather than a doer. He is also characterized, like Pilenz, by a fundamental sense of emptiness and a pronounced lack of wholeness and self-sufficiency. His unsent "love letters" to Tulla attempt retrospectively, and, once again, like Pilenz's narrative, to establish an intimate relationship that clearly never existed in fact but whose hypothetical reconstruction, however fictive, serves to provide at least some thread of meaning in a life starved of meaning.

Unlike Matern, who rejects any suggestion of complicity or guilt concerning the nightmare years of the Third Reich, Harry is deeply troubled by the thought of his own (real or potential) guilty connivance (*DY*, 318). Harry, we may note in this context, is a decade younger than Matern and Amsel, who were both born in 1917. Like Günter Grass, indeed, Harry was born in 1927 and conscripted into the army as an antiaircraft gunner at the age of 17. Harry's original career plan had been to become a historian; like Matern, he in fact becomes a radio announcer, a commentator from the sidelines on the events of the day. Like Grass, too, Harry is a writer, and "after the war I'm going to write a book" (*DY,* 349)—which we may take ourselves to be reading in the shape of his "Love Letters." If Harry is related to the aggressor Matern in his (voluntary or involuntary) collusion in crimes past, he is certainly also related to the victim Amsel in his attempt to shape those events through the medium of art.

Amsel, in his various metamorphoses, is the most ostentatiously polyvalent figure in *Dog Years,* parodically embodying the artist who is at once historically part of and imaginatively detached from the events presented and fictionally reshaped. That ironic detachment is not only entirely necessary for the artist but also inevitably ambivalent and at least potentially culpable. The essential ambiguity of Amsel's character is reflected in his own name: *Amsel* literally means "blackbird," but Amsel, first on a small scale as a schoolboy and later on a corporate scale as the entrepreneur Brauxel, specializes in the manufacture of scarecrows, designed to frighten birds away, just as he is frightened away from Danzig by the Nazi sympathies of his best friend. As the narrator, Brauxel, he ironically refers to himself in the German text as "der Federführende," a pun that is necessarily lost in its translation as "the present writer" (*DY,* 11), since *Feder* means both "pen" and "feather," and *Feder führen* thus parodically conflates "to write," "to bear feathers," and "to lead (*führen,* as in *Führer*) feathers (or pens)."

Even as a schoolboy, Amsel discovers that the artist who does his or her job too well may not always remain a popular member of society. One of his scarecrows, "the Great Cuckoo Bird" (*DY,* 93), is so extremely successful in scaring birds—and also people—that his ungrateful customers make a communal bonfire of it and, for good measure, of assorted other effects of the upstart young "sheeny" (*DY,* 93). The year is 1926, and change is in the air; for German readers the real-world reference to the Nazi book burnings of 1933 is patent. Change is also the preferred milieu of the artist Amsel, for his art is, above all, one of productive distortion. One of his early inventions is a schoolboy "secret language" that stands ordinary language on its head, scrambling and recombining its components so that while it retains an exact relationship to the everyday words it distorts, it is unintelligible to those uninitiated into the system of its refracted workings.

Amsel advances from stationary to mobile scarecrows, and his troubles increase proportionately. His mobile pièce de résistance is a whole squad of nine uniformed storm troopers whose built-in mechanism enables them to goose-step in stiff formation, to snap a precise eyes-right for their creator, and to greet him with the straight-armed Nazi salute (*DY,* 217). While his previous masterpiece merely led to a bonfire, this one almost costs him his life. The attack on Amsel by Matern and his thugs is partly the result of Amsel's Jewishness, but more importantly the result of what Matern, the now dedicated Party member, sees as a satirical desecration of National Socialist ideals. While there is undoubtedly a degree of social criticism implicit in Amsel's scarecrow Nazis, however, his own role is certainly not without ambivalence. For "who is being saluted? To whom are the eyes right addressed? What is the name of the Führer who is expected to look into all of their pasted eyes? Who looks, returns the salute, and passes them in review?" (*DY,* 217).

The answer, of course, is Amsel himself, Amsel as representative of the artist whose essential concern is less the ability to reshape the world of politics than the ability to reshape the world of forms. Just as in his schoolboy experiments with reshaping the language of everyday affairs, "he built with no adversary in mind, on formal grounds. At the most he wished to convince a dangerously productive environment of his own productivity" (*DY*, 189). As Amsel tells an unconvinced Matern, he "hadn't intended criticism of any kind, but merely wished, through his art, to create a hodgepodge of good guys and bastards, after the manner of life itself" (*DY*, 206). Like the work of his creator, Günter Grass, Amsel's artistic output is at once political and purely formal; at once involved and detached; at once a protest against the world he lives in, a celebration of it, and a collusion in its workings. After the war, Amsel alias Brauxel develops his scarecrow productivity into a major industry, a flourishing and, literally, underground economy that is at once politically critical of, formally reflective of, and inevitably in collusion with the society of the Economic Miracle in which, for better or for worse, it is firmly embedded. In this Amsel/Brauxel follows in the footsteps of Oskar—with whom Harry Liebenau claims to have seen Amsel once in earnest consultation (*DY*, 207)—who becomes a recording star after the war by dint of the same drumming that allows him both to lay bare its causes and reshape its history. Oskar and Amsel, alike, follow in the footsteps of their clear-eyed creator, Günter Grass, for what Ann Mason observes of Oskar is essentially applicable to all three: each one of them "engages in *all* his activities with a parodic consciousness of them as roles"; each one of them exemplifies the artist "watching by means of a wilderness of mirrors, himself participating in, yet satirically commenting on, the reality of the Nazi years" (Mason, 52–53).

The concept of a "wilderness of mirrors" aptly reflects the complexity of the narrative strategies at play in *Dog Years*. Grass's original plan was for a novel to be called "Kartoffelschalen" (Potato Peelings), narrated by a single potato-peeling housemaid (a motif that recurs more than a decade later in *The Flounder*). Other early drafts were called variously "Der Hund" (The Dog), "Die Vogelscheuchen" (The Scarecrows), and "Der Knirscher" (The Grinder). Interestingly, photographs of early drafts from 1959 show no mention of Amsel, who puts in a first appearance only in plans dating from May 1961. In its final shape, the narrative situation is constructed around the fiction of an authorial collective, three authors—victim, colluding witness, and aggressor respectively— writing three separate books that together will constitute a festschrift celebrating 10 successful years of Brauxel/Amsel's scarecrow factory. Brauxel is the organizer and guiding light of the literary undertaking and refers at various points in the first book to the progress that the other two authors are making toward the assigned deadline. The narrative is fictively composed over some six weeks, from mid-December 1961 to early February 1962.

The first book, as we have seen, is narrated by Brauxel, covers the years from 1917 to 1927, and is set in Danzig and its environs; the second is narrated by Harry Liebenau, covers the years from 1927 to 1945, and is set mostly in Danzig and later in Berlin; the third is narrated by Matern, covers the years from 1946 to 1957, and is set in various locations in West Germany and, finally, in Berlin and East Germany. All three authors—three differently angled mirrors, variously reflecting present and past—begin and end simultaneously (as Brauxel reports in his "last morning shift"), their narrative time of six weeks thus corresponding to a narrated time of 40 years, from 1917 to 1957. The interplay between these two time levels is strongly accentuated in the first book, is referred to much less frequently in the second, and is barely mentioned in the third.

It has been variously observed that in *The Tin Drum* there is a single focus of attention, Oskar; in *Cat and Mouse* there are two, Mahlke and Pilenz; and in *Dog Years* a central concern is the three-cornered narratorial relationship of Brauxel/Amsel, Matern, and Harry Liebenau. These latter three, however, may be read as three facets of a single narrative voice. Early critics tended to see the pervasive stylistic evidence of this single narrative voice as an inadvertent technical lapse on Grass's part, especially in the third book, where many of Matern's formulations seemed to them to belong all too obviously in Amsel/Brauxel's mouth rather than his own. More than one reviewer thus took Grass severely to task on the grounds that all three narrators were just puppets and that Brauxel/Amsel and Matern, in particular, were all too often simply interchangeable, whether in their actions, their experience, or their vocabulary. What these readings considered a debilitating flaw, however, was demonstrated by Michael Harscheidt's detailed analysis to be the central narrative strategy of Grass's fiction. That is, behind the three discrete narrative voices is indeed a single (and, strictly speaking, anonymous) narrative voice—an "implied" narrator, as one might put it—that projects itself variously, and in varying combinations and shadings, in the tones of the victim, the aggressor, and the culpable witness.[2] This ventriloquist technique may be read as a thoroughgoing attempt to give narrative form to the dilemma to which Pilenz gives voice in *Cat and*

Mouse: "If only I knew who made up the story, he or I, or who is writing this in the first place" (*CM*, 89). Though also tentatively adumbrated in *The Tin Drum* in the sparing use of Bruno and Vittlar as surrogate narrators, the systemic splitting of the narrative voice to such a degree as is evident in *Dog Years* is an important technical departure for Grass. He was to return to its multiple discursive possibilities in a number of subsequent works.

Like *The Tin Drum, Dog Years* situates itself firmly, if with parodic reflexivity, in a hallowed tradition of German literature, the *Künstlerroman* or artist novel. Rather than concentrating on the development of an individual artist, however, *Dog Years* focuses on the nature and role of art itself. In spite of the pronounced element of social criticism contained in Grass's narrative, he completely avoids any Brechtian dogmatism as to the educational role of the artist in society, just as he had done in *The Tin Drum.* Like Oskar, Amsel/Brauxel is marked by a flaunted polyvalence. As various critics have noted, Matern (reminiscent of Pilenz) is characterized, largely in realistic terms, by the ambivalence of his behavior. The same is true, by and large, of Harry Liebenau (likewise reminiscent of Pilenz), but Amsel (reminiscent rather of Oskar) is characterized by an ambivalence that is far more fundamental, an ambivalence that is less a matter of behavior than of his very being as an artist.

Art is essentially not about the world we live in, but about art. And, as one might summarize the "message" of *Dog Years,* art changes nothing, though it can certainly contribute to making it possible for *people* to change things, by making it possible for them to see things differently. This is essentially a Brechtian position shorn of its dogmatism. Art is no panacea for all ills, however, no refuge against the barbarity and brutality and unfairness of the everyday world. Amsel's role of artist (like Oskar's in *The Tin Drum*) is parodically reflected in several other artist and quasi-artist figures in the narrative. Felsner-Imbs, the concert pianist whose narcissistic pride is his great flowing artist's mane of hair, lives in a room that looks like an aquarium with his goldfish and a porcelain ballerina and plays Chopin against the scream of a buzz saw in the neighboring carpenter's yard. His art is no protection when he is savaged by Harras, egged on by Tulla. Jenny Brunies, Amsel's female counterpart, tempered in the fire of the same prejudice and brutality as he is, likewise metamorphoses from a fat little schoolgirl into a star ballet dancer—and ends up with both feet crushed as a random victim of Allied bombing. Her adoptive father, the toffee-loving teacher Brunies, lives in a fairy-tale world fantasized around the poetic vision of the late-

Romantic German poet Eichendorff, but it does not save him from dying in a concentration camp. Art is no antidote against reality, nor, as Grass's narrative is at pains to show, is art distinct from that reality. In *Dog Years*, to repeat Ann Mason's formulation, the tainted productivity of the Economic Miracle is ambiguously and self-consciously satirized by a productivity itself tainted, the artist ambiguously observing through a "wilderness of mirrors," at once actor and observer, participant and satirist.

The narrative world that is *Dog Years* is consequently characterized by a radical polyvalence. As in *The Tin Drum*, the grotesque plays a central role, and the intermingling of closely observed realism and extravagantly fantastic elements, variously characterized as "fantastic realism," has justifiably been seen as the fundamental stylistic principle of the narrative. All three books begin more or less realistically and end more or less fantastically. Everyday reality and narrative reality blur, each calling the other into question. One result (and cause) of this is a sense of great kinetic energy in the narration, objects and ideas continually merging and parting company and metamorphosing into something new and exhilaratingly unexpected. Michael Harscheidt views the stylistic heterogeneity—the rapid changes of formal presentation, of tenses, and of persons, as well as of types of discourse (especially reported and narrated monologue)—as all part of the expression of the central concept of "fantastic realism," a seamless web of the imaginative and the documentary, where each continually relativizes the other (Harscheidt, 65–85).

The theme of identity and transformation is a central one. Matern is continually shown, whether by his own account or that of the other narrators, to be an entirely hollow man, stuffed scarecrowlike with an ever-varying selection of ideologies, creeds, and cant phrases for all seasons, half-concealing and half-flaunting his guilty past: "Behold me, bald-headed inside and out. An empty closet full of uniforms of every color. I was red, put on brown, wore black, dyed myself red" (*DY*, 434). Harry Liebenau, the most realistically drawn of the three narrators, continually vacillates with perennially guilty conscience, ever-renewed indecision, and hypnotized inability to act, between his good and evil geniuses, Jenny and Tulla. Harry is a card-carrying member of the series of Grass's narrators with bad conscience that began with Pilenz and would reappear over the years in such figures as Starusch in *Local Anaesthetic* and the nameless narrators of both *The Flounder* and *The Rat*. As for Amsel, whose art consists centrally of taking things apart and putting them

back together again in entirely new and unexpected ways, transformation is the core of his nature, as reflected in the series of names he adopts
with his various changes of identity: Amsel, Haseloff, Goldmouth,
Stepun, Steppenhuhn, Brooks, Brauksel, Brauchsel, Brauxel.
Reality and its masks can rarely be distinguished with certainty:
Matern is an actor, whose profession demands a continuous experimentation with fictitious roles; Harry and Amsel, in their different milieus,
are both artists, whose profession demands a continuous reconstruction
and refiguring of reality. Symbols provocatively flaunt their overexcited
exaggeratedness, with the most obvious example being the parodically
overdetermined dog of the title. Representing everything from the
unexorcized ecstatic violence of Nazism to four-legged (and eventually,
in Matern's overheated imagination, 32-legged) conscience, this over-
worked pseudosymbol eventually self-destructs, polyvalently "connected with too many things to be taken seriously as a symbol" (Mason,
58). Amsel and Jenny, whose physical fatness graphically symbolizes
their shared otherness, are simultaneously beaten up and left individually entombed in complementary snowmen on either side of a hill over
which Harry scrambles back and forth all night watching the snowmen
melt and eventually witnessing the quasi-miraculous emergence of a
lithe young man and a slim young girl, reborn transformed through suffering wrapped in snow. (The whole episode can be read as a parodic
intertextual reference to Thomas Mann's canonic novel of 1924, *The
Magic Mountain,* in which the central character has a quasi-mystical revelation after being lost in the snowfields of the Swiss Alps.) When
Amsel/Brauxel and Matern finally meet again, their first confrontation
takes place in the surrealistic flames of a burning bar, tended by Jenny
Brunies, which leaves the three miraculously untouched. Their second
confrontation takes place in the equally surrealistic depths of the onetime potash mine that Brauxel has now transformed into an internationally famous production plant for scarecrows. The conclusion, entirely
inconclusive, can be read as evidence of a final reconciliation between
the two or as just one further proof that Matern has learned absolutely
nothing from his various experiences.

The exuberance of the plot is fully matched by an extraordinary linguistic exuberance. Harscheidt's detailed analysis catalogues an astonishing variety of linguistic and stylistic registers, reminiscent of the
range of Joyce's experimentation in *Ulysses* (Harscheidt, 124). A typical
bravura example of Grass's linguistic creativity is provided by the evocation of the real and symbolic blackness of the eponymous dog, ranging

from "umbrella-black, blackboard-black, priest-black, widow-black" via
"SS-black, Falange-black, blackbird-black, Othello-black, Ruhr-black"
to a final sequence of "violet-black, tomato-black, lemon-black, flour-
black, milk-black, snow-black" (*DY*, 513). Another is found in the
extensive and merciless parody of the tortured style of the philosopher
Martin Heidegger, especially in the episode where Matern attempts to
persuade himself, and anybody who will listen, that the pile of human
bones outside Stutthof concentration camp has at best only a theoretical
interest (*DY*, 304–16). Grass has been widely criticized for the attack on
Heidegger, but Harscheidt acutely observes that what is essentially
under attack is less the person of Heidegger himself (whose Nazi sympathies are certainly also satirized) than the similarities of thought between
Heidegger and Hitler (Harscheidt, 192), just as, in *The Tin Drum,* the
object of satire was the petit bourgeois perversion of Goethe's thought
rather than the person of Goethe himself.

Linguistic complexity is complemented by an extensively developed
system of numerical symbolism—which Michael Harscheidt has also
explored in extraordinary detail—dominated by innumerable references
to the numbers 9 and 32, the former the number of assailants in the
gang led by Matern that beats Amsel senseless, the latter the number of
teeth Amsel loses in that encounter and later replaces with the gold
teeth that give him his nickname of Goldmouth. As with much else in
this novel, the number symbolism is partly serious, partly play. Play is a
centrally important element in *Dog Years,* just as it was in *The Tin Drum,*
and we continually need to keep that in mind as readers, rather than
allowing ourselves to be led down a variety of inviting paths that
promise conclusive answers but invariably fail to deliver. *Dog Years* (like
The Tin Drum) is certainly "about" the accumulated guilt resulting from
one of the most massively reprehensible political systems the world has
ever seen, but it is also and just as centrally about art and creativity and
irrepressible inventiveness.

Dog Years is still generally and justifiably regarded as one of the most
difficult of all Grass's books because of the flaunted complexity and polyvalence of its narrative structure that frustrates well-meaning attempts at
linear interpretation. Even after more than 30 years, there is still no critical consensus on its overall "meaning," other than the obvious element of
social criticism. For the most part critics have preferred *The Tin Drum,* in
whose heavy shadow *Dog Years* has been unfairly neglected. Grass himself, it is worth noting, has repeatedly stated his opinion that *Dog Years* is
a stronger and more complex book than *The Tin Drum.*

Stylistically the most exuberant of the three narratives that constitute the Danzig Trilogy, *Dog Years* delights in its own self-conscious verbal and structural artifice, and it strongly resists the reader who is looking for a linear plot and a comfortably digestible bottom-line moral. This is by no means new in Grass's oeuvre, but it represents a definite intensification of what has been there all along. While Oskar's narrative is highly ambiguous and Pilenz's narrative is highly unreliable, the triply voiced narrative of *Dog Years* is strikingly more ambiguous and more unreliable than either. *Dog Years* is certainly a narrative of social criticism, as were both *The Tin Drum* and *Cat and Mouse*. To an even greater extent than either of them, however, it is also centrally a narrative about narrative itself and its concealments, its subterfuges, its slippages, and its creative possibilities. In the end, as Amsel tells Matern, "as long as we're telling stories, we're alive. As long as stories keep coming, with or without a point, dog stories, eel stories, scarecrow stories, rat stories, flood stories, recipe stories, stories full of lies and schoolbook stories, as long as stories have power to entertain us, no hell can divert us" (*DY*, 536).

Chapter Six
The Plebeians Rehearse the Uprising

After *Dog Years,* Grass was ready for new ways of looking at his material: by the time that novel appeared in print Grass had spent more than seven years working with narrators who all, in their varying ways, looked back at an unaccepted past and attempted to change it retrospectively. As he describes it in his autobiographical text *Vier Jahrzehnte* (Four Decades), he had had enough of the particular technique, had no wish to repeat himself, and was ready for something new (111). What he turned to was a dramatic rather than a narrative text, and to Berlin instead of Danzig. *Die Plebejer proben den Aufstand: Ein deutsches Trauerspiel,* a full-length play, was written between 1964 and 1966 and appeared in print in 1966. It was first produced in Berlin in January 1966. An English translation by Ralph Manheim, under the title *The Plebeians Rehearse the Uprising: A German Tragedy,* appeared in London and New York later that same year.

The play had its origins in an address Grass wrote for delivery to the Academy of the Arts in Berlin in April 1964 to mark the 400th anniversary of Shakespeare's birth. The address was entitled, tongue in cheek, "The Prehistory and Posthistory of the Tragedy of *Coriolanus* from Livy and Plutarch via Shakespeare down to Brecht and Myself."[1] In it Grass contrasts what he reads as Shakespeare's tragic presentation of Coriolanus as a great leader destroyed by his own arrogance and the fickleness of the mob with Bertolt Brecht's decision, when he set out in 1952 to adapt the play for his own East German Berliner Ensemble, to portray Coriolanus as a leader grown too big for his boots and eventually cut down to size by a politically aware working class. Grass also reveals that Brecht's own behavior during the abortive East German workers' uprising of June 1953—which Brecht did not allow to interrupt his scheduled rehearsals—has impelled him, in the light of the Coriolanus theme, to begin work himself on a play to be called *The Plebeians Rehearse the Uprising.*

The Plebeians deals with a fictionalized version of events surrounding the short-lived three-day uprising of June 1953, whose historical background is as follows. Faced with a continuing series of "voluntary" raises in work quotas, workers reached the breaking point when the East German government imposed a new, and no longer voluntary, 10-percent general increase in quotas. Workers on some construction sites in East Berlin began an illegal strike on June 15. Fanned by official paternalism and heavy-handedness, the unrest spread rapidly, and, in the course of a major street demonstration the following day, a general strike was proclaimed in Berlin. June 17 brought an escalation of the situation by politically fraught statements of moral support from the RIAS radio station in West Berlin, and a rash of sympathy strikes broke out all over East Germany. The Soviet military authorities, deciding that matters had gone far enough, declared a state of emergency in East Berlin and sent tanks into the streets. Despite stubborn resistance on the part of unarmed civilians, the abortive uprising was speedily quashed. Several people were killed, and thousands were arrested. The East German intelligentsia, as has often been observed, took very little part in the whole affair; after its failure, many of them quickly took the opportunity to express their solidarity with the Party and the government. The best-known and most internationally respected public literary figure of East Germany, Bertolt Brecht, who was director of the famous Berliner Ensemble theater, addressed a carefully phrased letter to the State and Party authorities in which two sentences of guarded criticism were followed by a third expressing his solidarity with the Party and its beliefs and aims. Only the statement of solidarity was published in the official East German newspaper, *Neues Deutschland.*

The central figure of *The Plebeians* is a well-known, if unnamed, poet, public figure, and theater director known only as the Boss, a character very overtly modeled on Bertolt Brecht. As the curtain rises, it is 17 June 1953, and the Boss is rehearsing the opening scene for a production of Shakespeare's *Coriolanus,* a scene in which a mob of Roman plebeians, armed with sticks and clubs and "hungry because the price of grain is climbing" (P, 8), clumsily plot an uprising against Coriolanus, whom they deem an enemy of the people. The Boss, who is intent on staging a Shakespeare for the times, is worried about the effectiveness for modern audiences of the dated stratagem by which the character Menenius defuses the abortive insurrection, namely, by relating the parable of the belly and the members. In this parable, the various bodily members or limbs plan to revolt against the lazy and voracious belly, who allegedly does nothing while they spend all their time working to keep it fed, only to be asked by the belly how exactly they think they would survive if their plan succeeded.

The moral is clear in the context—the belly is the power of the state as represented by Coriolanus, the limbs are the potential insurrectionists—but, says the Boss, the "wretched, limping parable" (P, 10) is entirely unlikely to persuade the real Berlin workers for whom he intends to stage his production. His aesthetic dilemma is interrupted only briefly when news arrives that an actual uprising appears to be about to take place outside. The Boss, a professional, has no time for amateur theatricals, and he curtly dismisses the whole affair as just a childish exercise in "unrehearsed incompetence" (P, 18). When several workers arrive to ask him to write a manifesto on their behalf, he taunts them condescendingly, mocks their awkward attempts to explain what they think they are doing, has them form various crowd-scene groupings in order to gauge the potential dramatic effect, and makes technical notes for his production of *Coriolanus* on the relevance of their gauchely unrehearsed behavior.

The workers have an ally in the Boss's leading lady (modeled on Brecht's longtime leading lady—and wife—Helene Weigel), who plays the part of Coriolanus's mother Volumnia. Together with other members of the cast, the leading lady unsuccessfully attempts to persuade the Boss, even using arguments from his own (which is to say, Brecht's) plays, that the reality outside the theater is just now infinitely more important than the dramatic fiction within. The Boss remains unpersuaded and rejects the workers' increasingly threatening demands for a written manifesto with the remark that he has spent his entire life writing for them: "But you forgot how to read before you even left school" (P, 27). When he accuses them of being typical German revolutionaries, allegedly wanting radical change but in fact not even daring to defy signs prohibiting walking on the grass, Volumnia, in turn, accuses him of having become not just a "miserable aesthete" (P, 47) but a self-inflated Coriolanus, "proud to the point of arrogance" (P, 5), a despiser of the common people with whom, for all his theorizing about the importance of theater for the people, he has completely lost contact.

The plot takes a new turn when the Boss is also approached by the despised Kozanka, a high-ranking official Party versifier, who calls on him to speak out on behalf of the authorities—a request that the Boss likewise promptly rejects. Kozanka's indignant departure is succeeded by the arrival of a group of much more radical workers, under whose threats the Boss does actually write a letter to Ulbricht as requested, but the result is so complexly equivocal that the new arrivals cannot even decide whether it favors or criticizes their cause. They angrily destroy the letter and resolve without further ado to lynch the Boss and Erwin, one of his assistant directors, as enemies of the people, "in the middle of their phony Rome" (*P,* 75). The Boss refuses to dignify the situation by protesting, and he escapes hanging only because Erwin saves the day by regaling the gradually intrigued workers with the same old parable of the belly and the members that had been the object of the Boss's professional disdain.

Further new arrivals bring dramatically related tales of heroic endeavors in the heat of combat. Together with the general euphoria of apparently decisive action—and especially the fiery rhetoric of one young woman who could, as the Boss observes, have stepped straight out of his (which is to say, Brecht's) play *Mother Courage*—these tales eventually combine to persuade the Boss to throw in his lot with the workers after all. Before he can even leave the theater, however, word arrives that the unplanned, unrehearsed uprising has quickly collapsed. "Almost with them for the time it takes / To breathe a poem" (*P,* 94), the Boss is left alone on stage. "The Holy Spirit breathed, and I mistook / It for a draft, and cried: / Who's come here to molest me?" (*P,* 94–95). Warned by a gloating Kozanka that he will lose his theater if he does not express his support for the State, the final act has the Boss laboriously writing a letter to the authorities in which guarded criticism is followed by a final paragraph expressing his formal solidarity with the Party. He wearily ignores Volumnia's protests that obviously only the statement of solidarity will be publicized. To the charge that he will at best be seen as merely sitting on the fence, he responds: "What better seat have you to offer?" (*P,* 108). Unable to congratulate either the "meritorious murderers of the people" or the "ignorant survivors of a feeble uprising" (*P,* 108), a chastened Boss is left "with fewer and fewer certitudes" (*P,* 110)—except that of a guilt he does not expect ever to be able to forget.

Shortly before the end of the play, the Boss realizes, too late, that Volumnia was right: he has slipped unwittingly into the role of Coriolanus rather than that of the plebeians he wishes to support in his adaptation. His guilt also has a more complex component, however. The Boss's last line is the last line of the play and a slightly altered version of the last line of a poem Brecht actually wrote after the abortive uprising: "You poor babes in the woods! Bowed down with guilt, I accuse you!" (*P,* 111). As Volker Neuhaus points out, the Boss's more complex guilt is not the result of his having failed to write the manifesto demanded by the workers; rather it results from the complete failure of his theatrical theory and practice.[2] All his life, as he himself tells the workers, he has been writing only for them. Yet it is now obvious that not a word he has written has been understood as he intended it to be, for if his revolutionary theater had been effective in its didactic aims, the workers would never in the first place have attempted an uprising so obviously doomed to failure. The guilt is, therefore, at least as much his as it is theirs; the accusation is leveled both against their ignorance and against his own failure to have prevented that ignorance. The Boss has indeed been right in theory all along, but while the workers at least had the courage of their instinctive convictions, he has allowed himself to be hypnotized by his own theory into a shameful inactivity.

The Plebeians is a far cry from the world of the Danzig trilogy. There is no fantastic realism, no incursions of the grotesque, no absurdly overinflated and idiosyncratic pseudosymbols. The time is the very recent past, the subject matter of immediate historical and political significance, the (apparent) central figure titillatingly familiar and famous. The play was neither a popular nor a critical success in Germany, however.[3] Most audiences considered that there was far too much discussion and far too little action. Many reviewers (especially in more radical circles) were incensed by what they read as a vicious and ungrateful attack on Bertolt Brecht. Grass himself protested, on many occasions, that the figure of the Boss, while certainly modeled on Brecht (and supported by many references to details of Brecht's life and work), is by no means an attack on Brecht the man or the writer. Instead, the Boss is an exemplary model of the enduring dilemma of the politically engaged artist who—like Grass himself—must always attempt to balance the competing demands of art and politics. To read the Boss as an experimental model in these terms certainly produces a much better play than does a reading of the work as a mere *ad hominem* attack. The wealth of reference to the historical Brecht, on the other hand, lends immeasurably to the play's allusive richness.

The play exploits to the full the possibilities of the play-within-a-play genre and contains a richly allusive weave of intertextual references to the Coriolanus theme in Shakespeare and Brecht, Livy and Plutarch, many of these references open, many more concealed. There is, likewise, a continuing flow of references to Brecht's plays and poetry and to his public career in the early 1950s as the foremost literary celebrity of the fledgling East German state. Many of the Boss's statements are only slightly altered versions of public statements Brecht made or of lines from his plays or his poetry. The language of the play is an intriguing and dynamic mixture: the colloquial and the vulgar continually shade over into (and continually retreat from) a highly formalized poetic usage based loosely on both the iambic pentameter of Shakespeare and the stylized free verse of Brecht. Lines by Shakespeare vie with lines by Brecht, and both with lines by Grass that read as if they must surely have been written by Shakespeare or Brecht. The end result sparkles with wit, irony, and not always subdued comedy.

For all its lack of popular success, *The Plebeians* is a major literary achievement—and certainly the most accomplished of all Grass's plays. Critics who look to the theater for action rather than ideas point to the basic flaw of *The Plebeians* as being the fact that, as Gordon Cunliffe puts it, "its plot, its whole conception preclude development of any real action."[4] Turning that accusation on its head, however, one could just as easily argue that this lack of action is the whole point of the theatrical exercise, just as it was in Beckett's *Waiting for Godot* a decade or so before. *Godot* has famously been described as a play in which nothing happens, twice (but only because there are two acts). In *The Plebeians,* nothing likewise happens, twice: the uprising comes to nothing, and the Boss's theory of didactic theater comes to nothing. What better way to memorialize nothing happening than in a play in which nothing happens—but manages to happen so intriguingly. Here we have the strongest and most interesting connecting link between Grass's early theatrical writings and the at first glance very different text *The Plebeians.* That is, nothing happens at all in any of them, but in this sophisticated rehearsal play about an unrehearsed uprising the stasis of *Waiting for Godot* is transposed into a political rather than an absurdist key.

Chapter Seven
Local Anaesthetic

Set in the Germany of the late 1960s, and originally conceived of as a drama under the working title "Verlorene Schlachten" (Lost Battles), the novel *Örtlich betäubt* appeared in 1969—and in Ralph Manheim's translation as *Local Anaesthetic* later that year. Eberhard Starusch, the first-person narrator, nicknamed Old Hardy by his students, is a disillusioned 40-year-old teacher of German and history in a Berlin high school. His narrative is presented in three parts.

The first and longest part recounts the progress of an extended dental treatment that Starusch must undergo in early 1967 to have a faulty bite corrected. During its course, he repeatedly receives the local anaesthetic of the title, half watches his up-to-date dentist's television set, half listens to the dentist's one-sided conversational efforts, and groggily reconstructs (or fantasizes) the course of a love affair he once had with Linde Krings, the daughter of a onetime Nazi general. Part two, set in a two-week break in the treatment, centers on the conflict between one of his students, Philipp Scherbaum, and Starusch himself. Scherbaum, as a protest against the American use of napalm in Vietnam, plans to set on fire his dachshund, Max, in front of the most expensive restaurant in Berlin; Starusch, as a good Social Democrat, espouses the position that radical action is never as useful in the long run as reasoned democratic process. Starusch's efforts to dissuade Scherbaum, however, are vigorously opposed by his fellow schoolteacher Irmgard Seifert, who welcomes the 17-year-old Scherbaum's gesture of public protest because it takes the place of the protest she herself never had the courage to make. Starusch, for his part, eventually involved in a lackluster affair with Irmgard Seifert, does not conceal the fact that, as a 17-year-old, he was himself the leader of a gang of juvenile delinquents in his native Danzig and that now, as a good teacher, he wishes to prevent Scherbaum from repeating his own mistakes. Starusch's good intentions are also opposed by Scherbaum's terminally bored girlfriend, Vero Lewand, whose main interest in the whole affair is to generate some excitement at all costs, and who eventually succeeds in seducing the conscience-stricken pedagogue on his own fireside rug.

In the end, Scherbaum simply abandons the idea and becomes the editor of the school newspaper instead. Ironically, however, he does so not because of Starusch's reasoned pedagogical arguments, but because he does not want to end up like Starusch, a 40-year-old has-been vicariously "peddling the feats of a seventeen-year-old."[1] The third book, much briefer, returns to Starusch's interrupted dental treatment and his increasingly violent fantasies involving his lost love, Linde. Scherbaum, who meanwhile has also had his bite corrected by Starusch's dentist, finishes school and goes on to study medicine. Vero finds her excitement by marrying a Canadian linguist. Starusch proposes to Irmgard Seifert, shortly before fantasizing a particularly vicious death by drowning for Linde. The final sentences send him back to the dentist to have a new abscess removed, an emergency operation that will necessarily have to undo much of what was so painfully achieved. "Nothing lasts. There will always be new pains" (LA, 255).

The narrative of Local Anaesthetic is in some ways much more "normal" than we are accustomed to from the Danzig trilogy. The element of fantastic realism has disappeared entirely, and the narrative is written in a much less flamboyant, more neutral style than either The Tin Drum or Dog Years, a style prefigured to some extent in Cat and Mouse. A new complexity is added in Local Anaesthetic, however. In each of the narratives of the Danzig trilogy there is an identifiable narrator-figure who declares himself to be writing an account of some sort. Starusch, on the other hand, never claims to be writing his story. He does claim at various points to be writing a story, but it is not the one we are reading. Starusch, a professional historian, has in his desk drawer a manuscript in progress on which he has been working in a desultory fashion for some time; its title is "Lost Battles" (LA, 23). As we gradually find out, it is intended to be a monograph on Field Marshal Ferdinand Schörner, Hitler's designated successor as commander in chief of the German Army. The manuscript makes little or no progress, however, and even in the last paragraph Starusch refers to it as being still only in the beginning stages. The narrative we read has a great deal to do with a Field Marshal Ferdinand Krings, however, who is the father of Starusch's onetime fiancée. Indeed, it quickly emerges that Starusch is completely obsessed with the breakup of his engagement to Krings's daughter.

"I told my dentist all this," Starusch begins his narrative. "Mouth blocked and face to face with the television screen which, soundless like myself, told a story of publicity" (LA, 8). Starusch, in other words, tells the dentist very little indeed. However gradually we may realize it, what we read in the first part of Starusch's narrative is an extended interior monologue in which he appears to be attempting to come to grips with the failure of his engagement and other assorted failures of his past. The account he constructs is more or less as follows. (The qualification is necessary, for many of Starusch's stories are frankly invented, others may well be invented, and some may conceivably be true; it is often extremely difficult if not impossible, however, to say which are which.)

Eberhard Starusch (like his creator Günter Grass) was born in Danzig in 1927. As a 17-year-old, under the name of Störtebeker (the name was originally that of a fourteenth-century local pirate), he became the leader of a gang of juvenile delinquents in a unfocused fight against all authority in the Danzig of the final year of the war. (This gang is, in fact, the same Dusters gang that adopts Oskar as its mascot in *The Tin Drum.*) At that time, Störtebeker learned to cultivate the pseudo-Heideggerean cant that he and no other taught to Walter Matern in *Dog Years.* When the gang was betrayed to the authorities, Störtebeker was assigned to a punitive battalion detailed to clear land mines (*LA,* 194). Surviving this, he was interned in an American prisoner-of-war camp in Bavaria (*LA,* 90). Discharged in August 1945 (*LA,* 26), he abandons his original interest in German literature and art to study mechanical engineering in Aachen, specializing (appropriately for the Germany of the Economic Miracle) in the properties of cement. Several years later, by now a qualified industrial engineer, he encounters Sieglinde (Linde) Krings at a cement producers' congress. By 1954 he is engaged to her and is employed by the Krings cement works in Andernach on the Rhine as a specialist in air-pollution control (*LA,* 27).

Their engagement is quickly disrupted, however, when Linde develops an interest in the plant electrician, Heinz Schlottau, who served as a soldier under her father in Russia (*LA,* 35). Ferdinand Krings, Linde's father, born in 1892, has by this time been in Russia for 10 years, one of them spent as a Nazi general, infamous for his determination to "fight-to-the-finish" (*LA,* 39) at all costs, the other nine as a Russian prisoner of war. After his return to Germany in June 1954, obsessed with the past and its failures, he cloisters himself in his suburban home with a specially constructed sandbox (wired by Schlottau with a system of indicator lights to represent the opposing armies) in which he triumphantly refights and wins battles once lost, whether by himself or by others. Schlottau cordially hates Linde's father, who demoted him from sergeant to private during the Russian campaign (*LA,* 86). This constitutes his main attraction for Linde, who (partly for personal, partly for political reasons) hates her father even more intensely. She matches her father's obsession with her own obsession to prevent him from reclaiming his lost battles. She gives up the medical studies Starusch had persuaded her to undertake, becomes an expert in military history in order to fight and beat Krings at his own game, and trades calculated sexual favors for information from Schlottau concerning her father's strategic planning for their next encounter (*LA*, 77). Too caught up in refighting her own lost battle with the father who abandoned her to have any further use for Starusch, Linde soon breaks off their engagement, largely because he tries to reason her out of her obsession with her father. It is not his only failure. Starusch, who, by his own account, suffers from a lasting "fear of not being taken seriously" (*LA*, 22–23), is a woeful failure as a fiancé and a complete disappointment in bed. In the end, his fiancée is even driven to getting rid of him by paying him a bribe of fifteen thousand marks to simply disappear (*LA*, 16). Starusch puts the money to good use by returning to his original interests and becoming a teacher of German and history.

Inconsistencies quickly emerge, however, from Starusch's account. After trying and failing to combine the various disparate versions into a single narrative, the reader begins to realize that Starusch's multiple tales constitute not so much a single coherent narrative as a series of narrative experiments, reflections not on how things actually happened but on how they might well have happened. Starusch's narrative experiments in restructuring the unsatisfactory past take place in 1967, 10 years after his engagement to Linde (allegedly) broke up (*LA*, 45). As befits a teacher of German and history, Starusch is an eminently reasonable man, with, as he assures us, a "deep-seated horror of violence" (*LA*, 32). He succeeds in overcoming his horror on numerous occasions in his various narratives, however, as when he graphically relates how he strangled Linde with a bicycle chain on one occasion (*LA*, 51); shot her, their three-year-old son Klaus (previously unheard of), and finally her mother on another (*LA*, 72); and drowned her, her husband Schlottau, and *their* two boys Wolfi and Ulli on a third (*LA*, 250–55). From the beginning, however, whether the details agree or not, Starusch reveals himself as totally obsessed by his lost Linde, whose corpse, the reader has already discovered in the first paragraph, is hygienically stored in the deep freezer being advertised on his dentist's TV, "lodged between veal kidneys and milk" (*LA*, 8).

All of this, as Starusch observes in his first sentence, he "tells" to his dentist, though with "mouth blocked" and face to face with a television screen as "soundless" as himself (LA, 8). From the opening sentence, in other words, the reader is warned—and immediately sets to work to ignore that warning—of the degree to which the entire narrative is a conglomeration of memory, reverie, and fantasy, an extended and experimental interior monologue rather than the series of conversations as which it is presented. In these alleged conversations, Starusch, in spite of the reasonableness he claims for his character, reacts to his failed past with a heady mixture of self-pity and self-loathing combined with a constant appeal to violence and sadistic brutality. The dentist, on the other hand, his alleged interlocutor, authoritatively takes on the mantle of reason and civilization so completely abandoned by Starusch.

Starusch repeatedly indulges himself in outbursts of uncontrollable rage, picturing whole armies of bulldozers obliterating entire cities, in an expression of "stored-up, accumulated, cork-popping . . . rage about and against everything" (LA, 115). The dentist, in his role as psychiatrist, talks (or is made to talk) of "a neurotic growth of hatred" resulting from "an old failure" (LA, 68), akin to the tartar that is slowly destroying Starusch's teeth. The dentist himself is married, has three children, "is in the prime of life and practices a profession that brings gaugeable results" (LA, 174). As a believer in unspectacular evolutionary change, he is contrasted to a Starusch who demands radical revolutionary change (LA, 99). Starusch's relationship with the dentist is a highly complex one. He relies on him completely as the provider of the local anaesthetics that keep pain at least temporarily at bay, but he simultaneously ridicules his "naïve faith in progress" (LA, 31). He continually phones him for reassurance and advice in his dealings with Scherbaum, and is disappointed that he is never asked to visit the dentist's home. He also fantasizes that the dentist and his assistant are really Schlottau and Linde—a small accidental burn on his lip becomes a deliberate attempt to brand him with a pair of red-hot electrician's pliers (LA, 115). He ridicules even their common enthusiasms: the dentist's utopian vision, as construed by Starusch, is "worldwide and socially integrated Sickcare" (LA, 81), replacing all existing systems, even all government (LA, 99); Starusch's own equally unworkable pipe dream is for a "pedagogical province expanded to worldwide proportions," where there are only learners and no teachers (LA, 81). Even the painful abscess with which the narrative ends is a triumphant (if Pyrrhic) victory for Starusch over the dentist's indefatigable faith in progress.

The relationship between Starusch and the dentist is partially reflected in the relationship between Starusch and Krings. Pain, physical and mental, is at the center of *Local Anaesthetic.* Both Krings and the dentist are admirers of the ancient Stoics and their doctrine of imperturbability in the face of inevitable pain. (It has frequently been observed that if the Danzig trilogy is informed by the spirit of Rabelais, *Local Anaesthetic* is informed by that of Seneca.) The dentist helps his patients to a version of this stoicism by the scientific use of the local anaesthetic of the title, while Krings anaesthetizes his own pain by replaying history to a more satisfactory conclusion. Starusch vacillates between keeping his pain alive by refusing to forget the past—"Ah, how pain keeps fresh in the deep freezer" (*LA,* 30)—and employing variations of local anaesthesia effected by keeping that past alive in conflicting versions over which he has at least narrative control. Starusch's sympathy for "Poor Krings!" (*LA,* 71) may well derive from his perception that Krings (like himself, of course) always had to fight defensively, usually against overwhelming odds (*LA,* 71).

The unnamed dentist's arguments for evolutionary, as opposed to revolutionary, change are presented so trenchantly that early reviewers of *Local Anaesthetic,* ignoring the warning of the first sentence, saw him as one of its chief characters, even the most intriguing one. Some critics sided with his views, others with Starusch's. The central irony structuring their relationship, however, is of course that *both* sides of the disputation are produced by Starusch as he sits openmouthed and silent in the dentist's chair. The dentist, during the extended treatment, may indeed have voiced one or two of the opinions attributed to him by Starusch, but whether he did or not, his views are also largely Starusch's views. The reasonableness that earns the dentist Starusch's contempt is the same reasonableness that earns Starusch Linde's contempt, just as the flaunted radicalism that earns Starusch the dentist's censure is the same radicalism that earns Linde—and later also Scherbaum, Vero Lewand, and Irmgard Seifert—the censure of the pedagogue in Starusch.

Throughout the first book, constituting almost half of the entire narrative, Starusch's thoughts frequently return to his favorite student, the gifted Philipp Scherbaum, whom he hopes to persuade to abandon his "juvenile anarchism" (*LA,* 14) and to edit the school newspaper, a project scornfully opposed by Scherbaum's radical girlfriend, Vero. In the second book, only slightly shorter, Scherbaum—who claims to have no interest in anarchism (*LA,* 192)—becomes a principle character. Disgusted by the apathy with which the American use of napalm in Vietnam is greeted in Germany, he conceives of the plan of publicly burning his beloved dog, Max, in front of the cake-eating ladies of the Hotel

Kempinski in Berlin. He has chosen this plan on the grounds that a city of dog-lovers is bound to be appalled by such an act, whereas if he set himself on fire people would have forgotten it by the next morning. Starusch's attempts to dissuade his student from his planned course of action take up the entire second book.

Scherbaum and Starusch are the chief protagonists in the drama, but Scherbaum's action also has consequences for three separate relationships, involving himself and his girlfriend Vero, Starusch and his friend Irmgard Seifert, and Starusch and his dentist.

We hear about Scherbaum's plan in one of Starusch's constant phone calls to the dentist. He and the dentist join forces in an attempt to dissuade the boy. The dentist's consistent advice to Starusch, now gratefully accepted, is that "dialogue prevents action" (*LA*, 140). Scherbaum's consistent response to Starusch's advice is that "as a teacher, you've got to talk like that" (*LA*, 141). Vero's consistent reaction is to warn against Starusch's intervention, for "Mao warns us against the motley intellectuals" (*LA*, 142). Starusch worries that Scherbaum may accept his diversionary offer to burn a dog himself, instead, but toys also with the idea of inviting Linde to witness such an event: "Now at last you'll realize that I'm not the affable, self-pitying underdog you insisted on turning into a schoolteacher, but a man, yes, a man of action" (*LA*, 143). It is the dentist who phones Starusch with the good news that Scherbaum has finally abandoned his plan, not as a result of any of the many arguments advanced but only because of Starusch's (negative) example: Scherbaum doesn't want to grow up to be the kind of man his teacher is, still dining out on his alleged feats as a teenager (*LA*, 219).

It is clear that Starusch is disappointed rather than jubilant when Scherbaum shows signs of giving up on his project (*LA*, 211). Starusch evidently sees his student as his own 17-year-old self, when he too wanted to protest against an unjust world without pausing to weigh up the advantages and disadvantages of his actions. Now he is just one more "has-been" who, as he puts it to Scherbaum, has "turned into something I don't want to be and that you don't want to be" (*LA*, 167). Starusch is not the only one who wants to shape Scherbaum's plan to his own needs. Scherbaum's girlfriend, Vero, delighted to be so closely associated with someone who approximates to her idea of the ideal Technicolor revolutionary, urges him to go through with his plan just as intensely as Starusch tries to talk him out of it; when Scherbaum abandons his plan, Vero immediately abandons him. The third person to leap on Scherbaum's bandwagon is Irmgard Seifert, like Starusch a teacher of

German and history—and like both Vero and Linde a natural protester. While Starusch thus reacts only with "disabused cynicism" (*LA*, 56) to the Great Coalition of the political left and right of the late 1960s and Kurt Kiesinger's chancellorship—both events that filled many middle-of-the-road German liberals with dismay and disbelief—Irmgard Seifert calls, typically, for "energetic and uncompromising protest" (*LA*, 56). Like Starusch again, however, her eyes are more firmly fixed on the past than on the present. As a 17-year-old squad leader in the League of German Girls, she twice denounced a local farmer to party headquarters for refusing to allow a tank trap to be dug in his field. Twenty-two years later, as an ardent antifascist, she is now obsessed by her own past: "sometimes I hope something will happen that will purify us; but nothing ever happens" (*LA*, 128). Starusch, with little success, repeatedly attempts to play the part of coolly rational adviser to Irmgard, as he does to Vero and Scherbaum. Irmgard, for her part, sets out passionately to encourage Scherbaum in an action that will redeem her own guilty past.

During the course of the encounter with Scherbaum's youthful idealism that constitutes the entire second book, Starusch's thoughts only seldom turn to his own troubled past at the Krings cement works. The brief third book, as his treatment resumes, returns immediately to Linde, but the old failures are now strongly colored by the new failures of the more recent past. Starusch now has difficulty in keeping Linde, Vero, and even Irmgard entirely separate in his mind (*LA*, 237). He likewise indulges in a lengthy fantasy in which, as an employee in the Krings works, he takes Scherbaum's place, immolates a dog, and is seriously beaten by a crowd of onlookers, but during which, however, he sees himself not as Scherbaum but as Krings, betrayed by a gloating Linde and Schlottau (*LA*, 239–41).

Shortly before the end of the second book, however, we learn something new about Krings and his daughter. Starusch has made a number of passing references to his Schörner project, mainly with regard to the lack of any progress. The actual name Schörner, however, is mentioned for the first time only toward the middle of the Scherbaum affair, in a mental note to himself concerning his own project: "stick strictly to the facts about Schörner" (*LA*, 163). "Leave a wide margin for insertions that will later be deleted," Starusch advises himself shortly afterwards, and "maybe say Schörner after all if we mean Schörner" (*LA*, 180). Starusch's interest in Schörner, it emerges, is that the latter was a war criminal who illegally executed soldiers under his command for desertion

(*LA*, 204)—and, like many other Nazi war criminals, is now living comfortably forgotten in the new Federal Republic of Kurt Kiesinger. The motto "There is no Arctic!," previously attributed to "fight-to-the-finish" Krings (*LA*, 39), emerges shortly afterward as having been coined for the benefit of his half-frozen soldiers on the Murmansk Front by "Fight-to-the-Finish Schörner" (*LA*, 210). Moreover, "on his return from Soviet captivity, Schörner, on the advice of the police, left the Hof-Munich express in Freising, where his daughter Anneliese was waiting for him" (*LA*, 217). Krings, when he returned home from Soviet captivity, left the Koblenz express a station earlier at Andernach, where his daughter Linde did not deign to wait for him, but accidentally met him anyway (*LA*, 42–47). All of the Krings episodes, in other words, are now revealed as simply Starusch's inventions, fictional spin-offs from the Schörner material on which he continues to work in a halfhearted fashion; regarding Linde, the reader is increasingly confused.

The relationship with the dentist, as reported by Starusch, begins to sour appreciably at this point. The dentist becomes increasingly testy, repeatedly challenges Starusch's version of events, and proposes other versions that show Starusch in a decidedly different light. The dentist tells Starusch it is time to abandon his "fuzzy fictions" (*LA*, 227) about his "Krings—or whatever he may have been called" (*LA*, 227). He suggests that Linde was not at all the monster Starusch makes her out to be, but rather "a level-headed but not unloving young girl who grew more and more displeased at her fiancé's hectically frequent escapades" (*LA*, 227). He even tells (or is made to tell) the story of a Frau Schlottau (not Linde) who falls for a flashy young Starusch in his Mercedes convertible and whose husband, a cement-truck driver, returning unexpectedly to find Starusch in his wife's bed, tips his entire load of already mixed cement into the shiny convertible (*LA*, 228); whereupon Starusch's fiancée indignantly breaks off their engagement, Starusch (who hasn't even finished his engineering degree yet) is fired, and her family pays him off in order to avoid further disgrace (*LA*, 229). Starusch counters with a second version of the story in which it is Krings who drives a Mercedes convertible and a group of disgruntled war veterans (possibly including Schlottau) who dump the wet cement into it (*LA*, 229). For good measure, Starusch also gives a third version: the convertible is Linde's, while the cement truck is driven by him (*LA*, 230). He does not appreciate his dentist's (alleged) new attempts to rewrite his rewriting of history—"I tried to hate my dentist" (*LA*, 234)—and vengefully pictures him secretly eating disgusting quantities of sticky candies while publicly preaching the virtues of dental hygiene (*LA,* 235). The dentist, for his part, has (allegedly) been carrying out investigations on his own and has now discovered, confirming our growing suspicions as readers, that Starusch was never an engineer. Moreover, while Starusch did have a summer job in a cement works in Andernach in 1954, there was never a cement works there owned by a family called Krings. Starusch seems to have had a girlfriend at that time called Monica Lindrath—whose family name may have supplied him with the name Linde and who now remembers him only very vaguely (*LA,* 237). Starusch this time offers no contrary narrative in rebuttal.

Three weeks after the successful completion of his dental treatment, Starusch proposes to Irmgard Seifert—and is accepted. The reader who likes happy endings might well assume at this point (with only 10 pages to go) that we are about to experience one; that Starusch has managed after all to overcome the effects of whatever traumatic disappointment he suffered in love some 10 years earlier, whatever the exact details; and that he is now ready to settle down in a new relationship. Within a few pages, however, Starusch launches into the longest and most sadistic of the many "murder plots" (*LA,* 250) he has in store, a voluptuously detailed account of how, two years earlier, while temporarily employed as a swimming-pool lifeguard, he viciously murdered Linde, her husband Schlottau, and their two boys (*LA,* 250–55).

Although *Local Anaesthetic* is written in a stylistic key that is very different from that employed in the Danzig trilogy, it shares with its predecessors a central vision of narrative as, above all else, ironic. That irony was largely lost on its original audience. There is an unusually high degree of dialogue in the narrative, reflecting both Grass's original conception of it as a play and its predilection, as in all three narratives of the Danzig trilogy, for unanswered questions rather than tidy solutions. Similarly, while there are obvious targets of political satire in the book— including, especially, Kurt Kiesinger, the onetime Nazi now become chancellor, at home, and American policy in Vietnam, abroad—the primary thrust of the novel is less satirical than ironic. This refusal to focus clearly on readily identifiable targets, together with the decision not to repeat the stylistic pyrotechnics of the Danzig trilogy, certainly contributed to the novel's failure to win popular approval in Germany at the time of its publication. *Local Anaesthetic* was greeted with general disappointment, critics openly charging that Grass, under cover of writing a novel, had merely written a political tract extolling the virtues of the Social Democrats. Grass had become a high-profile target for a mili-

tant New Left as early as 1967, a fact that became a major issue both in
the 1969 federal elections and in the reception of *Local Anaesthetic*. Especially the radical young, who had seized with enthusiasm on the drumming midget Oskar as an emblem of anarchic disruption, now impa-
tiently turned away from what they saw as the schoolmasterly
moralizing of the 42-year-old Grass's latest work. In the United States,
on the other hand, as already noted, *Local Anaesthetic* fared very well
indeed in Ralph Manheim's translation, and the novel has continued
ever since to be much more highly regarded abroad than in Germany.

Throughout *Local Anaesthetic*, the ambition to save the world by
preaching the virtues of reason and moderation—always Grass's own
political platform—is firmly ironized. For all its self-irony, however, the
general thrust of the narrative is clear. The dentist's practically applied
stoicism—the strictly local relief of pain by means of such purely temporary remedies as local anaesthetic—is highlighted in Grass's change of
title from the original "Lost Battles" to *Local Anaesthetic*. There will
always be new pains to endure, there will always be new battles to be
(inevitably) lost, there will always be old age and death. In the end, in
these terms, life itself is a battle we have no hope of winning: "We are
born into this life without prospect of mercy" (*LA*, 111), to quote Starusch quoting Krings quoting Seneca. For practical purposes, we are
clearly well advised to focus less on the major battles we are bound to
lose than on the day-to-day skirmishes we may have some limited
chance of winning, even if only temporarily and only provisionally.
Three years after *Local Anaesthetic*'s publication, this unspectacular credo
will become the central theme of Grass's next major narrative, *From the
Diary of a Snail*.

Max

The play *Davor* (1969)—literally "Beforehand," reminding us of the
axiom from *Local Anaesthetic* that "afterward begins beforehand" (*LA*,
226)—is a dramatized version of the Scherbaum plot. Like the novel, it
was not a popular success. It was translated in 1972 by A. Leslie Willson
and Ralph Manheim as *Max: A Play*.

The action of the play is almost exactly the same as that of the second
book of *Local Anaesthetic*. Unfolding in 13 scenes without an intermis-
sion, the presentation of the action is more concentrated and more stylized than in the novel. An open stage, without scene changes, makes
only minimal gestures toward realistic settings. The five actors are

symmetrically arranged: the two teachers, Starusch and Seifert; the unnamed dentist; and the two students, Scherbaum and Lewand. The two teachers talk about the same things they talked about in *Local Anaesthetic*. The two students frequently enter on bicycles, describe circles around their elders, and depart laughing. The dentist, while unstintingly contributing his professional opinions on the worldwide spread of caries, simultaneously serves as an ironic commentator on the obsessions of others. Cutting across the symmetry, however, Starusch is still firmly the central character, with by far the largest number of significant interactions with other characters.

One significant difference between narrative and play is that in the latter the action takes place in a vacuum, isolated from the larger context of the novel. Starusch's background, so crucial to the novel, is here barely sketched in, with no reference at all to Linde Krings or her Nazi father or to any engagement with Irmgard Seifert. The overall result of this stripped-down presentation is a major stylistic and tonal distinction between narrative and play, for Starusch's involvement is completely shorn of the richly contextualizing material presented in the first book of the novel. The audience is not privy to his murderous fantasies; neither is it aware of the degree to which the dentist's opinions are a projection of Starusch's imagination. In the play, although Starusch and the dentist are effectively played off against each other as academic pedants, the dentist and his ideas are by no means a projection of Starusch's mind; the dentist is as much (and as little) a realistic character as any one of the other figures.

As in all of Grass's plays, nothing really happens in *Max*. Scherbaum conceives a plan—and he is talked out of it, at some length. As in Grass's early absurdist plays, the presentation is closer to staged poetry than to theater in any conventional understanding of the genre. For all the theatrical schematism, however, which includes almost caricatural renditions of Irmgard, Vero, and the dentist, the relationship between Scherbaum and Starusch is in some ways more complexly realistic than in the novel. Starusch, for example, contradicts his own admonitions not to act rashly by silent exhortations to Scherbaum to act at all costs; Scherbaum contradicts his public rejection of Starusch's advice by silent pleas to him for support and understanding in his endeavor. Perhaps the most significant difference between the novel and the play is that the novel focuses on psychological stasis—Starusch's inability to escape from his private obsessions—while the play centers instead on an attempt (if an abortive one) at political action. It is indicative that in the play Vero has the last word. Scherbaum, much to her disgust, has accepted the editorship of the school newspaper, having abandoned his radical plan. When he invites her to an editorial meeting she indignantly refuses. Her "No!," as the last word of the play, is much more strikingly emphasized than in the novel, in which she likewise refuses, before settling down tamely as the wife of an academic. We leave the novel with an open question concerning the psychologically troubled teacher mired in an inescapable if entirely undecided past; we leave the play with an open question concerning a socially troubled younger generation on the threshold of an uncertain future.

Chapter Eight
From the Diary of a Snail

Grass's next major narrative, *Aus dem Tagebuch einer Schnecke,* appeared in 1972; it appeared in English the following year, in Ralph Manheim's translation, as *From the Diary of a Snail.* A highly complex piece of narrative art, *From the Diary of a Snail* resists classification. It combines a retrospective journal-like account of Grass's personal involvement as a highly active campaigner on behalf of the Social Democrats during the successful 1969 electoral campaign (as a result of which his friend Willy Brandt was elected Chancellor) with both historical data and a fictional story line concerning the fate of Danzig Jews during the war; snapshot portrayals of the role of a German father of four in the 1970s; a reflective essay on Albrecht Dürer's engraving *Melencolia I;* and a wealth of information, imparted in passing, on an impressive variety of snails and assorted gastropods (some 40 species of which are mentioned). In terms of content, *From the Diary of a Snail* thus clearly takes up and intensifies the political involvement of *Local Anaesthetic.* In terms of technique, experimenting as it does with the interaction of fictional and nonfictional forms of narrative, with the juxtaposition of novel, diary, history, autobiography, political tract, essay, and the lyric, it equally clearly points forward to the complex narrative structure of *The Flounder.*

In all of Grass's major works up to and including *Local Anaesthetic* (1969), the element of fictivity clearly predominated—even in *The Plebeians,* whose central character was quite openly modeled on Bertolt Brecht. In *From the Diary of a Snail,* Grass attempts a challenging new experiment in narrative form. Nearly 20 years later, in a 1991 interview, Grass still insisted on the central importance of *From the Diary of a Snail* in the formal development of his work as a whole, observing that he considers it to have been his boldest formal experiment, comparable perhaps only to *Dog Years.* Without *From the Diary of a Snail,* he continues, later experiments like *The Flounder* would not have been possible.[1]

The central nonfictional component of the *From the Diary of a Snail* is Grass's own first-person account of the seven-month electoral campaign of 1969, during which, traveling more than 30,000 kilometers in a Volkswagen van, he made an exhausting 94 public appearances throughout

West Germany. Grass conveys a convincing sense of the sheer hard work, the boring repetitiveness, the frequent discouragement, and the agonizing slowness involved in nudging voter figures just a notch or two higher on the scale. His political beliefs are practical and unheroic: "I am a Social Democrat because to my mind socialism is worthless without democracy and because an unsocial democracy is no democracy at all."[2] The central symbol of the narrative is that of the lowly snail of the title, symbolizing the excruciatingly slow, thoroughly unexciting, highly vulnerable but nonetheless steady and reliable evolutionary reformism that Grass sees as typifying the kind of socialist democracy he and the SPD alike espouse. Grass stylizes his political involvement, "aiming at small gains" (DS, 33), "grimly" pulling "the weeds of German idealism" (DS, 33) wherever they are to be found, balancing a need to move on and get things done against a "tendency to dwell, hesitate, and cling" as "gradually evolving into the snail principle" (DS, 63). The snail may not be the most exciting or glorious of chargers to ride into battle in the name of progress, but "Many overtake me and later fall by the wayside: / Object lessons in unsteadiness" (DS, 42).

The entire narrative, which is ostensibly designed to serve as an explanatory setting for Grass's role in the electoral campaign, is addressed to his four children, aged from 4 to 12 (and is dedicated to the children of his friend Vladimir Kafka, a Czech artist who died in 1970). The children will inherit the future Grass and his fellow politicians (as well as others with very different ideas and values) are attempting to prepare for them, just as they unwittingly inherit the weight of the past. Grass reflects on the kind of persons they will turn out to be, the kind of world in which they are likely to live, and the kind of world in which they might well have lived. The writer's task is to prevent the past from being conveniently forgotten, so that it will not have to be repeated in the future: "A writer, children, is someone who writes against the passage of time" (DS, 141). For their part, the children's cheerful irreverence for his eternal "talktalktalk" and their continual impatience for something new and more exciting guarantees a regular alternation between the narrative strands, few episodes lasting more than a few pages before being succeeded by something quite different.

The second major nonfictional element of the narrative is an account of the historical facts surrounding the expulsion of Jews from Danzig during the war years. Grass, as historian, recounts the results of the numerous interviews he conducted with relatives and descendants of the victims in the process of piecing the story together. The present of the election campaign and its aftermath is thus continually seen in (and relativized by) the light of the past, as when the 42-year-old Grass revisits the concentration camp in Dachau—now preserved as a monument—that he had first seen (and been devastated by) as part of an American reeducation program when he was a 17-year-old prisoner of war (*DS,* 146).

The central fictional character of the narrative—though based to some extent on the real-life experiences of the literary critic Marcel Reich-Ranicki (*DS,* 18)—is Hermann Ott, nicknamed Doubt (*Zweifel*) by all who know him because of his cautious, instinctive, and unfailing skepticism. Born in Danzig in 1905, Ott worked during his student vacations at the Jewish transit camp on the island of Troyl near Danzig, where Jewish emigrants, on their way from persecution in Russia and Poland to a new life in America, were lodged while waiting for their visas. Later, a high-school teacher like Eberhard Starusch, he is hounded out of his school in Langfuhr because of his quiet refusal to go along with the growing persecution of Jewish fellow citizens from 1933 on. Though not himself Jewish, he briefly becomes a teacher in a Jewish private school instead.

The biologist Ott's passion in life is snail collecting. His pet aversion (and Grass's) is the heroically galloping Hegelian *Weltgeist*—suggested for Hegel by the equestrian statue of Napoleon in Jena—that is, the abstract spirit of history storming irresistibly toward a glorious future that must be achieved regardless of the cost in human misery (*DS,* 42–43). (In *From the Diary of a Snail,* Hegel, or at any rate the excesses to which his philosophy of history has led, provides the target for Grass's mockery, much as Heidegger does in *Dog Years.*) Even Ott's fiancée eventually abandons him for his unpatriotic doubt, his lack of belief in the golden future promised by National Socialism (*DS,* 121). In the end, after beatings by both the Hitler Youth and the police, Ott sees that there is no choice but to resort to flight—which he does typically undramatically, by bicycle, taking with him little more than a change of clothing and reproductions of two engravings, one of a snail carrying its house, one of Dürer's *Melencolia I* (*DS,* 115). After only a few miles, more or less by accident, he finds shelter in the cellar of a more or less friendly bicycle dealer, one Anton Stomma, an unpredictable Kashubian giant who alternately beats him for his own good and sweats anxiously over lessons from him in reading and writing.

Ott spends more than four years in the cellar, tended by Stomma and his daughter Lisbeth. Lisbeth has become so weighed down by melancholy over the death of both her husband and her son in the first days of the war that she is generally considered to be no longer right in the head and spends most of her time in cemeteries, talking to the dead. Since Ott is in hiding, Stomma refuses to be convinced that he is not a Jew and, especially after Ott's money runs out, weighs at length his patriotic duty to hand him over to the Germans against Ott's usefulness as proof of his own anti-German activities if the Russians should win. Stomma never quite makes up his mind, and as a result, more or less by accident, Ott is allowed to remain in relative peace.

Lisbeth, meanwhile (who, at her father's orders, regularly but entirely mechanically goes to bed with Ott), discovers his passion for snails and brings him various specimens that Ott, to pass the time, uses for elaborate snail-racing experiments. In a flash of the fantastic realism that we have not seen since the Danzig trilogy, one of these snails, when placed on Lisbeth's body, magically draws all her melancholy out of her, growing inky black in the process and turning Lisbeth into a normal young woman with normal desires and appetites. Far from kissing the now revolting gastropod and discovering that it was a prince all along, Lisbeth promptly squashes the hideous reminder of a past she would now rather forget. "Nail the slug to the cross" (*DS*, 264), the text comments tersely, for few good deeds escape appropriate punishment, as various saviors throughout history have discovered to their cost. The implication on a personal level is also clear: Grass, too, has therapeutically drawn much "melancholy" (literally, in Greek, "black bile") out of the German system, not entirely to general applause, and might well also one day find himself trodden upon for his pains. The following page brings an account of anonymous death threats—"the bullet's ready" (*DS*, 265)—telephoned to his home and passed on by his children.

Lisbeth's magical cure, we are given to understand in an ironic coda, also turns her into an indefatigable shrew who (like Dürer's wife Agnes, we are assured, and anticipating the insatiable Ilsebill in *The Flounder*) drives her newly acquired husband Ott to distraction. Two years after the war she commits the increasingly melancholy Ott, still vainly searching for the magical snail that can cure melancholy, to an institution. There he spends the next 12 years brooding in almost complete silence. In the late 1950s, however, now cured, he and his wife and son leave Poland for West Germany—as Grass assures his children, who have their doubts about the happy ending and sensibly accuse him of having just made it all up (*DS*, 280). The accusation teasingly reminds us that Ott's nickname, Doubt, also lends his story an allegorical character, as Volker Neuhaus has aptly pointed out: Doubt flourishes dangerously in a Jewish school during the rise of Nazism, survives only underground during the war years, comes into its own again briefly toward the end of the war, is relegated to a mental institution in communist Poland, and is grudgingly tolerated in the Germany of the 1960s (Neuhaus, 119). During his work on the election campaign, Grass tells his children, Doubt was not only "silently present at every speech" but played a major part in writing them, too (DS, 275).

The fourth major strand of the narrative is a continuing essayistic reflection on the nature of melancholy and its relationship to the concept of utopia. This reflection is derived from the fact that Grass agreed, toward the beginning of the election campaign, to give an address in Nuremberg two years later, in May 1971, on the occasion of the 500th anniversary of the birth of Dürer. Grass decided to talk on the engraving *Melencolia I*, completed by Dürer in 1514 following the death of his mother—and his address, "On Stasis in Progress," is printed as the final chapter of *From the Diary of a Snail*. Working notes on the topic are interjected throughout the narrative: Dürer "apparently regarded them as sisters. How Melancholy and Utopia call each other cause. How the one shuns and disavows the other. How they accuse each other of evasion. How the snail mediates between them" (DS, 91). The deepest melancholy is the equally dangerous opposite of utopian idealism, à la Hegel: "Everything sounds hollow in her ears, and she tots up a hollow list: absurdity, the eternal cycle, the futility of all effort and the recurrence of the same" (DS, 116). Utopia, on the other hand, is "a gullible little thing, always on the road" (DS, 117), always looking for new absolutes to follow. Both melancholy and utopia, in moderation, are necessary components of the healthy personality, whether individual or national—"As though progress had stasis as an echo. As though melancholy were the inner lining of utopia" (DS, 92)—each keeping the other in balance, the desire for progress and change held in check by the realization that all progress is relative. Either of the two, on the other hand, unchecked by the other, can lead to disaster.

Melancholy provides the connecting link between Grass the writer and politician; his fictive alter ego, Hermann Ott; and the real-life Manfred Augst, the most disturbing figure in Grass's account of the election campaign. The encounter with Augst took place in July 1969 at the Evangelical Church Congress in Stuttgart, where Grass had agreed to give a reading and take part in the discussion. The unfortunate Augst, a 56-year-old pharmacist, served briefly in the SS during the war before being invalided out for ill health, became a convinced pacifist after the war, but never recovered the sense of absolute purpose and comradeship the Nazi years had brought him. Finding no alternative satisfaction in family, friends, profession, or religion, he has given up any pretense of hope in himself, in today's Germany, and, especially, in the younger generation. He makes an incoherent and rambling speech to this effect from the audience, ending with a provocative salute to his old SS comrades; is booed off the floor by an unsympathetic crowd; and promptly, in an act of "ritualized protest" (*DS,* 164), swallows a lethal dose of cyanide brought along for the purpose.

Augst, as reconstructed by Grass, who was deeply affected by the incident, is the complete opposite of Ott—and of Grass himself. While Ott's (and Grass's) guiding principle is Doubt, and Grass writes of his "disgust at the absolute and suchlike thumbscrews" (*DS,* 142), Augst is a fervent believer in absolutes, a man who is unable to resort to compromise as a safety valve, a man emblematic of an endangered society "on whose fringes groups were beginning to take desperately extreme attitudes of resignation or euphoria" (*DS,* 287). Augst's right-wing fanaticism is, for Grass, just another version of the left-wing fanaticism he sees as dangerously on the rise in the Germany of the late 1960s. For Augst, "everything was black or white" (*DS,* 232); for Grass, gray is always preferable to either black or white—"Of all flowers my favorite is the light-gray skepsis, which blooms all year round" (*DS,* 71)—and "melancholy and utopia are heads and tails of the same coin" (*DS,* 287). Ott, alias Doubt, likewise a believer in complementary relationships, is particularly interested in the mating practices of hermaphroditic snails. He even plans at one time to write a treatise "On the Happiness of Hermaphrodites" (*DS,* 234), on the relationship between hermaphroditic species of snails on the one hand, that is to say, and on "melancholy and utopia on the other" (*DS,* 234).

Structurally, *From the Diary of a Snail* is a highly interesting narrative experiment. Although part of that experiment consists in its resistance to classification, it is clearly more adequately judged as a work of creative fiction incorporating nonfictional elements than as a factual journal larded with fictional episodes. The nonfictional novel, as a literary form, had by this time already been popularized in American fiction by Truman Capote and Norman Mailer. But while Capote, in *In Cold Blood* (1959), limited himself to an evocative structuring of empirical facts, and Mailer, in *Armies of the Night* (1968), experimented primarily with ironic third-person autobiographical narrative, Grass goes much further.

He first introduces himself—politician, family man, celebrity, writer-at-work—as first-person narrator and then proceeds, in addition, to fictionalize himself in the course of a parallel narrative by evocatively slipping into the personality of Hermann Ott. He is thus able to maintain a structural tension in which the real-author-as-character and the fictive character interrogatively illuminate each other and serve as mutual balances and question marks. This new possibility of fictionalized autobiography is developed extensively in his next major book, *The Flounder,* where the authorial persona as narrator and protagonist is reflected in a panorama of fictional counterparts through four millennia of history. The same technique, in a variety of applications, becomes a central trademark of Grass's narrative practice right through the 1980s, up to and including *The Call of the Toad.* To this extent, simultaneously pointing backward once again to Danzig and the war years, firmly anchored in the West German present like *Local Anaesthetic,* and pointing forward technically to *The Flounder* and later narratives, *From the Diary of a Snail,* as Volker Neuhaus observes, is a key text in the development of Grass's work (Neuhaus, 114).

For all its formal innovation, however, *From the Diary of a Snail* met with little more than, at best, a polite response in either Germany or the United States. Once again, political factors obviously played a major role in the response in Germany, and Grass was widely vilified for having produced yet another political pamphlet. On both sides of the Atlantic, there were suggestions, by no means always free of malice, that the 45-year-old Grass had by now clearly passed his prime and was merely attempting to use the provocative juxtaposition of fiction and nonfiction in *From the Diary of a Snail* to disguise the fact that his narrative genius was exhausted. In his personal life, too, significant rifts were beginning to appear. In late 1972, after the long-drawn-out stress of the election campaign, with his first marriage by now an admitted failure (various echoes of which can also be found throughout *From the Diary of a Snail*), and with a new relationship under way, Grass made a determined attempt to escape the limelight. He bought a medieval half-timbered retreat, protected by a historical preservation order, in the village of Wewelsfleth, near Itzehoe in Schleswig-Holstein, where he, too, might at least temporarily be protected against the unwelcome incursions of the outside world. *From the Diary of a Snail* marks a turning point not just in technical terms: after it, the tentative optimism of the 1960s begins to give way to the sustained melancholy that will infuse Grass's work with an increasing bleakness from the early 1980s on.

Chapter Nine
The Flounder

During the five years that separated *From the Diary of a Snail* from Grass's next major narrative, *Der Butt,* which appeared in 1977 and was translated the following year by Ralph Manheim as *The Flounder,* the suggestion continued to be heard that Grass had nothing more to say.[1] When the new novel finally appeared, after a lavish and carefully orchestrated advance program, such suspicions were shown to be entirely unfounded. The determinedly low-key style of *From the Diary of a Snail* gave way again to the robust fabulation that his readers remembered from the Danzig trilogy—and by now demanded. A present to himself to mark his 50th birthday (as he characterized it for the journalists), a new beginning, and a major media event, the almost 700-page novel marks a return to Danzig and Grass's narrative wellsprings. It also can be read as in many ways an interim summation of his previous narrative work. In formal terms, *The Flounder* combines the baroque fullness of the Danzig trilogy with the relative severity of *Local Anaesthetic* and *From the Diary of a Snail,* while its twin thematic concerns, the ethos of protest, action, and revolution on the one hand and the snail-like pace of historical progress on the other, are prefigured respectively in the latter two texts.

In *The Flounder,* Grass turns his primary attention from the philosophy of historical progress and the trials of local politics, as explored in *From the Diary of a Snail,* to the politics of the war of the sexes. The flounder of the title is borrowed from the Grimm brothers' well-known (and frankly misogynistic) tale of "The Fisherman and his Wife." In the Grimms' version, the fisherman's wife accidentally catches a magical fish, a flounder, who in exchange for his freedom promises that she shall have her heart's desire. Wishing to be rich, she is soon dissatisfied at not being richer; wishing to be king, she grows unhappy at not being emperor; her desire to be emperor granted, she wishes to be pope; and once she is declared pope she decides that what she really wants is to be God—whereupon the magical flounder disappears and she finds herself back in the same miserable fisherman's hut she started out from. In Grass's version, the fisherman, rather than his wife, catches the magical flounder at some point in the Stone Age—and at that very point on the Baltic coast where the city of Danzig will eventually rise. The fisherman, become immortal like the flounder himself, is guided through history by the magical fish, whose first and most urgent task is to release the male sex from the bondage of a primeval matriarchy. Down through the centuries the fisherman graces the pages of history in a variety of typically male roles, but he is also perennially troubled by the nature of these roles. Or so he tells us, at any rate, for the onetime fisherman is also our narrator. His worldview has recently been severely shaken, for the magical flounder has allowed himself to be caught again, this time by a group of 1970s feminists who promptly bring the male chauvinist fish before a Women's Tribunal in Berlin to answer, if he can, for the millennia of insidious advice he has been providing to men and for the resultant mess they have succeeded in making of things.

All of this our (not entirely dependable) hero also relates to his wife, for *The Flounder,* on at least one of its many levels, is structured around the deeply troubled relationship between the nameless narrator and his pregnant wife "Ilsebill," whose disparaging nickname he borrows from the Grimms' conveniently angled tale. Weak and ineffectual, shaken and resentful, the narrator takes continual flight into his various ingenious fictions, elaborately ringing hypothetical changes on his and Ilsebill's relationship by constructing other possible relationships that might have obtained between other possible versions of themselves throughout history. There is little to suggest that the eventual birth of their child will in any way signal a rebirth of their relationship—indeed, they separate before the child is born.

Ostensibly a novel, *The Flounder* stretches this elastic term as far as it has ever been stretched. The central narrative strand covers four millennia, depicted in a virtuoso variety of styles ranging from the lustily Rabelaisian to outraged intensity, journalistic reportage, vigorous satire, and tongue-in-cheek self-parody. In addition, there is much historical documentary; an interspersed cookbook with, by all accounts, workable (if decidedly Germanic) recipes; and a respectably sized intercalated collection of 46 lyrics, all set against the autobiographical backdrop of the author's own comings and goings as public figure and private person over the preceding five years or so. Autobiographical material is particularly interestingly deployed: the narrator and his wife live in Wewelsfleth, near Itzehoe in Schleswig-Holstein, where Grass himself had been living since 1972; the novel is dedicated to Grass's own daughter, Helene, named for his mother and born in the summer of 1974, while work on the novel was underway. The suggestion of immediate autobiographical relevance, as in *From the Diary of a Snail,* enriches the narrative by implicitly inviting readers to indulge their curiosity by speculating as to the various degrees of fictionality involved in the narrative they are reading. A cycle of more than a hundred graphics, based on the various themes of *The Flounder,* also came into being during the five years of work on the novel.[2]

Grass has outlined the genesis of the resulting meganovel in various interviews. The initial concept centered on the history of food, always personally important to Grass and now a major question in global economics. The history of food inevitably began to involve the history of women, and this in turn suggested the fable of the flounder and its enthusiastically antifeminist account of the archetypal shrew. The rewriting of the Grimms' tale, the revelation of "the other truth," is cast in nine books (or "months," as they are titled) that correspond to the nine months of a pregnancy that the aggressively feminist Ilsebill intends will produce the birth of a new man, an "Emmanuel," a savior.[3] The novel opens with the copulation that is to engender the new man, shortly before which the fairy-tale flounder, an amalgam of male *Weltgeist* and God the father, Mephisto and male superego, is placed on trial before the Women's Tribunal. The trial also lasts nine months. With the exception only of the first chapter, which deals with three separate female figures, each of the nine chapters, simultaneously related both by the narrator to his wife and by the flounder to the tribunal, deals with a single female figure, giving in all 11 women, more specifically 11 cooks from the Neolithic Age to 1974, each of them associated with a particular favorite dish of the narrator. Each of these historical women has a present-day counterpart who serves on the feminist tribunal sitting in judgment on the flounder and on a history dominated and written by males. Each of them, moreover, has a male counterpart, or several male counterparts, representing the narrator through history in various guises and a variety of relationships. The narrator in turn, by his own account, has had carnal relations, real or fantasized, with almost all of the members of the tribunal. His projected selves through history, finally, have each at least one male counterpart, who is much more what the world expects of a "real man," lusty, aggressive, decisive, extroverted, and certainly not prey to the all-pervading melancholy and self-doubt that characterize the narrator from the beginning.

Behind all the mock-apocalyptic fables of the narrator as latter-day Scheherazade, we find the same founding confrontation of a man and a woman, the narrator and his "Ilsebill," always changing and always the same. From the opening sentence—"Ilsebill put on more salt" (*F,* 3)—to the closing "I ran after her" (*F,* 547), Ilsebill is therefore central. She is both the narrator's wife, whom he at once loves and hates, and the rhetorically projected receiver of his narrative soliloquy. She is the central woman in the novel, and she is all women—though her predominant mask for the narrator, profoundly shaken and filled with an all-encompassing sense of loss by their growing estrangement, is that of the castrating feminist witch. Women's rights are at the heart of the novel, and this is crystallized in the terse opening sentence. Woman's role as cook, sustainer, lover, wife, and mother is the unwritten dark side of history. Ilsebill, for the narrator, adds salt to a male collective consciousness shaken by the new self-understanding of women and tormented at once by a half-admitted guilt and by a deep-seated fear of abandonment. Ilsebill is also the fairy-tale shrew, infuriating, indomitable, insatiable, castrating. Not surprisingly, some reviewers found *The Flounder* to be "shrilly partisan," filled with an "anti-feminist sermonizing that runs through the book like a bitter thread."[4] The novel, however, can much more fruitfully be read as offering not sermons of any sort but what one might call a narrative phenomenology of women through history—reminiscent of the scarecrow phenomenology of Brauxel's mine in *Dog Years*—as evoked by a narrator whose judgment and dependability are as overtly questionable as those of any narrator we have met in any Grass text.

The most intriguing structural feature of this huge and complex novel is the intricate network of correspondences that is set up between the various female figures, as the narrator's troubled confrontation with one woman provokes his narration of the stories of 11 "other" women down through history. The first book—or, rather, "The First Month"— deals with three of them, the parodic trinity of Awa, Wigga, and Mestwina, charting the development from Awa's divine gynocracy by way of Wigga's semidivinity to Mestwina's aberrant priesthood in the service of an upstart male god in the shape of a flounder. Awa—a variation on whose character we have met before under the name of Anna Bronski, Oskar's grandmother in *The Tin Drum,* and whose name in German, Aua, is a cry of pain—is the *magna mater,* the great mother. Her three breasts are inexhaustible sources of food, comfort, sexual gratification, and existential security. In the early Christian era, we are told, her worship shades imperceptibly into the cult of the Virgin (*F,* 49). Awa is "related to Demeter, Frigga, Cybele, Semele" (*F,* 105) as well as to the

Virgin—but she is also related to "black Kali" (*F,* 175), the destroyer, and thus to Oskar's Black Witch. Wigga's leadership is a weakened version of Awa's, and male "wanderlust" (*F,* 11) begins to manifest itself as the young men of the tribe climb "tall trees . . . to see if something was coming, if something new was coming" (*F,* 11), the beginning of a cycle we see beginning again in the lesbian Maxie's climbing "the phallic pine" (*F,* 475) in the "Father's Day" episode.

The tenth-century Mestwina is the most complex member of the triad. As gynocratic culture draws to a close, Mestwina begins to sacrifice first to one male god, the Hegelian flounder, then to another, likewise symbolized by a fish, Christ. Finally, she acts like a man rather than a woman in killing "me" (*F,* 12), alias Bishop Adalbert, who then, as a nameless shepherd—again a Christian reference—in turn betrays her. Like Pilenz and like Matern, the narrator preserves the memory of this primal betrayal undimmed, and Mestwina (like Niobe in *The Tin Drum*) is characterized by her amber jewelry, the amber of an uncomfortably persistent memory. Her uncertainty in the face of a world she no longer understands finds expression in her addiction to mead and storytelling—which introduces both the recurrent hallucination theme and the Scheherazade motif. Unlike Scheherazade, however, Mestwina's stories cannot save her, and she is eventually executed for the murder of Adalbert. Mestwina's death thus completes the symmetry of the opening triad: the divine Awa dies a ritual, sacrificial death—killed and eaten by the tribe, "she didn't taste especially good" (*F,* 261); the still semi-mythical, Iron Age Wigga dies an accidental death of blood poisoning caused by a rusty iron nail; and Mestwina, who cannot accommodate herself to male hegemony, is executed.

This triadic pattern continues throughout the series. A second triad encompasses the saint Dorothea of Montau, the hedonistic nun Margarete (Gret) Rusch, and the convicted witch Agnes Kurbiella. A clear parallelism is established between the two triads. Awa and Dorothea are both associated with the sphere of the divine; Wigga and Gret adhere very definitely to earthly pleasures; and Mestwina and Agnes are both used by men for their pleasure and then discarded. Awa and Dorothea die ritual deaths; Wigga and Gret die accidental deaths; Mestwina and Agnes are executed. If the first triad demonstrates the waning of primeval matriarchy, the second explores the extremes of the sexual confrontation. Dorothea masters men by starvation, in terms of both food and sex, and does this in spite of the fact that she bears nine children (the parodic number symbolism continues throughout the novel). Gret masters men by a superabundance of both food and sex. Agnes is woman as the eternal victim.

Dorothea of Montau, based on a real fourteenth-century ecstatic of the same name, is clearly nonetheless related to the Black Witch of *The Tin Drum*. Dorothea "inspires fear" (*F,* 12)—and does so precisely because of her ability to withdraw so completely from the world inhabited by her husband, the narrator-projection Slichting, to strip it of all importance, to castrate. Devoting herself body and soul to the ecstatic rigors of a sexual-mystical Christolatry, she allows eight of her nine children to die of neglect. The ninth is almost boiled alive when she falls into the family cooking pot and her screams prove insufficient to attract the attention of her mother, rapt in contemplation of the crucifix. But Dorothea is also a tragic figure, a victim of history, a would-be liberated woman in an age when such was not possible for a woman of her class, and she is left only with the choice of being considered a witch or a saint. Slichting considers her a witch, popular opinion considers her a saint, and when she dies immured, her death is partly murder, partly sacrifice (in both senses), and partly the ultimate escape of suicide.

Margarete Rusch is no less a personification of the Black Witch in her Earth Mother manifestation, the mother that is both womb and tomb. Although her only opportunity for public position is clerical—she is the sixteenth-century abbess of a convent—this does not prevent her from highly effective manipulations behind the scenes. The one occasion on which she traumatically fails is when she proves unable to prevent her father's execution, although even here she is able to exact appropriate vengeance: one of those responsible she murders by overfeeding for many years, the other she smothers in bed between her ample breasts. Overtly modeled along Rabelaisian lines, Fat Gret, as she is called, is as much a free spirit as Dorothea, as capable of being a leading public figure in her age, and, as a representative of female counterhistory, she is at least as important as Vasco da Gama, whose explorations were necessary, the narrator claims, primarily because of Gret's need for pepper in large quantities. A overabundance alike of food, sex, and Rabelaisian laughter constitutes her proper milieu: "she drowned the pope and Luther in her laughter" (*F,* 13). Her vitality is that of life itself, and so is her inscrutability. "She sheltered me with her fat," the narrator claims (*F,* 14), but she also castrates one lover and murders two others. However different from Dorothea's her approach to the war of the sexes may be, her enforced role also kills her in the end: she chokes on a fishbone, her death thus establishing the similarity of her final defeat to that of Wigga and Mestwina.

Agnes Kurbiella, the final member of the second triad, is also, mathematically and otherwise, the central figure of the 11. A seventeenth-century kitchen maid, she lives through the Thirty Years' War, a period especially suited to exemplify the vision of history as chaos. There is a particular poignancy about this episode, in regard both to Agnes, perhaps the most sympathetically drawn of all the women, and to the narrator-projection Opitz, certainly the closest in spirit of all the narrator-projections to Grass himself.[5] Agnes is "one of those women who can only love comprehensively" (F, 15). She is consumed by her devotion to the four men she successively loves, the Swedish cavalryman Ludström, who abandons her; the painter Möller and the poet Opitz, who use her as maid, mistress, muse and nurse; and the visionary Kuhlmann, who fills her head with the incoherent dreams that eventually lead her to the stake as a witch. A victim of her own good nature, she counts for nothing in a world where goodness is a liability. Agnes, as eternal victim (and as nurse), may be read as an echo of Agnes Bronski of *The Tin Drum,* whose suicide in the first book of that novel is echoed by the murder in the second book and the surrealistic suicide in the third of her other namesake, the nun Agneta. Although there is an obvious affectionate wistfulness in the portrait of Agnes Kurbiella, she is not merely a romanticized ideal woman. Rather, we have a poignant portrait of a woman whose human richness is squandered in a thankless age—an age whose boundaries are certainly not fixed by the limits of the seventeenth century.

A third triad follows, consisting of three characters of distinctly modern mold and political turn of mind: Amanda Woyke, a farm-kitchen cook but nonetheless a thoroughgoing product of the Age of Enlightenment; Sophie Rotzoll, a Romantic revolutionary; and Lena Stubbe, the socialist compiler of a cookbook for the working classes. Once again there are correspondences with the first triad: Amanda's storytelling, Sophie's hallucinations, and Lena's violent death link them all with Mestwina's defeat. They are all three idealists, all three make a historical contribution, and all three, to a greater or lesser extent, are nonetheless thwarted and repressed throughout their lives by the very society they attempt to serve.

Amanda, with her "potato face" reminiscent of the "wurzel mother" Wigga, is an avatar of Awa the provider, of Anna Bronski in the Kashubian potato field. In historical terms she is the most successful of the women: she introduces the potato into Prussia. "Though only a woman, she made history" (*F,* 16), the Hegelian flounder dryly observes. An enlightened proto-Maoist (*F,* 322), "from the reality of the farm kitchen she derived a utopian West Prussian potato soup that would be dispensed the world over" (*F,* 300); mothered Frederick the Great ("Ole Fritz"); is tied by marriage to the reactionary and dim-witted narrator-projection Romeike; and cherishes her lifelong illusion of the eventual worldwide conquest of hunger "up to the reason-transfigured end" (*F,* 324). After her death, still unstoppable, Amanda even introduces her potato soup in heaven. While Grass's account celebrates the introduction of the potato as being an event of far greater significance than the self-erasing victories of the battlefield, and likewise celebrates Amanda's dogged endurance, her unshakable belief in progress (similar to that of the irrepressibly optimistic dentist in *Local Anaesthetic,* at least as portrayed by Starusch) is in the end firmly, if gently, ironized.

Sophie Rotzoll, Amanda's granddaughter, retains all of Amanda's visionary idealism and none of her practical energy. Similar in nature to Dorothea and Ilsebill, she is a thwarted revolutionary who would much rather have been born a man. Her self-effacing love for the similarly thwarted revolutionary Bartholdy echoes that of Agnes for her Ludström, and his eventual imprisonment turns her into an extremist whose would-be revolutionary fervor is chiefly expressed in Jacobin songs and an addiction to the drug muscarine. Her attempt to assassinate the French governor of Danzig fails but results in six accidental deaths, and her one possibly successful action as a revolutionary may have been her participation in the destruction of the town's food supply depot— Amanda's idealism thus ironically canceled out by Sophie's.

Lena Stubbe, the final member of the political trio, continues the revolutionary tradition in a sobered form dear to Grass's own heart: she is a socialist. Political agitation does not appeal to her, however, and she contents herself with spending her entire life in public soup kitchens, ladling out soup to the needy. She conceives of her would-be magnum opus, a cookbook for the laboring poor, as her enduring contribution to the socialist cause. The cookbook is rejected as politically embarrassing even by the father of socialism himself, August Bebel, the theoretician more specifically of the role of women in the socialist movement. The project is abandoned, the manuscript is lost, and Lena herself is eventually beaten to death, many years later, in Stutthof concentration camp. Her life is grey on grey, its unassuming tragedy summed up in her laconic response to Bebel's refusal to support publication of her book: " 'It don't matter' " (*F,* 438). Nonetheless, Lena is closer to political reality than either Amanda or Sophie. She is neither carried away by unrealizable idealism nor is she destroyed by the failure to materialize of her vision of historical progress. In line with the unassuming pragmatism of Grass's own snail philosophy, Lena goes on ladling out soup till the end.

We thus have three interconnected triads whose dominant tone throughout is one of unrealized capabilities and that lead up to the presentation of the last two women of the 11, Sibylle (Billy) and Maria. These two, together with the narrator's "Ilsebill," form the final triad, composed this time of contemporary women of the 1970s. It is worth noting that the narrator does not invent these characters in the same sense that he does the series from Awa to Lena—he was engaged to Sibylle in the early fifties, he tells us, and Maria is his cousin. The levels of fictionality are nonetheless blurred by the postulation of blood relationships between Billy, Maria, the narrator, and the historical series of women as far back as Dorothea (who, to confuse the matter further, is historically verifiable), for, "after all, we Kashubians are all related by way of a country lane or two" (*F,* 500).

In this final triad we find in Billy's story a combination of the ritual deaths of Awa and Dorothea, the executions of Mestwina and Agnes, and the casual murder of Lena, and we may note that *Sibylle* is an almost exact anagram of *Ilsebill.* The narrator's wife is depicted as being at the same stage of unreflected ideological enthusiasm as Billy was passing through, even if hesitantly, before the denouement of Father's Day. But Ilsebill is also Everywoman. The unhappy Billy becomes the model for oppressed womankind searching for a new identity, for suffering humanity trapped between inhuman ideologies. Billy's hesitant experimentation with militant feminism ends traumatically when she is gang-raped by her lesbian feminist friends. Abandoning militancy, Billy belatedly and tearfully attempts to return to "normality," only to be gang-raped once again, and this time brutally murdered, by a motorcycle gang celebrating Father's Day. This episode, astonishingly, has been decried by some critics as viciously antifeminist. In its obsessive intensity, however, matched in Grass's work only in the climactic "Faith, Hope, Love" chapter in *The Tin Drum*—which centers on another victim and another ideology—it is the most truly feminist episode in the novel. But the feminism argued for here—as the implicit argument advanced in every single case from Mestwina to Lena culminates in a powerful climax—is a true liberation of women that would also be a true liberation of men, rather than a one-sided quasi-liberation that would merely reverse the direction of age-old injustice. Such an emancipation would be so sane and reasonable that it is just as unlikely ever to be realized as is Amanda's utopian dream of food for all or Sophie's utopian dream of freedom for all. Ilsebill intends her pregnancy to produce a new man, an "Emmanuel" (*F,* 515). The enthusiastically lesbian Maxie goes one better and vows to engender an "Emmanuel" (*F,* 473) all by herself, without benefit of male intervention. It is all too clear, however, that this metamorphosed man of the new age, this putative savior, would be a product of castration rather than androgyny. (And saviors are notoriously unpredictable—Ilsebill's baby turns out to be a girl.)

The next-to-last scene of the novel shows the flounder as *Weltgeist,* as the spirit of history, his favor finally transferred from the male to the female sex as he leaps out of the Baltic into the arms of 25-year-old Maria Kuczorra. Unlike Billy and Ilsebill, Maria is uninterested in institutionalized feminism; also unlike them, she lives in the Danzig where all the other historical cooks have lived. Maria, too, is a victim of men and utopias—her husband was shot in the Danzig food-prices insurrection of 1970. She lives quietly as a canteen cook, with her two young daughters, "still alive, getting harder and harder" (*F,* 415). The heir to thousands of years of victimization, oppression, and injustice, her character indelibly stamped by the resilience of Agnes and Lena, Maria's central characteristic is simply that she quietly and undemonstratively endures in the face of all hardships. The last scene of the novel has Maria speaking with the flounder on the shore of the Baltic, and Maria has become Everywoman: "Then slowly she came to meet her footprints. But it wasn't Maria who came back. It must be Dorothea, I thought with alarm. As step by step she grew larger, I began to hope for Agnes. That's not Sophie's walk. Is Billy, my poor Sibylle, coming back? Ilsebill came. She overlooked me, overstepped me. Already she had passed me by. I ran after her" (*F,* 547).

This intricate interweaving of myth and reality, past and present, tragic and comic, is held together by the nameless narrator who projects himself under so many names. The narrator's voice is simultaneously, though not all of the time, the voice of Günter Grass as autobiographer and as poet, the anonymous voice of male exhaustion and self-doubt, and the contrary voice of progress and male self-assurance. Centered on the motif of fabulation as flight, narration in *The Flounder* is presented as simultaneously obligation and escape, the obligation to remember in spite of the desire to forget, evade, repress. The narrator veers continually between aggression and capitulation. He at least occasionally indulges himself—in a manner reminiscent of Starusch's fantasies in *Local Anaesthetic*—in vicious antifeminist outbursts and bouts of sadistic imagination, such as the hallucinated torturing and burning at the stake of Ilsebill (*F,* 285). These excesses alternate with lachrymose self-accusation, culminating in the masochism of a lengthy hallucinated trial (*F,* 383–95) that is reminiscent of the likewise hallucinated trial of Leopold Bloom in Joyce's *Ulysses*. This particular axis of oscillation is crossed by another: the constant interaction of tragic and comic, the deeply felt and the parodic. We are already familiar with such alternation of self-acceptance and self-rejection from all three works of the Danzig trilogy, but only in *Dog Years* is anything of the same scale attempted. The destabilized narrator is simultaneously the opponent of and identical with the Hegelian flounder. His primary projections through history are almost all melancholiacs, self-doubters, self-accusers, onlookers rather than actors. In each case, as already noted, they are complemented by at least one counterprojection, a hypothetical alter ego who is unproblematically active, unambiguously aggressive, and completely unburdened by the doubts and self-doubts of the traumatized narrator.

Clearly this multiply fractured narrative consciousness reflects a deep-seated crisis of male identity, but at least equally compellingly revealed is the narrator's horror in the face of a history that, for him, can only be read as a meaningless sequence of meaningless acts. The "snail philosophy" (*F,* 330) of the narrator (and of the author) lends itself easily to satire, and Grass deprives us of that pleasure by continually satirizing it himself: "My (his) absurd dislike of ideology had become an ideology with me (him)" (*F,* 388). Yet this same dogged pragmatism that was celebrated in *From the Diary of a Snail* is defended once again in the face of chaos and ideology alike, and it manifests itself throughout in a deep-seated respect for fundamental human values—in spite of everything, most especially their own complete insufficiency. Either to accept or to reject that such fortune-cookie wisdom constitutes the narrative's "answer" to the nightmare of history that is so compellingly evoked, however, would be equally misguided. As always, Grass's text does not aim to provide answers, only more interestingly shaped questions. Scheherazade goes on talking: "The book goes on, and so does history" (*F,* 453).

The Flounder is linked to Grass's earlier works by an extended network of thematic and formal threads. The emphasis on food and its ambiguous properties is present in Grass's work from as early as the mysterious soup of *The Wicked Cooks,* to the noxious soup Susi Kater forces Oskar to choke down, the fish Oskar's mother gorges herself to death on, the unripe gooseberries that Mahlke crams desperately into his mouth before his final retreat to the barge, the frogs that the schoolboy Amsel swallows live in order to prove his schoolyard manhood. The potato-peeling motif of the Amanda Woyke chapter reminds us that Grass originally intended to call *Dog Years* "Kartoffelschalen" (Potato Peelings) and to use a potato-peeling housemaid as narrator. A narrative cookbook was promised in *From the Diary of a Snail*—as was the eighth book of *The Flounder,* "Father's Day," though mentioned there as a projected book rather than as an episode in a longer fiction (thus reversing the genetic process of *Cat and Mouse* and *The Meeting at Telgte*). *Local Anaesthetic* contributes several motifs, as well as the painter Anton Möller, whose "Last Judgment," as we may remember, plays a significant role in that novel. But the most interesting thematic link with the earlier works is certainly provided by the treatment of female characters. The series of "black witch" figures in *The Flounder* clearly evokes and expands the similar series in *The Tin Drum,* already expanded upon in *Cat and Mouse, Dog Years,* and, especially, *Local Anaesthetic.* The characters Linde, Vero, and Irmgard from the latter novel, as portrayed by Starusch's narrative, are clearly close kin of Ilsebill's. Vero Lewand in particular, an impetuous would-be revolutionary (modeled in turn along the lines of Susi Kater, Lucy Rennwand, and Tulla Pokriefke from the Danzig trilogy), serves as a preliminary study of Ilsebill. (Grass originally intended to call Ilsebill Veronica, as newspaper accounts of his public readings from the unfinished manuscript indicate.)

The formal connections with Grass's earlier works are also immediately evident, most obviously in the verve and enthusiasm with which the novel returns to the flaunted inventiveness of the trilogy. *The Flounder* also reverts to one of the central preoccupations of the Danzig trilogy in its scrutiny of the inevitably questionable processes of writing (and rewriting) history. The element of narrative unreliability that characterizes the earlier work returns in full force. The impotence of the narrator is clearly prefigured in Starusch, his shiftiness in Pilenz, his capacity for outrageous invention in Oskar, his evasiveness in Amsel's ability to surround himself with a narrative hall of mirrors, to play with simultaneous involvement in and disengagement from a reflected reality. Experimenting with the provocative juxtaposition between the same covers of novel, history, autobiography, cookbook, essay, tract, and lyric, *The Flounder* continues to explore that same confrontation of literary and nonliterary forms that was first undertaken in *From the Diary of a Snail*. In terms of its narrative technique, in short, *The Flounder* emerges as a synthesis of the Danzig trilogy and *From the Diary of a Snail*. It is a synthesis whose productive possibilities Grass would continue to develop in each of his subsequent major works.

Chapter Ten
The Meeting at Telgte

Das Treffen in Telgte was published in 1979, only two years after *The Flounder;* it appeared in an English translation by Ralph Manheim, under the title *The Meeting at Telgte,* in 1981. Unlike most of Grass's narratives, it is an almost entirely straightforward tale (at least on the surface), recounting the meeting of a score or so of German poets in a small town in northern Germany in May 1647, just as the Thirty Years' War is drawing irresolutely to a close. The Treaty of Westphalia that will finally end hostilities is still some months off. The country is completely devastated by war and plague, towns everywhere lie in smoking ruins, law and order are just a distant memory from an almost forgotten past. The poets, summoned by one of their number, Simon Dach, congregate not only from all over Germany, but from as far away as Königsberg in the east and London in the west. Their aim is both literary and political, hoping both to "rescue their cruelly maltreated language," "giving new force to the last remaining bond between all Germans, namely, the German language they held in common, and—if only from the sidelines— uttering a political word or two." [1] They arrive footweary and irritable, in some cases having been assaulted and robbed along the way, comforted only by the knowledge that "they, not the powerful, were assured of immortality" (*MT,* 23), to find that the accommodation they had originally reserved in the village of Oesede, near Protestant Osnabrück, has been commandeered by Swedish troops.

Only through the good graces of a swashbuckling rogue in Imperial (and therefore nominally Catholic) colors do the (strongly Protestant) poets eventually find suitable lodgings in the Bridge Tavern in the small town of Telgte, near the Catholic city of Münster, in Westphalia. There they spend the next three days reading their work aloud to each other (and to frequently bitter criticism), hotly debating the theoretical niceties of metrics, vigorously refreshing old feuds too good to forget, incessantly squabbling, and continually belaboring one another "with stones transmuted into words" (*MT,* 37). Toward the end of their meeting they make common cause long enough to compose what starts off as a contentious and elaborately pompous document and ends up as a simply worded manifesto appealing for peace and tolerance in the devastated fatherland. Celebrating their modest accomplishment with a final (and for the first time harmonious) meal together, they barely escape with their lives when the tavern suddenly goes up in flames. The scrupulously wrought manifesto is forgotten in the panic and likewise goes up in smoke. "And so, what would in any case not have been heard remained unsaid" (*MT,* 136).

In *The Plebeians Rehearse the Uprising,* Grass borrowed the historical Bertolt Brecht as a template for the protagonist of his play, and in *The Flounder* the historical seventeenth-century poets Gryphius and Opitz put in a brief but memorable appearance. In *The Meeting at Telgte* he extends this technique considerably, for the great majority of the 20 or so characters in the narrative are based on well-known seventeenth-century German writers, 2 or 3 others are based on historically verifiable publishers of the time, and another is based on a well-known German musician, Heinrich Schütz, a major precursor of Bach. The poets whose fictional counterparts turn up at the meeting in Telgte include the greatest of the German poets of the time, such as Andreas Gryphius (again) and Johann Scheffler, and a crowd of lesser but still well-known poets, such as Georg Philipp Harsdörffer, Christian Hofmann von Hofmannswaldau, Paul Gerhardt, Friedrich von Logau, Georg Rudolf Weckherlin, Simon Dach (the fictional organizer of the meeting), and numerous others. The discussions of the fictional poets contain a great deal of gossip, intrigue, and backbiting based in the majority of cases on the known relationships between their historical counterparts and in some cases on mischievous fabrications on Grass's part.

As always in Grass's texts, however, the past and the present are inextricably interlinked, and the Telgte poets also have their twentieth-century context. The narrative is a tribute to Grass's friend and mentor Hans Werner Richter, to whom it is dedicated in celebration of his seventieth birthday in November 1978. Richter was the German writer who convened the first meeting, in 1947, of what was to become famous as Group 47, a loose association of writers, critics, and publishers who gathered once a year to read and discuss the writers' latest work and whose avowed (and very successful) ambition over the next three decades was to rekindle the ashes of German literature after the devastation of the Second World War. Grass himself received the Group's annual prize for his reading of a chapter from the still unpublished *Tin Drum* in 1958, and *The Meeting at Telgte* is a tribute both to the Group (whose final meeting took place in 1977) and, especially, to its founder.

Grass's narrative is based on the central fiction of a founding Group 47 meeting in the seventeenth century, in 1647, one year before the end of the Thirty Years' War, rather than in 1947, two years after the end of the Second World War. German readers were naturally interested in the degree to which the narrative could therefore be considered a roman à clef. Certain correspondences were obvious—especially Simon Dach as a seventeenth-century version of Hans Werner Richter—and readers sought eagerly for others. Some reviewers, several of whom were themselves members of Group 47, even chose to treat the search for disguised parallels as if it were the real point of the book. Various readers proposed various correspondences, most of them mutually contradictory.

Non-German readers, understandably, had (and have) little or no interest in whether such teasing contemporary correspondences exist or not. The narrative can be read with just as much enjoyment (and perhaps less reductively) without any such specialized information, however. To the degree that twentieth-century biographical parallels can be shown to exist, they are certainly primarily parodic rather than necessary for an understanding of the text (much as the flaunted numerological symbolism in *Dog Years* is largely parodic rather than prescriptive of meaning). Similarly, in regard to the play with historical seventeenth-century counterparts, readers who are familiar with German Baroque poetry (and this includes by no means all of Grass's German readers, of course) will certainly have the additional pleasure of recognizing names with which they have long been familiar in a different context and of enjoying "insider" status in doing so. For this kind of reader, indeed, the book is a delight, and Grass's publisher capitalized on this fact by issuing a paperback edition in 1985 that included some 70 pages of poetry written by the historical poets whose names and personalities Grass had made use of. Many non-German readers will be glad of the sort of help that is provided in the Penguin Books edition of Ralph Manheim's translation, to which the British scholar Leonard Forster contributes an afterword and a biographical glossary of the historical poets who are fictionalized in Grass's text, making clear the amount of historical research Grass had put into his ostensibly artless tale. But it should be stressed that *The Meeting at Telgte* can stand entirely on its own without any such academic background, for what is primarily important about the book, to quote S. S. Prawer in the *Times Literary Supplement* for 26 June 1981, is not its impressive, if lightly carried, learning but rather that it is a "brilliant entertainment."[2] *The Meeting at Telgte*, indeed, as even the most inveterate of Grass's habitual critics were driven to acknowledge, is nothing short of a minor masterpiece.

A central intellectual thrust of the narrative emerges in the provocatively paradoxical opening sentence (stylistically not at all typical of the narrative as a whole): "Yesterday will be what tomorrow has been" (*MT,* 9). German history, European history, world history have been and are and will no doubt continue to be a never-ending and unchanging state of war, violence, and destruction in which past, present, and future are essentially indistinguishable, an entropically featureless *Vergegenkunft* or "paspresenture" ("past-present-future"), to employ the neologism Grass later coins in *Headbirths.* The consistent thrust of Grass's work, however, is that, rather than simply capitulating to this entropic vision, we must always keep the past in mind in order to have at least some minimal possibility of shaping the present and future, even if at best only very locally and always without any hope of enduring success. "Our stories of today need not have taken place in the present. This one began more than three hundred years ago. So did many other stories. Every story set in Germany goes back that far" (*MT,* 9). Simon Dach's conference meets with an abrupt end because of an unforeseen disaster, and his assembled poets disperse, never to meet again. The dedication of *The Meeting at Telgte* to Hans Werner Richter, whose assembled group of poets three hundred years later continued to meet over three decades and put German literature triumphantly back on its feet after an even more destructive war than the Thirty Years' War, is certainly an indication—taking up the central theme of *From the Diary of a Snail* from a decade before— that sometimes, at least, there can be a limited degree of local and temporary progress after all.

The Meeting at Telgte grows out of the episode in the fourth month of *The Flounder* in which the poets Opitz and Gryphius meet and dispute, and it bears a similar relationship to its predecessor as did *Cat and Mouse* to *The Tin Drum,* restrained conciseness taking over in each case from baroque luxuriance. *The Flounder* had emphasized, at great length and with enormous complexity, the degree to which the German present is, inevitably, a product of the German past. *The Meeting at Telgte,* in a different key and on a much smaller scale, does very much the same thing. The central theme is the relationship of writing and political commitment, and more overtly than most of Grass's other books, indeed, *The Meeting at Telgte* thematizes their interaction. Written by one politically engaged writer for another, *The Meeting at Telgte* explores, tongue in cheek, the role of writing in history, a role it self-ironically situates some-where between vital importance and total impotence.

Telgte is situated between the Protestant town of Osnabrück and the Catholic town of Münster, which for the three years preceding the poets' meeting have been the respective focal points of continually interrupted negotiations for an end to the long-drawn-out hostilities, while the hostilities in question have continued unabated by the good intentions. Between the warring factions, only very roughly identified by the religious labels, Grass situates his fictional meeting of poets as representatives of the intellectual life of the almost exhausted fatherland, a hypothetical "third force," as Leonard Forster aptly calls it in his afterword to Manheim's translation, assembled for a meeting "that never took place, that never could have taken place," Forster observes for "it can be shown that none of the participants could have been in that place at that time" (*MT*, 139). The impossibility of the meeting ever having taken place, however, is of course irrelevant: *The Meeting at Telgte* is a *Kopfgeburt*, to anticipate the title of Grass's next work, an imaginative "headbirth," an improved (or potentially improved) version of German literary history as it might (or should) have been.

As the avatar of Hans Werner Richter, the fictive Simon Dach plays a key role in Grass's narrative. The historical Dach is perhaps best known for an ironically playful (and much anthologized) poem that he wrote on the destruction of a cucumber bower he had cultivated in his garden. The destruction of the bower, in whose shelter he and his friends used to read their poetry to one another in the cool of the evening, symbolizes the destruction of poetry and culture and peace and tranquillity every-where, the civilized idyll of the flowering garden overrun by noxious weeds and thistles. For the assembled poets, indeed, the embattled fatherland is aptly symbolized by the thistle they place on the second day of their meeting beside the ceremonial chair in which each in turn sits to read from his works. The thistle is only a weed, disdained by all, rooted out and destroyed where possible—but it is enormously resilient and, for all its thorns, it is also capable of beauty.

It is the inspiration of the thistle, surviving unscathed when one of their number smashes the pot that contains it, that eventually impels the fractious poets to put aside their petty squabbles and animosities and collaborate on their abortive manifesto against violence and barbarism—even if in doing so they still frequently "spoke contentiously of peace, intolerantly of tolerance, and penny-pinchingly of God" (*MT*, 128). But the thistle is doubly emblematic, not just of the fatherland, but of the poets themselves, conscious as they are of their own inadequacy in the face of political forces of which they know little and over which they have little hope of exerting any influence. That the writer's words may possibly never be heard, however, can be no excuse for not attempting to utter them. Like the thistle among the rocks, the central political task of the writer in society, whether heard or unheard, is essentially to endure, to keep writing, in spite of all obstacles. Grass's own cover illustration makes this doctrine the emblematic point of the book: a hand clutching a quill pen, poised to write, rising undaunted from a sea of stones. Grass's own career as a writer has been entirely exemplary of the political role assigned to the writer in *The Meeting at Telgte*.

The Meeting at Telgte is rich in deft thumbnail sketches of the assembled poets: the anxious father-figure Dach, who, like his twentieth-century parallel Richter, provides a roof (*Dach,* in German) under which the assembled poets gather; the intimidating Schütz; the pious Gerhardt; the swaggering Greflinger; the bashful but brilliant Scheffler; the supercilious Hofmannswaldau; and the thundering Gryphius, who "could thunder even when he lacked lightning" (*MT,* 38). It is particularly interesting, however, in its oblique portrayal of a writer whose name is mentioned directly only as a future nom de plume of the roguish Gelnhausen. For *The Meeting at Telgte* is a tribute not only to the twentieth-century writer Hans Werner Richter but also to the seventeenth-century writer Hans Jakob Christoffel von Grimmelshausen, who is one of Grass's own most important literary ancestors. Grass has more than once been called the most extravagant imagination the German literary tradition has had to reckon with since Grimmelshausen.

One of the central ironies of *The Meeting at Telgte* is that the illustrious poets who, by literary proxy, crowd its pages are thoroughly upstaged by two entirely fictional characters. When the poets fail to find accommodation in Oesede, they are helped by "a red-bearded fellow who called himself Christoffel von Gelnhausen" (*MT,* 12) and who emerges as an amalgam of Grimmelshausen himself (who was born in the town of Gelnhausen, near Frankfurt am Main) and, more importantly, the eponymous picaresque protagonist of Grimmelshausen's most celebrated narrative, *Simplicius Simplicissimus* (1669), a highly colored tale of the fortunes and misfortunes of an innocent abroad in the Germany of the Thirty Years' War. "In his green doublet and plumed hat he looked like something out of a storybook" (*MT,* 12). It is Gelnhausen who helps the beleaguered poets (whatever their moral reservations as to his methods) to find alternative quarters in Telgte, and it is Gelnhausen who, when food runs low, almost miraculously replenishes their table—initially to their enthusiastic applause, but later engendering lasting horror and ecstasies of guilt, when it emerges that he has fed them so sumptuously only by virtue of robbery and looting and quite possibly even worse. Gelnhausen occasionally takes part in their discussions, often to shrewd effect, and is regarded by most of the poets with a mixture of cautious revulsion and guarded admiration. He arouses the scandalized indignation of the more fastidious and self-important among them when he reveals that his intention is also to become a writer, but not of "well-behaved rhymes for church congregations. No, he would let every foul smell out of the bag; a chronicler, he would bring back the long war as a word-butchery, let loose gruesome laughter, and give the language license to be what it is: crude and soft-spoken, whole and stricken, here Frenchified, there melancholicky, but always drawn from the casks of life" (*MT,* 118). The result, of course, will be Grimmelshausen's *Simplicius Simplicissimus*, the greatest German novel of the seventeenth century, which fulfills all these promises and more. Nearly three hundred years later, Günter Grass adopted very much the same artistic credo in what is arguably the greatest German novel of the twentieth century, *The Tin Drum*.

The second major figure of the narrative who is not modeled on a historical person is the redoubtable landlady of the Bridge Tavern, Libuschka, nicknamed Courage, who turns out to have been an old flame of Gelnhausen's. Seven times married, she has buried seven husbands and is still going strong. "An aging woman under a layer of face paint, she was wrapped in a horse blanket and wore soldier's breeches, but spoke with refinement and claimed descent from the Bohemian nobility" (*MT,* 16). Her nickname, as Ralph Manheim's translation informs the reader in a helpful footnote, bears a double meaning, since in the bawdy context of the Grimmelshausen novel from which she, too, is borrowed (namely, *Courasche*, published in 1670, one of several sequels to the popular *Simplicius Simplicissimus*) "courage" denotes not only physical boldness but also (with heavy male irony) the female sexual organ. "Though undoubtedly a trollop" (*MT,* 21), however—and a camp follower who boasts shamelessly of the rich pickings she acquired in the destruction of Magdeburg, looting the bodies of the slain—she flatters and charms the assembled writers by quoting fluently from their own works and "might have been made to order for a meeting of poets" (*MT,* 18).

Gelnhausen and Courage, onetime lovers, are still joined by "a very special cement" (*MT*, 49) that is a volatile mixture of love and hatred. Shortly before the end of the narrative the two quarrel bitterly and eventually come to blows—ironically because Courage laughs at Gelnhausen's ambition to become a writer. (Ironically, here, because Courage, of course, owes her very existence to the fact that "Gelnhausen" eventually "becomes" the writer Grimmelshausen.) Gelnhausen, wounded in pride, abruptly departs, leaving an embittered Courage, wounded both in pride and in body, to watch, "grey with hatred" (*MT*, 119), over the poets' final sessions. The narrator's closing sentence claims that he has no idea who can have set the tavern on fire, but the reader is clearly invited to hazard an educated guess. When the tavern goes up in flames, Courage, already wrapped in her horse blanket and showing suspiciously little emotion, turns her back without a word and sets off grimly, mounted on a mule and leading another carrying a few quickly salvaged pots and pans, to join a recently arrived troop of gypsies on their wanderings. Here Grass also ironically nods in passing to Bertolt Brecht, who similarly borrowed Grimmelshausen's Courage as the title character of his best-known play, *Mother Courage* (1941)—in which, indomitably but self-destructively, eventually losing everything she possesses and everyone she loves, she trudges relentlessly from defeat to defeat through the chaos of the Thirty Years' War.

The levels of fictionality at play in *The Meeting at Telgte*, to summarize, are thus complexly and playfully interwoven. The various fictional poets who meet in Telgte may or may not be modeled (or partially modeled) on real twentieth-century writers—many of whom will themselves have been readers of the book. The fictional poets (and their guest of honor, the composer Heinrich Schütz) are certainly based on real historical personages bearing the same names. The most colorful character in the narrative, however, is only partly modeled on the real writer Grimmelshausen (who, unlike a number of other seventeenth-century poets whose fictional proxies do not attend, is never mentioned by any of the poets present) and much more immediately on a fictional character borrowed from Grimmelshausen. Libuschka is entirely modeled on a fictional character likewise borrowed from Grimmelshausen. While the fictional Simon Dach corresponds to the real seventeenth-century poet Simon Dach and also, more or less overtly, evokes the twentieth-century writer Hans Werner Richter, Gelnhausen simultaneously evokes both the real writer Grimmelshausen and one of his characters. Libuschka is borrowed here just as she had been borrowed by the playwright

Brecht—whom, to add one more layer of complexity, Grass had in turn borrowed as a character in *The Plebeians Rehearse the Uprising.*

Finally, of course, there is the narrator, a nameless and marginalized figure who refers to himself only as I and presents himself as contemporaneous both with the seventeenth-century poets at Telgte and with his twentieth-century creator. In *The Meeting at Telgte*, that is to say, Grass once again, as in *The Flounder*, plays with an overtly divided and transtemporal I. The narrating I is initially presented as identical with Grass the twentieth-century writer and member of Group 47: "If I am writing down what happened in Telgte, it is because a friend, who gathered his fellow writers around him in the forty-seventh year of our century, is soon to celebrate his seventieth birthday" (*MT,* 9). As well as this, however, the narrated I makes frequent and more or less peripheral appearances (beginning in the fourth of 23 chapters) as a witness, as an unnamed member of the group of seventeenth-century writers that meet at Telgte: "How do I know all this? I was sitting in their midst, I was there" (*MT,* 88).

As befits a birthday present from one writer to another, *The Meeting at Telgte*, a story about writers and the triumphs and defeats of writing, is suffused by a tone of good humor. *The Meeting at Telgte* is centrally about the relationship of writing and politics, and the role of the writer is far from being overestimated. When the poets first assemble, as we have seen, they find their quarters unceremoniously requisitioned by Swedish soldiers; much worse, not a single one of the Swedish officers has even heard of the illustrious visitors, whose indignant and self-important protests are greeted with the laughter of people for whom their accomplishments simply do not exist (*MT,* 11). Arrived at Telgte and heartened by their own numbers, by their own togetherness, and by the sound of their own voices, the assembled poets shake off this initial disappointment and soon wax eloquent once again on the centrality of poetry and poets in the affairs of nations.

The one success of the fictional meeting at Telgte is that the assembled poets eventually climb back down from these Olympian heights and realize in all sobriety "that poets were without power, except to write true if useless words" (*MT,* 74). Grass does not exclude himself from this ironically delivered lesson in humility, for *The Meeting at Telgte* also parodies his own views on the German language and German literature as the last meaningful bond between the two parts of a then still divided Germany, a theme he will nonetheless return to on many occasions over the next decade. Conceived of as both celebration and critique of the writer and the writer's trade, *The Meeting at Telgte* is carried throughout by an optimism, however ironically tinged, that is increasingly rare in Grass's later work. This optimism was not present in *The Flounder,* and it will certainly not be present in the products of the 1980s, in what Grass calls "Orwell's decade."

Chapter Eleven
Headbirths

Grass's first fictional text of the 1980s, *Kopfgeburten oder Die Deutschen sterben aus,* appeared in 1980 and was translated by Ralph Manheim, in 1982, under the title *Headbirths, or The Germans Are Dying Out.* On one level the journal-like account of an extended voyage of discovery taken by its writer, *Headbirths* is reminiscent of *From the Diary of a Snail.* Grass first visited India in 1975, and the experience of that journey was fictionalized in the Vasco da Gama chapter of *The Flounder.* Four years later, in 1979, the newly divorced and remarried Grass, together with the filmmaker Volker Schlöndorff (with whom he had recently collaborated on the film version of *The Tin Drum*) and their respective wives, the musician Ute Grunert and the filmmaker Margarethe von Trotta, embarked on a reading and lecturing tour of China and Indonesia sponsored by the Goethe Institute, the organization of German cultural institutes abroad. *Headbirths* was written mainly in late 1979, shortly after their return to Germany and shortly before the German elections of 1980. The title refers on one level to the birth of the goddess Athene from the brow of Zeus, a parable about the power of the imagination. (The title also puns on "brain child" and—by implication at least— "head presentation" in childbirth, appropriate for a narrative dealing with both the population explosion and a baby conceived mentally but not physically.) Grass's text is centrally about the power of the (artistic) imagination, the "what if," the hypothetical scenario, alternative realities—in short, about *choices,* as Gabriel Josipovici aptly points out.[1]

Headbirths is a book of many themes. Surrounded by hordes of cyclists in Shanghai, Grass (or his narrator-persona) conjures up various hypothetical scenarios. What if the First and the Third Worlds were reversed? What if there were a billion Germans and only 80 million Chinese? How does the Berlin Wall compare to the Great Wall of China? Or to the wall of death rays that would have to be constructed to keep the hungry masses from the East from invading Europe in a new *Völkerwanderung* or Great Migration of Peoples? How does German efficiency compare with Chinese efficiency? Could the billion Germans feed

themselves as efficiently as they could undoubtedly wipe themselves out
with sophisticated weaponry?

In spite of the fact that *Headbirths* is centrally concerned with conditions in the Third World, Germany is thus never far from its central
characters' consciousness or its author's mind. Grass's own trip to China
had included presentations in various cities of an essay on German literature as the essential (and only remaining) force holding the two otherwise so different German states together in one cultural nation, as the
poets of *The Meeting at Telgte* had also argued. He returns to this essay in
Headbirths, calling for a National Endowment—"Admitted. It's a wide-
awake daydream. (Another headbirth.)"—that would impose a "common roof, our indivisible culture" over the inimical states, "lest we continue to stand in the rain like fools." [2]

Headbirths is certainly also a "contribution to the election campaign,"
as Grass anticipates outraged critics protesting (*H,* 111). The principal
contenders in the 1980 elections were Helmut Schmidt, the incumbent
Social Democrat chancellor of the Federal Republic, and the challenger
Franz Josef Strauss, the Bavarian Prime Minister and head of the opposition party, the Christian Democrats (CDU). The Social Democrats, supported as always by Grass, carried the day. (Two years later, the Christian Democrats had their revenge when continued economic difficulties
in Germany led to the fall of the Schmidt government and the return to
power of the CDU under Helmut Kohl). Grass vigorously attacks
Strauss's scare-mongering tactics that assert that the low birthrate
among Germans combined with the increasing influx of non-German
workers and their families would lead eventually to the Germans "dying
out." Grass sees such tactics as a completely irresponsible contribution
to a growing swell of hostility in Germany against foreigners—and "fear
in Germany has always had a high rate of increment" (*H,* 3). He enthusiastically seizes the opportunity to lambaste Strauss, whose pronounced
right-wing sympathies had some time earlier incautiously led him to
characterize writers (especially those who disagreed with him) as no better than "rats and blowflies" (*H,* 46). The English translation omits 10
pages of the German original in which the attack on Strauss is pleasur-
ably elaborated (*H,* 147).

Other "headbirths" considered at greater or lesser length include
Grass's hypothetical plan of action if he were to become dictator for a
year and the putative course of his own biography if he had been born
10 years earlier, in 1917 rather than 1927, when his stories and poems,

instead of recalling an unexpiated past, might have been concerned with his perhaps even enthusiastic involvement in shooting partisans or destroying Ukrainian villages (*H,* 69). *Headbirths* is dedicated to another writer, his friend Nicolas Born, whose lingering death of cancer shortly after Grass's return from India is one of the interlacing story lines of the text.

The various essayistic themes of *Headbirths* are offset against a central fictional strand not yet mentioned. In *From the Diary of a Snail* Grass's journal of his own political comings and goings was interleaved by the fictional story of Hermann Ott, alias Doubt. In *Headbirths* the account of his experiences in the Far East and his various social and political concerns are likewise interleaved by the fictional story of a very serious-minded (and rather boring) couple who similarly undertake a cultural journey to the Orient. Harm and Dörte Peters, former radicals of the 1960s, are now respectable high-school teachers in their thirties—he of English, she of French—in the northern German town of Itzehoe, near Grass's second home in Wewelsfleth. The Peterses are professionally all too aware of the multiple disasters that potentially threaten the survival of the planet—world hunger, overpopulation, environmental pollution, nuclear holocaust. All of these factors enter into the decision they are trying to make as to whether to have a baby. (Dörte has already had one abortion on these grounds.)

To bear or not to bear a child becomes a central question of the narrative, set in two quite different contexts: on the one hand, the disastrously overpopulated squalor of the Far East; on the other, the dire warnings of a Franz Josef Strauss that Turks and other "undesirable" foreigners will assuredly overrun the country if Germans fail to do their patriotic duty and procreate. The headbirths of the title ring multiple variations on this central opposition of "too few Germans" and "too many foreigners," contrasting the inward-turning parochialism of the German and European past and the global citizenship that will be required if there is to be a future of any sort. Harm and Dörte's story is set in the near but nonetheless still hypothetical future: in 1980, while Grass is writing in late 1979. That already puts them into "Orwell's decade" (*H,* 71), with its attendant overtones of impending catastrophe—the most immediate of which, for Grass, may be the triumph of a resurgent right-wing fundamentalism under the aegis of a Strauss or his like.

With *The Meeting at Telgte* Grass already broaches what we may call the realm of alternative realities—alternative, hypothetical worlds in time and/or space, involving stories that might conceivably happen or have happened. In a sense, of course, this is exactly what Grass—and indeed any writer of fictional texts—always deals in, but in Grass's work of the 1980s, the "hypotheticality," as we might say, the flaunted fictionality of the stories presented is increasingly strongly marked. The adventures of Harm and Dörte are presented as material for a hypothetical film script (to be called *Headbirths*) for his friend Volker Schlöndorff. With *Headbirths*, indeed, Grass once again revisits the stylistic experiment he had begun eight years earlier with *From the Diary of a Snail* (1972), namely, the blending of fictional narrative, autobiographical narrative, and the essay. *Headbirths* is thus an example of a genre—the narrative essay— that Grass has more or less invented and made his own, allowing a sort of literary "double exposure" of the subject matter, as Fritz J. Raddatz deftly put it in a review of the book, and experimenting with a variety of styles without settling definitively for any one of them.[3] John Leonard, writing in the *New York Times Book Review,* called *Headbirths* "part fiction, part travelogue, part screenplay, and part political pamphlet."[4] The essayistic moment is less obviously in evidence in his next major work, *The Rat* (1986), but returns strongly to the fore in both *Show Your Tongue* (1988) and *The Call of the Toad* (1992).

Harm and Dörte have strong views on a wide variety of subjects and seldom refrain from making them known. In their thinking, indeed, Grass parodies the role of the committed intellectual—even if their thinking reflects positions he once shared or continues to share—for Grass's satire of his well-meaning teacher couple is, of course, also self-satire. On several occasions Harm and Dörte are made to speak Grass's own lines, as already revealed to the reader a few paragraphs or pages before—as when Harm, revealing his putative political platform if he were dictator, "solves the energy problems of the eighties along my lines" (*H,* 79), or inveighs against Strauss (*H,* 91), or is portrayed, as Grass will portray himself on the following page, as Sisyphus, rolling various stones to the top of various political mountains only to have to start at the bottom all over again (*H,* 85). Both characters agree with Grass's vehement opposition to the building of a new nuclear power station at Brokdorf, near Itzehoe (*H,* 116). Conversely, in a humorous exercise in dialogism, Harm and Dörte are occasionally made to disagree with Grass, as when they reject with one voice his mock proposal to convert the West German army, the Bundeswehr, into a more flexible and much less expensive part-time army of partisans to be called upon as needed to demoralize the enemy of the day (*H,* 78).

The narrative of Harm and Dörte in the Orient is made to reflect continually on its own fictionality and provisionality. The result is to some degree less a story told than the negotiated residue of a multiplicity of potential other stories likewise not told. The account of their ostentatiously invented doings is teasingly larded with suggestions for directions it might have been made to take—hypothetically involving Dörte in an impulsive affair with a handsome young Balinese rickshaw driver, for example, or both of them in involuntary gunrunning because of Harm's desire to visit an old friend from Itzehoe who lives in Bali. This old friend is also the intended recipient of a large vacuum-packed liver sausage that Harm buys as a gift before their departure from Itzehoe. The liver sausage accompanies them throughout their entire trip—growing steadily more demoralized and less edible as it goes—and parodically symbolizing the inevitable baggage from back home that accompanies even the most open-minded explorer of foreign climes. In the end, the "plot-fostering" liver sausage ostensibly triumphs even over Grass as narrator, who, tongue in cheek, claims finally not to know what to do with it any more: "Another unsolved problem" (H, 105).

The Peterses' trip is arranged by the Sisyphus Travel Agency, which also provides a tour guide, one Dr. Wenthien, "always unchanged and seemingly sexless" (H, 59), who seems to speak all the languages of the Orient, whose apparently universal knowledge recalls the omniscient dentist of Local Anaesthetic, and whose worldly-wise cynicism is parodically reminiscent of Mephistopheles in Goethe's Faust. On more than one occasion, as "great guru and world-crisis specialist" (H, 99), Wenthien speaks unabashedly in the words of his creator Grass, as when he talks of capitalism and communism, for all their surface differences, as "one pair of shoes" (H, 97). Wenthien's role in the narrative is left teasingly undeveloped. The names of Grass's fictional couple, Harm and Dörte, likewise parodically hint at Goethe's bucolic idyll Hermann and Dorothea (1797)—which was also an experiment in literary and narrative form, incongruously portraying in resounding classical hexameters the tribulations and eventual triumph of young love in a modern-day, petit bourgeois Rhineland milieu. The nine chapters of Headbirths, a text balancing population explosion and pregnancy postponed, echo the nine chapters of The Flounder, keyed to the nine months of a pregnancy. They also echo the nine books (each named for one of the Muses) of Hermann and Dorothea.

Harm and Dörte, as Grass himself observes, are two more examples, parodically drawn, of his "thing with teachers" (H, 108), which began with Oskar's teacher Fräulein Spollenhauer in *The Tin Drum* and continued with Mahlke's nemesis Klohse in *Cat and Mouse*, Papa Brunies in *Dog Years*, Starusch in *Local Anaesthetic*, Hermann Ott in *From the Diary of a Snail*, and "even the Flounder turns out to be a pedagogue" (*H*, 108). Teachers, as any one of these texts makes clear, do not necessarily have all the answers. In one narrative headbirth Dr. Wenthien joins Harm and Dörte in their electioneering efforts on their return to Germany: "In every language at his command, Hindi, Tamil, Indonesian, even in Mandarin Chinese, he proclaims the new world order: 'The continents have joined into one family. Southeast and Northwest are one. Willingly—indeed, as we now see, happily—Europe is dissolving into Asia. . . .' " (*H*, 138). The final paragraph of *Headbirths* takes up this theme (to which Grass will also return in *The Call of the Toad*). Back home in Itzehoe, Harm and Dörte, still childless and still indecisive, almost run down a small Turkish boy who darts in front of their well-preserved Volkswagen. They manage to stop just in time, and the boy's friends rush into the street en masse to "celebrate his survival" (*H*, 148). Soon the entire street is filled with children, all of them "foreigners"— Indian, Chinese, Turkish, African—and all of them also now "Germans," joyfully celebrating their friend's (and their own) survival, laughing and waving to the physically and intellectually becalmed Harm and Dörte, who, "foreigners" themselves in such company, don't even know "what to say in German" (*H*, 148).

Headbirths, balancing the Berlin Wall and Bavarian politics against the Great Wall of China, middle-class western scruples against the third-world population explosion, and the tidy-mindedness of half-timbered German villages against the chaotic human clutter of Bombay, is centrally about the abrupt, almost instantaneous transition from one civilization to another made possible by late-twentieth-century technology. Like *The Meeting at Telgte*, it is one of Grass's shortest narrative texts, less than 150 pages in its English translation. Gabriel Josipovici, writing in the *Times Literary Supplement*, saw the Grass of *Headbirths*, "an exhilarating performance," as going on from strength to strength, "becoming, with each new work, at once more German and more international, more personal and more universal" (Josipovici, 455).

Headbirths, indeed, as we have seen, is "about" many things: the quizzically ironized concerns of Harm and Dörte, once radical sixties flower children, now middle-of-the-road liberal democrats like their creator Günter Grass; the anticipated disaster of a threatened world population explosion; the potential menace of a reborn right-wing funda-

mentalism in German politics; the appalling misery of the interchangeable and omnipresent slums of India; the shameful confrontation of
first-world luxury and third-world desperation; world hunger and overpopulation; the agony of Grass's writer-friend Nicholas Born, dying
slowly of cancer; Grass himself, now in his fifties; and, like *The Meeting
at Telgte,* centrally also writing and the writerly imagination.

Headbirths marks the beginning of what has been called Grass's ecological phase, as environmental concerns in the broadest sense come to
be central to his imaginative work, both graphic and literary. But it is a
good deal more than that. Grass began by writing of the legacy of the
past in the Danzig trilogy; turned, in *Local Anaesthetic,* to the problems
of the present; and moves in *Headbirths* not just to a hypothetical future
but to what he calls "a fourth tense, the paspresenture. That's why my
form gets untidy. On my paper more is possible. Here only chaos fer-
ments order. Here even holes are contents. And loose threads are
threads that have been left radically untied" (*H,* 112). The "paspresenture" (or "past-present-future"—Grass's neologism in German is *Vergegenkunft*) is the hypothetical tense in which past, present, and future are
simultaneously present and inextricably interactive. This tense is most
productively at home in the hypothetical worlds, at once intertextual
and intertemporal, of the literary text. Past, present, and future—
"There once was: there once is. There will have been once again"
(*H,* 131)—inevitably shape each other in shaping themselves, and the
problems of each are always at least potentially the problems of the others. The temporal telescoping of the "past-present-future," in turn, finds
a parallel in the ever-shrinking spaces of the global village and its problematic new definitions of here and there, ours and theirs, belonging and
foreignness.

The problems continue to be legion, while the answers continue to be
painfully slow in coming: "I made a mistake in banking on the snail.
Ten and more years ago I said: Progress is a snail. The people who
shouted at the time, 'Too slow! Too slow for us!' may recognize (as I do)
that the snail has slipped away from us, has hurried ahead of us. We'll
never catch up. We're way behind. The snail is too quick for us"
(*H,* 121). Despair is by no means the order of the day, however: "I am
not chucking it. Every time I try, I (only seemingly elsewhere) slip back
into my old commitments from a new direction" (*H,* 131). Camus's
Sisyphus—"The absurd man says yes, and his labor will know no end"
(*H,* 140)—is the patron saint of Grass's *Headbirths*—"All headbirths,
including mine, are absurd" (*H,* 140)—written on the threshold of

Orwell's decade: "I'm curious about the eighties: a meddling contemporary" (*H*, 131).

Like almost everything that Grass has written, *Headbirths* is firmly grounded in ambiguity rather than dogma. This is a book of hypothetical scenarios, a book where no final decisions can be reached. *Headbirths* is a short and deceptively simple text, and it is easy to underestimate its importance in the development of Grass's writing. In many ways, however, it occupies a key position in that development, much as the similarly multiplex *From the Diary of a Snail* did a decade earlier. *Headbirths*, however, while specifically looking back to *From the Diary of a Snail*, also clearly points forward as well, introducing the apocalyptic (or, more accurately, mock-apocalyptic) tone that characterizes Grass's major writings of the 1980s, including most obviously *The Rat*. It also looks even further ahead, namely, to the central concern of Grass's work during the 1990s, the revisited question of German national identity, as developed in both *The Call of the Toad* and *Too Far Afield*.

Chapter Twelve
The Rat

In November 1982, in Rome, Grass delivered an address on the occasion of his being awarded the Antonio Feltrinelli Prize. The address, "The Destruction of Mankind Has Begun," struck a decidedly unfestive note: "Our present makes the future questionable and in many respects unthinkable, for our present produces—since we have learned above all to produce—poverty, hunger, polluted air, polluted bodies of water, forests destroyed by acid rain or deforestation, arsenals that seem to pile up of their own accord and are capable of destroying mankind many times over."[1] A little more than three years later, in early 1986, this doomsday scenario found literary expression in a 500-page narrative entitled *Die Rättin*. Preceded by lengthy extracts in major newspapers, the new novel was an instant best-seller in Germany and remained so for several months. By early August 1986, according to newspaper reports, translations were being prepared in 20 different languages; Ralph Manheim's English translation, *The Rat*, appeared in 1987.

"At Christmas I wished for a rat," begins the narrator of *The Rat*, and thereby hangs a tale—indeed a whole collection of them, for *The Rat* is less a novel in any traditional sense than a collection of latter-day and decidedly grim fairy tales.[2] Very much latter-day, in fact, for Grass's narrative focuses on no less final a scenario than the nuclear Big Bang that obliterates all traces of human life on earth. No one is quite sure who finally pushes the button or why, but somehow it happens anyway, as if by the sheer weight of inertia. Humanity perishes, a victim of its own stupidity, and disappears as completely as the dinosaurs once did. But even though humankind fails to survive, there are other survivors—the rats— and they are legion. So, at least, the narrator is informed, as he in turn tells us, for the basic narrative structure of the book establishes itself very quickly: the gift rat under the Christmas tree metamorphoses into a voice of doom inexorably relating the imminent, inevitable, and apocalyptic end of human affairs, while the narrator, once again a Scheherazade, spins and juggles tale after tale, narrative against narrative.

The Rat very overtly invites interpretation as an apocalyptic text, prophesying, with apparent gloomy relish, a scenario of ultimate and inevitable disaster. Those readers who like their message this neat, however, predictably tended to reject *The Rat* for the same reason they also rejected *The Flounder* nine years earlier. Grass, for all his obvious good intentions, so the argument goes, has in both cases produced monstrous farragoes of ineffectual satire that eventually drown in their own diffuseness and narrative self-indulgence, failing signally in the process to achieve their ostensible aim.[3] A more productive reading of *The Rat,* however, locates the central emphasis on apocalyptic prophecy as a process of exploratory interrogation rather than the product of authoritative assertion. The plot, in this reading, constitutes an unresolved narrative duel—a contest of stories, worlds, and realities—as the rat's monolithic No is relativized and held uneasily at bay by the narrator's continually restated efforts at saying Yes. The resulting balance of conflicting narrative hypotheses illustrates prophecy as purely deictic, apocalypse as purely revelatory, without any implied confidence in the power of prophecy to prevent or correct human folly, the restorative moment of traditional satire deconstructing into the reflexivity of self-consciously postmodernist fabulation.

If the talking flatfish of *The Flounder* parodically embodied the spirit of Hegelian optimism in history, the rat, as voluble as the flounder ever was, equally parodically incorporates the spirit of Spenglerian pessimism in a West caught up in the last throes of historical decline. Her tale (for, perhaps not surprisingly after *The Flounder,* she is a female rat) is a straightforward one, and its point simple: ultimate disaster is inevitable, or rather, *was* inevitable, for, as far as the rat's narrative is concerned, the whole affair is not a matter of the future but of the past—humanity *has* ceased to exist.[4] As far as the narrator is concerned, the nightmare scenario is, at worst, in the perhaps postponable future, or, even better, in a purely hypothetical world whose validity can be challenged and relativized by the construction of other, different, narrative counterworlds.

The narrator has a whole collection of narratives, and they are related not one after the other in a linear sequence, but all together, interweaving in a complexly shifting narrative construct. There is, first of all, the story of the five women who set out to forestall disaster in the Baltic, for the life of the Baltic as an ecosystem is endangered not merely by anything as mundane as industrial effluents or acid rain, but by a population explosion of jellyfish. The five women, one of them a marine biologist, undertake a research trip in an old converted freighter to measure the extent of the damage. Their voyage turns out to be a continuation of *The Flounder;* indeed, at one point their captain, Damroka (a church organist, like Grass's wife Ute), consults with the mythical flounder himself, cross-eyed as ever and still espousing the feminist cause. The nameless first-person narrator (by his own account) is not only in love with Damroka but, Edek-like, has also had relations of one kind or another with each of the others as well, though each of them in turn has written him out of her life. The boat is called *The New Ilsebill,* and no men need apply. All five of the women (except one, the cook) are impassioned knitters, "as though determined that their yarn should never break off" (*R,* 25).

But if the yarn is the story of feminism, the narrator implies, it has already broken off, for in the Germany of the 1980s feminism has come to nothing, all the real power is still firmly in the hands of men, the flounder's promises were lies, and nothing has changed. The optimism of the 1970s is a thing of the past, and the future now holds only the threat of nuclear holocaust. The research trip is redirected by Damroka into the search for a promised land in the form of the legendary sunken city of Vineta, a feminist Utopia, an Atlantis beyond the reach of men and their apparently unquenchable thirst for self-destruction. The women are miraculously guided to the site of Vineta jointly by the flounder and a supernatural chorus of jellyfish, only to find, as they gaze down on the towers and steeples of the city, that it has already been recolonized: the streets are swarming with rats. The women's discovery coincides with the moment of the first nuclear strike against nearby Danzig that vaporizes them instantaneously, terminating both their quest and their story.

The narrator's tale of the women who try to escape turns, whether he wants it to or not, into a self-reflective demonstration of the universal impossibility of escape, even into a world of fiction, a dream world. The women's attempt to take cover, to go under in a sunken city of the mind, may well remind the reader of Mahlke's attempt to dive to safety in the sunken minesweeper of *Cat and Mouse* or Oskar's attempts to emulate his grandfather and disappear under his grandmother's skirts. And that is exactly where we find Oskar at the moment the five women are vaporized, for both Oskar and Anna Koljaiczek reappear as characters in *The Rat,* 30 years older than when their careers were temporarily suspended at the end of *The Tin Drum.* Anna Koljaiczek is now no less than 107 years old, and it is to celebrate her birthday that Oskar returns to Danzig in 1984 in a chauffeur-driven Mercedes, the chauffeur none other than his old keeper, Bruno. Oskar himself is approaching 60 and has grown prosperous and respected as the director of a film company

called Post Futurum Productions. After making his fortune in pornographic movies, Oskar has astutely moved with the market into educational videos, under the proud slogan "We Produce the Future." The
narrator and he are on cautiously friendly terms, and Oskar is interested
in producing one or two of the narrator's scripts in due course and even
collaborates with him on the plot, since he suspects the narrator of being
totally out of touch with marketing trends. Oskar has considerable
reservations about making the trip back to Danzig, or rather Gdańsk,
for that, as Oskar sees it, is just the problem. There can be no real going
back, and to attempt to do so, he feels uneasily, may be to court disaster.
He is, of course, more right than he can imagine, for his trip to Danzig
is simultaneously a voyage into both a fictive past and a hypothetical
future, and the dangers of both are unknown. At the height of the birthday celebrations the world ends, and Oskar ends with it, vainly fleeing
in his last seconds to curl up, as of old, in the ineffectual shelter of his
grandmother's skirts.

Or, at any rate, that is one version of what happens. In another version Oskar remains blissfully ignorant of his own demise and travels
back through Poland and East Germany tormented not by regret for his
own untimely passing but by an acute prostate problem. Oskar,
unaware that he has already been written out of the script, will later
accuse the narrator of trying to do so by having him die prematurely as
a result of his prostate condition—a fate averted, as Oskar somewhat
bitterly notes, only by quick thinking on the part of Bruno in getting
him to a hospital as quickly as possible. Dead or not, Oskar in due
course celebrates his sixtieth birthday, the occasion marred only by a
telegram announcing the death of Anna Koljaiczek, who also chooses to
ignore her previous death of radiation poisoning and obstinately dies all
over again of natural causes. The narrator is an invited guest at Oskar's
party but is treated with some coolness; on the other hand, Oskar seems
favorably disposed toward the narrator's striking companion, Damroka,
who, no longer dead either, has returned home safe and sound from her
research trip. She is glad the trip is over, sick of canned food and count-
ing jellyfish, eager to get back to her music, and has not mentioned a
word about Vineta (R, 340).

The world of *The Rat* is the world of *Märchen*, the world of the fairy
tale, where all reality is relative, where Little Red Riding Hood will be
found safe and sound inside the wolf, none the worse for having been
devoured. In Grass's version of the Grimms' story, indeed, the threshold
between disaster and escape is modernized and mechanized: the wolf

comes already equipped with a zipper to facilitate escape, and Red Riding Hood courts disaster for kicks. *The Rat* reanimates the world of the Grimms as well as that of *The Flounder* and *The Tin Drum,* and among the dramatis personae we find not only Little Red Riding Hood and the wolf, but also her grandmother, who reads aloud to the wolf for pedagogical reasons from the 32 volumes of the Grimms' other masterpiece, their monumental historical dictionary of the German language. We have Snow White and her seven (lascivious) dwarfs, we have Briar Rose and her (overamorous) Prince, we have Rumpelstiltskin, Rapunzel, the Frog Prince, and Hansel and Gretel and their (buxom) Witch. For good measure we also have the brothers Grimm themselves, now members of the federal Ministry of the Environment in Bonn.

There is need of them there, for the woods of Germany are dying, and with them the *Märchen.* Desperate measures are necessary, and they are invoked by Hansel and Gretel—who in reality, in another reality, are not Hansel and Gretel at all but Johannes and Margarete, the runaway children of Federal Chancellor Helmut Kohl. The children run away into the deep woods in search not of gingerbread houses but of an alternative to the creeping devastation of the natural environment. Hansel and Gretel succeed in radicalizing the fairy-tale world they find still intact there, to the point where a protest march on Bonn is planned, to be followed by the abduction of the government and the seizure of power. Success seems momentarily assured when the brothers Grimm are declared leaders of the revolutionary government and the world of *Märchen* guaranteed a voice in all future government decisions. Ultimately, however, their demands—clean air and water, uncontaminated fruit and vegetables—are so outrageously unrealistic that they provoke a counterrevolution, and the world of the Grimms, the world of metamorphosis, transformation, and the possibility of changing direction, is crushed out of existence by the combined forces of church, capital, army, and riot police. The only survivors are Hansel and Gretel. Once again they flee into the deep woods, "as though fairy tales were still in existence" (*R,* 344), the dead forest this time bursting into life around them as they run. At a crossroads, a carriage with four white horses is waiting, and the children join its occupants, the brothers Grimm, as it moves slowly, pulling the white horses behind it, into the shelter of the past, into a time when woods were still woods and magic was magic. The ending is Oskar's contribution—for the whole story of the dying forests turns out to be a scenario by the narrator for one of Oskar's educational videos. "Somebody has to get away. Nobody wants to be entirely without fairy tales" (R, 343).

The past is the abode of *Märchen* in more ways than one, for while changing what will happen in the future seems to be beyond the powers of human imagination, changing what happened in the past is within the reach of all. Oskar, that master himself in the art of creative reinterpretation, is less interested in the story of Hansel and Gretel than in the career of his contemporary, the East Prussian painter and master forger Lothar Malskat. Lübeck was the site of Malskat's rise and fall, for when the rubble had been cleared away after the British bombing of the cathedral there, and while masons were discreetly removing the swastika chiseled above the high altar on the orders of a Party-minded bishop, Malskat, to the delight of the chapter and art experts alike, succeeded in uncovering mural after mural that clearly dated back to the heyday of Gothic art. When Malskat eventually tires of the game and admits that the murals are his own work, nobody wishes to acknowledge that what was so convenient as truth could be anything but truth. Only when Malskat retains a lawyer and proves beyond all doubt that he is indeed guilty of forgery are the sanctions of law and order duly, if belatedly, invoked.

Appearances are deceptive, however, the narrator observes. Malskat was no forger. His paintings were genuine Gothic; what was a forgery was the times in which he was forced to paint them. Other forgers, however, the narrator goes on, were at work in those days, the early 1950s, and everybody knew they were forgers—but, happily, since they, unlike Malskat, never chose to draw attention to the fact themselves, nobody else had to either. The master forgers were Adenauer and Ulbricht, "The Great Pretenders" (R, 348), who chiseled away the swastikas so cleanly in their respective states that no one had to remember ever again that the nightmare of Nazism once did really happen. Forgery has become the norm. Malskat's originals, however, are whitewashed over, leaving ugly stains as reminders on the walls, as much casualties of a forged reality as were the devastated woods and the devastated world of the *Märchen*.

History is not a record of what really happened, it is a narrative of what may have or what might have happened, for facts die without fictions to perpetuate their reality, and fictions can be contested by other fictions perpetuating other realities. Not just Orwell's year and the year of Oskar's sixtieth birthday, 1984 is also the 700th anniversary of the

Pied Piper's seduction in 1284 of the rats of Hamelin, lured to their death in the river Weser by the sweet sounds of the flute. According to another version of the legend, however, it was not only rats that were lured to destruction but also children—130, to be precise, in the narrator's version of the story. For the narrator is able to give us the truth of what really happened in Hamelin. The year 1284, like 1984, had its punks, too, High Gothic punks, dropouts and protesters like their future counterparts, complete with chains and safety pins and pet rats dyed violet or pink or green to match counterculture hairstyles.

In Hamelin, it turns out, things got a little out of hand when first the mayor's daughter and later other young ladies, too, allowed their pet rats increasing liberties. A crisis point was reached when Gret, the mayor's daughter, gave birth after an unusually short pregnancy to triplets, three tiny infants whose only peculiarity was their tiny rats' heads. The other 129 Gothic punks of Hamelin are delighted with this miraculous conception and delivery, but the common people, unsettled by the intrusion of fairy-tale happenings into the solidity of their everyday world, seem in imminent danger of beginning to wonder just how solid that world might be. With civil disturbances, strikes, even riots rumored, the authorities must move quickly to contain the situation. A piper is engaged, for a certain number of pieces of silver, to entrap the punks in their own love of dancing and carousing. Hans and Gret (for the rat's name is Hans) and their three infants (duly baptized Kaspar, Melchior, and Balthazar) have fled for safety to a cave in the hillside. There they are joined, on the feast of St. John, in June 1284, by the remaining 129 Gothic punks and their 129 pet rats, led by the piper. The night passes in dancing and merrymaking, until at dawn the piper slips away unnoticed. Thereupon, the cave mouth, according to plan, is quickly walled up by skilled masons, hidden under loads of sand, sprinkled with holy water—and everything returns to normal.

All of the narrator's tales, individually and in their interrelationship, explore the possibility of escape—escape from the future, escape from the present, escape from (and to) the past—and in each case the possibility is exploded. The rat as counternarrator, on the other hand, tells a single, relentless tale of the impossibility of escape—and can do so only because she and her fellow rats have always escaped, always managed to survive. Their abilities as escape artists have been honestly come by over the course of millennia, for always, the rat complains, they have been hunted down and exterminated, feared and loathed as carriers of disease, plague, and death, held to be responsible for all ills: "The rats and the

Jews, the Jews and the rats are to blame" (R, 99). The injustice goes
back to earliest times, for even Noah, according to the rat, disobeyed
the express command of the Lord and refused rats alone entry to the
Ark, although that did not prevent them from surviving the Flood.
Then, as later, they were able to dig in and wait out the storm, for a key
factor in their survival mechanism is to be able to spot a sinking ship in
good time, to recognize disaster when they see it coming, an ability
humankind has never managed to emulate. The signs of humankind's
final death throes were far too obvious to be missed toward the end:
hunger, warfare, overpopulation, and massive unemployment worldwide; seas, rivers, woods, fields, and air poisoned and dying; humankind
choking on its own garbage—and itching for the delicious release of
self-obliteration. Which side finally pushed the button is no longer of
any interest—maybe it was even the rats themselves who eventually
gnawed their way into the central computer systems.

After the decades of fire storms and dust storms, radiation poisoning
and nuclear winter, the rats, unchanged except for their new bright
green coats, venture forth again and establish their own civilization in
the Danzig area. After initial genocidal religious strife among warring
sects, harmony is established and agriculture flourishes under a fertility
goddess and the divine infant discovered by the rats under her skirts—
for the deity and her assumed offspring are none other than the
shrunken and mummified remains of Anna Koljaiczek and Oskar.
Rumors still circulate about a savior or a race of saviors still to come,
however, and in due course a derelict hulk appears in the harbor. From
it, to the tolling of all the bells of Danzig (spared out of cultural considerations by the neutron bombs that obliterated all human life), the mes-
siahs climb ashore. "There were five of them, then seven, and finally
twelve" (R, 307), they are blonde, blue-eyed, the size of a three-year-old
child, perfect little human beings with perfectly proportioned rats'
heads. The hulk is the remains of The New Ilsebill, whose five feminists
(previously planned, says the narrator, as being 7 in number, reduced
from an original 12) had returned from a brief shore leave unwittingly
accompanied by some escaped laboratory rats on whom Swedish scien-
tists had been conducting gene-splicing experiments. The desired result
is Ratman, a comic-book millennial synthesis of human rationality,
smurflike industry, and the rat's ability to survive; a postmodern cen-
taur; a neogothic grotesque à la Malskat—one of whose more inaccessi-
ble miniatures, as it happens (and if fuzzy photographs can be trusted),
contains a map showing the site of Vineta, while nearby another shows

three small ratmen playing flutes over a legend referring to St. John's day in Hamelin (*R,* 327). The miracle product, like all millennial ambition in Grass's world, is a failure, however, for the quickly multiplying ratmen have all too little of the rat's ability to survive and all too much of the human thirst for military expansion. Having lived through human history before, and with no desire to repeat it, the rats resolve to wipe the ratmen out. The last five survivors of the ratmen make a vain attempt to escape on *The New Ilsebill,* still lying in the harbor, but are eaten alive by the victorious rats, whose coloring has now reverted from green to black. The last of them to die is the one in whom the narrator claims to recognize his Damroka.

The relationship between the narrator and the also narrating rat is the driving force of *The Rat,* and that relationship hinges on the possibility of escape. The rat's voice, like that of Death or the Devil in a medieval morality play, drones the inescapable reminder that escape is impossible, while the narrator extravagantly explores the possibilities of conceivable and inconceivable flights, whether in romantic visions of his Damroka's flowing hair, in the fairy-tale forests of yesteryear, or in whatever other games with alternate realities he can construct to hide among, like Briar Rose behind her hedge of impenetrable thorns. Like Oskar and the talking flounder, the narrator, too, can be said to have been "borrowed" from another text, for the narrating *I* of *The Rat* is the same *I* we are familiar with from *The Flounder:* cowed, defeated, helpless, ineffectual. It would, of course, be simplistic to identify this *I* with the writer Günter Grass; but we also need to be careful in calling this *I,* without further qualification, the narrator, as we have been doing so far for simplicity's sake. Behind or beside the narrator who calls himself *I* there is another voice, whom we might distinguish by a capital as the Narrator, whose role is precisely the balancing and juxtaposition of the two narrative voices, that of the narrating *I* and that of the rat, yea-sayer and naysayer, one against the other. The narrator continually refers to the rat as "the rat I dream about," but who is dreaming whom?

> I dreamed of a man, / said the She-rat of my dreams. / I argued with him until he thought / he was dreaming about me and said in his dream: the She-rat / of my dreams thinks she is dreaming about me; / we read each other in mirrors / and question each other. // Could it be that both of us, / the She-rat and I, / are being dreamed, that we are the dreams / of a third species? (*R,* 311)

To be dreamed is to be without responsibilities, as when the narrator—reminiscent of the ineffectual Starusch in *Local Anaesthetic*—visualizes himself orbiting the devastated earth in a space capsule, listening to the rat over the communications system, but unable to affect the situation in any way, for better or for worse. To be a member of society demands the acceptance of responsibilities, and it is the rat's voice, rather than the narrator's, that we hear reiterating that demand throughout. The rat is a pedagogue, and her message is a simple one: be afraid, forget dreams of immortality, acknowledge that you are indeed going to die, and, just possibly, you may live a little longer (*R,* 122). The rat, to this extent, is precisely the "footnotes and commentary" (*R,* 6) on human idealisms and ideologies, the shadow side of all human endeavor, Mephisto's No to Faust's dreams of Yes. The rat, in a word, is Oskar's bête noire, the Black Witch, the boring truth the narrator refuses to face when he talks of his "graying fear that all untrue stories will be exposed and that only the boring truth will prevail" (*R,* 68). The Narrator (with a capital), however, knows better: "Children, we play at getting lost / and find one another much too quickly" (*R,* 129). And, knowing better as he does, he goes on playing anyway, for if the narrator deals in narrative escape, the Narrator deals in narrative play.

The responses to impending destruction that one can glean from *The Rat* are powerless platitudes: love thy neighbor, abandon arrogance, learn from our mistakes, be reasonable, tolerant, and kind—the standard maxims of eighteenth-century Enlightenment thinking, perfectly sound advice, and perfectly useless. But the point of *The Rat* is hardly to offer us a hitherto unsuspected path to salvation. The narrator is well aware, for example, that his film on the death of the woods, even if Oskar produces it, will be quite powerless to save the forest, or anything else either, for that matter. The point of Grass's art—which for all its overt political engagement has, in this respect at least, been solidly postmodernist from its very beginnings—has always been not to provide us with neatly packaged real-life solutions to real-life problems, but to present us with new and often startling ways of reenvisaging the reality we inhabit. We may, if we wish, take the rat's warning at face value, but we must not forget that the warning is constructed as a *Märchen,* not a treatise; we may deduce a moral, if we wish, but we need to be constantly aware of the element of parodic play involved as well.

From the opening sentence, with its ironic allusion to other earlier and fruitless attempts, such as Lessing's, at educating humankind—"At

Christmas I wished for a rat, in the hope, no doubt, of stimulus words for a poem about the education of the human race" (R, 1)—Grass implicitly pokes ironic fun at his own pedagogical ambitions and efforts over the years.[5] More than that, the very notion that art *can* educate or achieve change is parodied, and the parody is strengthened throughout by the flaunted inappropriateness, even for Grass, of the chosen vehicle for the ostensible message. *The Rat* is very far from being the sort of cultural Third Program that the narrator listens to on the radio, where a troublesome world is tidily packaged into neat explanatory commentaries, interspersed with baroque music. The element of self-parody has been strongly present in Grass's work from its very beginnings: in *The Rat* it becomes the paramount consideration. *The Rat* parodies not only the pedagogical aspirations of a Brechtian concept of writing but also writing itself; not only the processes of constructing historical fictions but also the subsequent inability to break away from those fictions; not only the practice and process of searching for conclusive answers in life as in literature but also the very idea that there may be any final answers to look for in the first place.

This kind of all-encompassing parody has, of course, an element of satire in it, but the relationship is a distant one. Traditionally the satirist has written authoritatively, from a position of knowledge: he or she knows what is right and castigates, with a greater or lesser degree of mercilessness, any deviations from that unassailable norm. There are episodes in *The Rat* that are still satiric in this sense (the Malskat narrative is an obvious example), in which an implicitly corrective attack is launched on a relatively sharply focused target. When the focus becomes so diffuse as to encompass human impotence itself, there is little point in calling it satire any more, for the satirist's optimistic trust in the power of corrective medicine is exposed as itself a fraud and a fiction. It is possible to read a number of Grass's earlier books, *Local Anaesthetic,* for example, or *From the Diary of a Snail,* as belonging to this latter category; it is difficult to read *The Rat* as anything else. Humanity disappeared, says the rat, because it was incapable of change (R, 265). *The Rat* is a book crammed with changes, transformations, and metamorphoses, but in the end nothing changes either. Just as Oskar's film of his grandmother's birthday eventually turns into the film of itself (R, 232), so the end of *The Rat* runs into its beginning in a vicious circle, the discussion marking time rather than developing, narrator and rat frozen in a narrative stasis.

In the massive headbirth that is *The Rat,* not just the Germans are dying out, everybody is. The Danzig trilogy, in J. P. Stern's memorable phrase, matched an unbelievable past with unbelievable metaphors; *The Rat* performs the same task for an unbelievable future.[6] If Oskar can escape his predestined end, can we? Is it possible that common sense, peace, brotherhood, and all the other similarly outmoded virtues could still save us in the end, against all the odds? "A beautiful dream, said the She-rat, before dissolving" (*R, 371*). Whether the dream will become reality may still, we hope, be up to us. *The Rat* trades in dreams and realities; shows how fluidly each can metamorphose into the other, just as future and past can reverse their roles; speculates on the multifarious disintegration of order and on whether entropy may yet still be reversible. Its speculations, however, are always conducted in terms of fictional rather than extrafictional realities, and their relevance to the extrafictional world is left to the reader to determine.

Apocalypse Variations

The Rat was followed over the next five years by three shorter texts in a similarly apocalyptic mode that ring a series of minor variations on the theme of humankind's apparently irresistible urge to destroy itself. A striking feature of this group of texts is the increasing degree to which Grass the writer yields center stage to Grass the graphic artist.

Between August 1986 and January 1987 Grass and his wife Ute spent five months in India, mostly in Calcutta. The result is *Zunge zeigen,* published in 1988 and translated by John E. Woods, in 1989, as *Show Your Tongue.*[7] In this attempt to come to grips artistically with what proved to be a harrowing experience, Grass combines three separate strategies: the book consists of just under 100 pages devoted to a journal of his stay; more than 100 pages filled with brooding neo-Expressionist drawings in charcoal and heavy inks; and a 20-page poem in 12 stanzas likewise entitled "Show Your Tongue," whose (German) text the reader has by then already encountered in often barely legible scraps overwriting each of the hundred pages of drawings. In *Show Your Tongue* Grass portrays his horrified fascination with a radically deromanticized twentieth-century version of the once "mysterious East," with Calcutta, "the real capital of the world," the ultimate symbol of extreme poverty and total desolation.

Show Your Tongue is both a bravura performance and a very personal reflection on this far from brave new world—and, just as in *Headbirths,* a reflection simultaneously on the differences between it and the too-well-fed world of the Germany and the Europe he has left behind. Grass's instinctive sympathy for suffering humanity, for the underdog, the man and woman all too literally in the street, is evident on every page, as is his sustained rage that one half of the world can bear to let the other half exist in such conditions. His horror and rage, however, are uncomfortably accompanied by the realization (and even the guilty relief) that there is absolutely nothing he can do, in his role of globe-trotting cultural tourist, to make any real difference.

Compounding the guilt is the fact that what appalls the man and the moralist intrigues the artist—a theme of Grass's that we are familiar with from the days of *The Tin Drum* and *Dog Years*. *Show Your Tongue*, for all its moral indignation, is also one more testament to the artist Grass's continued fascination with his own role as artist and writer, as literary voyeur. Harm and Dörte in *Headbirths* dragged their European and German baggage along with them to Asia in the shape of the vacuum-packed liver sausage; the twentieth-century German writer Grass takes a collection of the nineteenth-century German writer Theodor Fontane's novels along with him. How Fontane would have or might have reacted to the reality of Calcutta becomes a recurring theme in *Show Your Tongue*, allowing Grass one more refracting lens through which to view his subject matter, one more contrast in a series involving the familiar and the foreign, here and there, then and now. (Almost a decade later Fontane would resurface in Grass's work as the central figure around whom the novel *Too Far Afield* is constructed.)

Calcutta is a strange new world, a world of troubling contrasts where black and white blur into a worrying grey. It was the home, for example, of Subhas Chandra Bose, a Bengali hero and freedom fighter, but one who was prepared to embrace the doctrines of Fascism during the Second World War as part of a larger project to undermine British rule in his country. It is a world of new and unsuspected opportunities: Grass's play, *The Plebeians*, unperformed in Germany for 20 years, is seized upon by a local theatrical group who enthusiastically stage it in a Bengali version. Most of all, it is a world of ubiquitous garbage, slums, hovels, stench, poverty, human misery, and death in all shapes and sizes: it is the world of Kali, whose portrait, tongue extended, graces the cover of the volume. The very name of the city of Calcutta—originally Kalikata—contains that of the goddess Kali, whose name means "the black one" (once again evoking Oskar's Black Witch) and who plays a central symbolic role in the text. In Hindu mythology Kali the Destroyer is the female emanation of Shiva the Destroyer, the great and terrible god of destruction and death. In traditional iconography Kali is portrayed as a dancer, richly arrayed and beautiful, but one of her four arms grasps a bloody sword and another a severed head, she wears a necklace of human skulls, and her tongue hangs obscenely from her mouth, red with the blood she has drunk in her fury.

The tongue of the title is strikingly polyvalent. It can be read as an invitation to its readers to be ashamed for their part in permitting the human tragedy of the Third World to continue, for in India, as the text tells us, extending one's tongue is an indication of shame. It can likewise be read as an invitation to its readers to admit that they simply don't care, for in the affluent West, sticking your tongue out indicates scorn. It can be read as playing with the possibility of a solution, as when a doctor invites patients to show their tongue. It can also be read as admitting the complete incurability of the disease, evoking the bloody tongue of Kali. *Show Your Tongue* is a disturbing book, obsessively peopled by horrifying images. The graphic images in particular have a (literally) darkly threatening power that openly invites the reader to turn away; to escape to the (even if only relatively) less threatening environment of the cooler, more distanced print medium; to close the book. Having returned to all too prosperous Germany, Grass promises himself that from now on Calcutta will be his yardstick. A recurring theme in the book, however, is how quickly one yearns—and learns—to forget.

The German original of *Show Your Tongue* was followed just two years later by *Totes Holz* (Dead Wood), consisting primarily of some 50 oppressively dark lithographs of, literally, dead wood. The collection, drawn between summer 1988 and winter 1989, is accompanied by ironically deployed texts, some poetic, some autobiographical, some official texts by government bodies on the demise of the German forests. In *Totes Holz,* equally ironically dedicated to Jacob and Wilhelm Grimm, so many of whose tales take place in the romantic depths of dense German forests, Grass returns to the theme he had already broached four years earlier in *The Rat,* namely, the apparently irreversible destruction of Germany's (and Europe's) forests. *Totes Holz* is also directly related to *Show Your Tongue,* the devastation of Germany's forests reflecting the devastation of India's people.

Composed (sketched, drawn, written) just before and published just after the fall of the Berlin Wall, the dead wood of the title is also a symbol for the devastation that Grass sees as having been (and continuing to be) visited on East Germany in the name of monopoly capitalism by its triumphant West German neighbor, now master. A key expression in *Totes Holz* is *Kahlschlag,* the technical term for clearcutting in forestry management. This term carries the strong connotation in German of "devastation," not just of the forests but also in the heads and minds of the German people, east and west, clearcut by the ideological and the financial power of a victorious capitalism.

Grass expands upon this theme in *Brief aus Altdöbern* (A Letter from Altdöbern), which appeared in 1991, a series of drawings (mainly charcoal) of familiar Grassian fauna, produced for a bibliophile series devoted to the work of graphic artists who are also writers. The windfowl of the early poems, the optimistic rooster of SPD days, the philosophical flounder, the apocalyptic rat, the dead owl that comes to symbolize the desolation of *Totes Holz*, the double-headed snail of self-erasing progress, and finally, summing the series, the man-eating Kali of *Show Your Tongue* are set against the devastated moon landscape of the exhausted Altdöbern coal pits of the formerly East German Lausitz region, a victim of industrial progress in the form of unregulated coal mining. The drawings (reprising the style of *Show Your Tongue*) are accompanied and overwritten by the actual "letter from Altdöbern," the central thrust of which, ironically placed in the mouth of the fairy-tale flounder, is that the Hegelian charger of progress has failed us once again, been overtaken once again by the snail of doubt.

The moonscape of the Lausitz area significantly recurs four years later in the major novel *Ein weites Feld* (*Too Far Afield*), which Grass was already writing by this time and which centers on what Grass, defying popular opinion, persisted in seeing as the unmitigated disaster of German unification. The devastation of the forests portrayed in *Totes Holz*, largely drawn in the Oberharz and Erzgebirge regions—both in the former East Germany—is overtly presented by Grass as corresponding to the political and social devastation that has befallen East Germany since the forced marriage, as he sees it, with a victorious West Germany, a process that, for Grass, was likewise the result of the unreflected pursuit of a vision of material progress fatally narrowly defined.

Chapter Thirteen
The Call of the Toad

The novel *Unkenrufe* appeared in 1992, as did Ralph Manheim's translation, *The Call of the Toad*. (It was the last of Grass's works to be translated by Manheim, who died in September 1992, shortly after finishing it.) The dust jackets of both carry an illustration by Grass of a large toad squatting behind a fountain pen. Toads, the latest addition to Grass's parodic artistic menagerie, are, we are told, common in the swampy lowlands surrounding Danzig, where the novel is once again set. The title has a self-ironic overtone: in many German fairy tales the call of the toad presages disaster, and the expression "Unkenrufe" thus has the colloquial connotation of a Cassandra's warning, an unheeded prophecy of doom. Grass's fiction, as the author himself was well aware, had been becoming increasingly Cassandra-like over the previous two decades.

The story begins (just days before the Berlin Wall finally began to crumble) in St. Dominic's Market in what was once German Danzig, now Polish Gdańsk, on 2 November 1989, the Feast of All Souls, which commemorates the dead. It begins with the chance meeting of a West German widower and a Polish widow, both preparing to visit a cemetery, he for professional reasons, she to visit her parents' grave. Both in their sixties, he is a somewhat bumbling professor of art history at the University of Bochum in West Germany, specializing in tombstone inscriptions and given to impromptu lectures, she a somewhat scatty conservator and restorer of ecclesiastical carvings, specializing in gilding and gifted with shaky but effective German-language skills. He grew up in Danzig, it emerges, she "in Wilno, as Vilnius or Wilna is called in Polish."[1] They even have a common first name: Alexander Reschke, Alexandra Piatkowska. Encouraged by these signs, he buys her some asters, then some mushrooms, which leads to a meal, which leads eventually to bed. "They seem to have mastered the art of making love. At their age patience is needed and the kind of humor that ignores the possibility of defeat" (*CT,* 63).

Both more than middle-aged, both divorced, and both enthusiastic devotees of the arts, Alexander and Alexandra are clearly soul mates, fated by the laws of narrative convention to meet and fall in love. Their grand passion, however, turns out to be less of a romantic than of a historical nature, as their shared interest in the richness of Danzig's cultural history develops into a growing obsession with a visionary scheme to repatriate Danzig's dead, to reverse the *Völkerwanderung* or Great Migration that had seen thousands of its citizens flee to the West as Russian troops advanced at the end of the Second World War. Driven out of Poland like many others by the vicissitudes of war, their parents, it emerges, also shared an unfulfilled desire, namely, to rest eventually in Polish earth. The pair gradually develop the idea—its germ conceived in a graveyard on All Souls' Day—of a "German-Polish Cemetery Association" that will enable the return of the exiled dead to Danzig, a reconciliation in death of the political divisions imposed during their lifetimes and a contribution to a new friendship between Germans and their eastern neighbors.

Their endeavors are blessed by beginners' luck, and the scheme, after some initial difficulties, proves to be surprisingly popular—so popular, indeed, that, like many a visionary scheme before it, the ambitious plan to reunite in death what life had put asunder quickly outgrows its naively idealistic founders and falls into more opportunistically entrepreneurial hands. German-Polish reconciliation was to be cemented by the lovers' funereal scheme, but capitalism soon displaces idealism. A Board of Directors of the Cemetery Association is carefully selected, chosen on grounds of political correctness, German and Polish, male and female, clerical and lay. Shortly after the initial success of the endeavor, soon renamed the Cemetery of Reconciliation, and shortly after Reschke has resigned from his university position to devote himself full time to the undertaking, which he characterizes as "the ultimate in international understanding" (*CT*, 115), Alexandra abruptly declares that they should stop while everything is still going well (*CT*, 118). They don't, and soon everything begins to go far too well. Corporate and government funding rolls in, legal advisors are retained, bank balances soar dizzyingly into the millions, assets are diversified, cremation services are added to coffin burials. Comfortable retirement communities are soon under construction, shortly followed by geriatric clinics, as a wave of "burial-ready" expatriates, some 30,000 of them, relocate from Germany to Danzig (on payment of DM 1,000 each) in order to die and be buried there. The most significant achievement, however, is the introduction of an executive reburial option, involving the bodies of displaced Danzigers being flown in from Germany—a service which, as the ultimate in German-

Polish reconciliation, could obviously be made available only at a significantly increased rate (*CT,* 160).

Horrified at the thought of one more German invasion of Poland, this time by ghoulish armies of exhumed corpses, Alexander and Alexandra indignantly resign their positions as members of the Board of Directors. Their indignation is shared by one of the most memorable characters in the novel, Erna Brakup, a token appointment to the Board, one of the very few Germans who remained in Danzig when it became Polish, and a rough diamond in her eighties reminiscent of Oskar's grandmother, Anna Bronski. She discourses folk wisdom to all who will listen in an outmoded dialect of German that will die with her—and likewise resigns in disgust from the Board of Directors of the Cemetery Association shortly before she dies, an outmoded relic of a rapidly disappearing past. Their departure is politely regretted—though not before certain barbed comments are made concerning Reschke's unorthodox methods of bookkeeping—and the reburial program continues to prosper hugely and thrive mightily. Whole chains of cemeteries of reconciliation are soon mushrooming in formerly German cities throughout western and northern Poland, now frequently accompanied by lakeshore vacation bungalows and immaculately groomed golf courses for younger relatives wishing to spend a few days or weeks relaxing before returning home, not to mention maternity clinics "for sudden confinements and premature births" that will produce "New Danzigers" (*CT,* 223).

The nature of the satire here is immediately reminiscent of Oskar's postwar career as a celebrity drummer in *The Tin Drum* or Matern's postwar career as ostensible unveiler of Nazis in *Dog Years.* The whole novel, indeed, can be read as an extrapolation of the episode in *The Tin Drum* where Oskar drums variations on the ambiguous title of the Polish national anthem, "Poland Is Not Yet Lost," prophesying new and more efficient invasions of Poland, more efficient for being corporate rather than military. The tone is entirely different, however, as the undisguised outrage of the earlier works now yields to a far more quizzically ironic form of satire. Neither *The Tin Drum* nor *The Call of the Toad*—nor any other of Grass's works, for that matter—displays any identifiable belief in the power of satire to change the world. But where the consciousness of this inevitable failure leads in *The Tin Drum* to Swiftian savagery, in *The Call of the Toad* it leads instead to something closer to an ironically detached resignation.

The *Völkerwanderung* unwittingly unleashed by the lovers' scheme is reflected in another grand (and equally harebrained) vision in the novel, that of the Bengali Mr. Subhas Chandra Chatterjee. Also a victim of political partition, Chatterjee is obsessed by his plan to flood the western world with fleets of rickshaws in order to save it from inevitable self-destruction by carbon monoxide poisoning—a vision hearkening back to *Headbirths* and its evocation of a Germany overrun by foreigners. Since Chatterjee's arrival in Danzig in the 1980s, he has contributed greatly to reducing both unemployment and environmental pollution. Other cities have gone even further: Madrid and Rome have even banned automobiles altogether and ordered great numbers of bicycle rickshaws.

The now-dying twentieth century—the Century of Expulsions (*CT*, 69), as Reschke calls it—marks the birth of a new multicultural Europe in the course of a new and irresistible *Völkerwanderung,* as already parodically anticipated in *Headbirths.* Reschke (like Grass) is German but grew up in what is now Poland; Alexandra is Polish but grew up in Lithuania; Chatterjee regards himself as a Bengali, though he grew up in Pakistan, studied in Cambridge, and carries a British passport. The possibility of all of Europe one day speaking Bengali cannot be simply dismissed out of hand: "As the ancient Greeks knew, all is flux," Chatterjee lectures Reschke. "We shall come. We will have to come, because it's getting a little cramped over there. Everybody pushes everybody else; the end will be one great push that will be impossible to stop" (*CT*, 36). The anticipated submergence of the by now newly unified Germans in this increasingly international and multicultural Europe is echoed in the multilingual street signs to be found in the newly prosperous Danzig of the booming Cemetery Association and Chatterjee's rickshaw empire, signs on which German still appears, but only in the company of English, Polish, Russian—and Bengali. "Regard me, if you please," Chatterjee advises, "as a forerunner or billeting officer of the future world society, in which the egocentric worries of your compatriots will be lost" (*CT*, 37).

The phenomenal success of Chatterjee's philanthropic and environmentally friendly endeavor is of course also a caricature of the sort of thing that Grass himself has been advocating for decades. Much as *Local Anaesthetic* had ironized the Worldwide Sickcare scheme of the enthusiastically reforming dentist, *The Call of the Toad*—reminiscent of Flaubert's equally parodic late novel *Bouvard and Pécuchet* (1881)—ironizes all such grand visionary schemes, whether Chatterjee's salvation by rickshaw, the aging lovers' afterlife repatriation, the latter-day euphoria of German reunification, or its author's own earnest efforts as politician and concerned citizen to educate and enlighten his not always enthusiastically grateful compatriots.

Reschke and Chatterjee are two sides of a coin. Reschke, a left-liberal from the sixties, adds ecological convictions to his worries in the eighties (*CT,* 84), and his diary broods with conscientious glumness over global warming, the aftereffects of Chernobyl, "the future, the weather, the traffic, reunification, and so on" (*CT,* 85). His determined gloom—which earns him his students' nickname of Jeremiah (*CT,* 85)—is balanced by the unshakable optimism of Chatterjee and his belief that "the future belongs to the bicycle rickshaw" (*CT,* 46). Both are, of course, faces of Grass himself, a relationship parodically emphasized when Reschke prudently decides to invest surplus profits from the cemetery business in Chatterjee's competing millennial rickshaw vision (*CT,* 135). "While our obligation is to the dead, he is aiming at the survival of the living" (*CT,* 136).

The Call of the Toad tells the story of a "beautiful idea and its ghastly incarnation" (*CT,* 150). It also tells a touching (if ironically portrayed) late-in-life love story, for Alexander and Alexandra are indeed deeply in love. "The Pole and the German! I could fill a picture book with them: no quarrels, congenial in every way, too good to be true" (*CT,* 142). Fittingly, therefore, this is a book clearly directed to the reader as senior citizen. Alexander and Alexandra both have grown children—she a son, he three daughters—all living in Germany and all completely out of sympathy with their parents, whose idealistic doings they contemplate with a mixture of amused cynicism and thinly veiled contempt (*CT,* 80). Alexander is an old-fashioned liberal democratic thinker like his creator, a veteran of 1968 like Harm and Dörte Peters in *Headbirths.* Alexandra was a committed and idealistic communist in her youth, one who had the opportunity to become disillusioned first with communism and then with capitalism. Alexander (whose brothers were killed during fighting at the end of the war) is high-minded (but decidedly stuffy); Alexandra (whose brother was shot by the Germans during the war) is goodhearted (and good fun). Their resignation from the Board is explained in detail (Alexander's idea) in a tape-recorded message backed by locally recorded toad calls. Soon afterward they marry, but since this is a novel about death—Reschke proposes at Erna Brakup's funeral—there can be little doubt in the reader's mind that, when they set off on their honeymoon journey to fulfill a lifelong wish of Alexandra's to see Naples, they will indeed see Naples and die. And they do. Their car, under unexplained circumstances, goes off the road and over a precipice somewhere in southern Italy, and their bodies are charred beyond recognition. "Only two wooden crosses mark their double grave. I won't have them reburied. They were against reburial" (*CT,* 248).

The Call of the Toad belongs to the group of Grass's more formally restrained texts, thus joining *Cat and Mouse, Local Anaesthetic,* and *The Meeting at Telgte.* As usual in Grass's work, *The Call of the Toad* delights in detail, frequently employed to overtly ironic effect, such as the three-note bell imitating the call of the yellow-bellied toad on each of Mr. Chatterjee's fleet of bicycle rickshaws—a sound that, we are given to understand, eventually replaces the blaring of horns in many cities of Europe (*CT,* 176). The "so-called plot" (*CT,* 2) begins when each of the two later lovers unsuccessfully attempts to assemble a bouquet of rust-red asters at the cemetery and the widower gallantly surrenders his slim pickings to the widow, converting two failed bouquets into one acceptable, "unified" (*CT,* 4) bouquet. The scene has multiple parodic overtones: the aging lovers brought together by death, the two parts of a very soon to be "unified" Germany, the economic poverty of eastern Europe as represented by Poland and its "currency so rich in zeroes" (*CT,* 4). From the opening scene of the Polish cemetery in which the lovers meet to the closing evocation of the Italian cemetery in which they finally rest, the novel luxuriates in the imagery of death, from the autumnal colors of the asters the pair assembles and the carefully catalogued Baroque coffin nails Reschke collects as a hobby (*CT,* 108) to the final irony of seeing Naples and then dying.

The fictionality of the narrated world of *The Call of the Toad* is suggested in the first sentence: "Chance put the widower next to the widow. Or maybe chance had nothing to do with it, for the story began on All Souls' " (*CT,* 1). After two paragraphs, in which, moreover, the reader is aware of only a single narrative voice, the third opens with the revelation that this narration is itself based on another narrative: "His diary confirms All Souls' " (*CT,* 1). From that point on, the double narrative voice is present throughout, the idealistic hopes and fears of Alexander Reschke relativized by the skeptical irony of the unnamed narrator—who bears an unmistakable resemblance to Günter Grass. The suggestion that someone should write a history of the Polish-German Cemetery Association, it emerges, is mooted at the wedding of Alexander and Alexandra. Reschke, doubting his own literary skills, mails the package of materials to the narrator from Rome, as the newlyweds, finally liberated from their brainchild, set off for Naples. The narrator—in a parodic recycling of one of the oldest devices of realist narrative—thus has all of his material delivered to him in the form of notes, journals, photographs, and tape-recordings scrupulously assembled by the scholarly pedant Reschke, who also turns out to have been an old schoolmate. The narrator, ostensibly, merely has to reinterpret and reassemble the accumulated documentation, which he does with all the irony appropriate for the naive enthusiasms of an otherworldly old friend and his comically misguided schemes.

The narrator, on several occasions, vents his alleged annoyance that Reschke has saddled him with the task of conveying to posterity the boringly moral tale of the German-Polish Cemetery Association. Reschke and he, it emerges, were once classmates at St. Peter's High School in Danzig, though the ostensibly irritated narrator initially plays down any significance this chance connection might be deemed to have. As the story progresses, his fondness for Reschke is allowed to become more evident. The relationship between the two, as presented by the narrator, likewise shifts from skeptical distance to parodically obvious affinity. Reschke—born, like Grass, in 1927 (*CT,* 38)—is fascinated by toads and their minatory croakings and drags Alexandra along on trips into the wetlands to record their mating calls; the narrator, as Reschke reminds him in his covering letter, attained celebrity status among his schoolboy peers for swallowing not just live frogs (like Amsel in *Dog Years*) but, on one historic occasion, even a live toad, "a hundred percent with no returns" (*CT,* 33). The narrator's reporting of this alleged feat is interestingly reminiscent of the evasiveness we associate with Pilenz in *Cat and Mouse:* first as an unsubstantiated "claim" on Reschke's part (*CT,* 29), then as being "possible" (*CT,* 33), and finally, "if you insist," as having in fact taken place (*CT,* 47). The narrator's relationship to Reschke, indeed, is distinctly reminiscent of Pilenz's relationship to Mahlke. The narrator on this as on several other occasions wavers between initial denial, subsequent grudging admission, and eventual nostalgic glorification of Reschke's memories of their schoolboy doings together and their later friendship in the Airforce Auxiliaries (of which Grass had also been a member).

Dealing with the relationship of the past and the present in the context of an unknowable future, *The Call of the Toad*—like its immediate predecessor in Grass's work, the autobiographical account *Vier Jahrzehnte* (Four Decades)—is centrally about time and its passage. This central concern is largely responsible for the ironically elegiac tone characterizing the narrative. The treatment of time itself is also striking. Reschke's account, as transmitted by the narrator—"I'm not Reschke" (*CT,* 196)—increasingly operates in the "paspresenture," the conflated tense in which past, present, and future are all simultaneously present. The reader initially has no way of assessing the significance of Reschke's having postdated to 19 June 1999 the covering letter he sends to the narrator (*CT,* 9). The account of the rise and fall of the originally envisaged Cemetery Association is increasingly dotted with proleptic episodes, "leaps in time" (*CT,* 25, 214) in which Reschke, exercising his "special gift of seeing in retrospect things to come" (*CT,* 35), projects himself into the role of a future historian and looks back at his present and more immediate future from a further distance of 5, 10, or 20 years (much as the narrator of *The Rat* projects himself into a future beyond apocalypse). Key events, such as the couple's resignation from the Board or Erna Brakup's death, are recounted not once but several times, each telling superimposed on its predecessors like successive washes of color—or like the successive microthin coats of gold leaf that Alexandra, the professional gilder, painstakingly applies to an angel's wing.

The Call of the Toad is a latter-day German parable, an allegory about good intentions and what can become of them, about misguided idealism and barefaced greed. German reviewers were in general not amused, the graveyard scheme far too obviously satirizing the German reunification that was taking place simultaneously in creating a new *Völkerwanderung* of the dead that too overtly matches that of the living between what was once the two Germanys. Few German critics paid any attention to the fact that Alexander Reschke, a long-winded, self-important bore, in his sixties, sporting a beret and a salt-and-pepper mustache, can clearly be read as an ironic self-portrait of Grass as savior, teacher, and unappreciated prophet of his people. Most German critics—choosing the now long familiar route of (mis)reading his literary work as political tract—were (or professed to be) outraged at Grass's prophet-of-doom presumption in satirizing national reunification. The book and its author thus took a predictable thrashing in the German press for lèse-majesté—but met with a much more friendly reception in the English-speaking world, where reviewers tended to see the novel as less an immediately focused satire than an ironic meditation on the tendency of (especially German) visionary schemes to fall victim to Murphy's Law. English-language reviewers also noted the similarity between the central thrust of the novel and Evelyn Waugh's macabre satire on the Californian way of death, *The Loved One* (1948), namely, the trade in the dead as commodity and the resulting grotesque boom in cemeteries.

Alexander and Alexandra's quixotic scheme is doomed to failure from the beginning—as the narrator, more skeptical than they, does not fail to observe on several occasions. The motif of failure is emphasized when the pair die an accidental and pointless death and, compounding the irony, are buried in alien soil. Many of Grass's texts center on failure, of course, and failure is certainly the primary focus in the apocalyptic series that begins with *The Rat* and continues with the texts of the later 1980s that center on the ecological destruction of Central Europe. *The Call of the Toad* marks a return from the darkly pessimistic tones of these works to a more whimsically ironic key; it also marks a return from the wider perspectives of global disaster to specifically German concerns. These concerns become increasingly central in Grass's work during the 1990s.

Chapter Fourteen
Too Far Afield

Shortly after the publication of *The Call of the Toad,* Grass issued a terse political statement entitled *Rede vom Verlust* (1992; On Loss). In it he paints a grim picture of postunification Germany, where, as he sees it with a distinctly jaundiced eye, rampant capitalism disastrously combines with rampant xenophobia, racism, and renewed right-wing extremism. He laments the growth of a radically conservative new nationalism and the loss of any true federalism in Germany, now replaced by an aggressive centralism and political monopoly; he bitterly regrets the loss of a true humanitarianism, as exemplified by the increasing difficulties put in the way of those seeking political asylum; and he attacks the loss of true democracy and free speech signaled by the increasing monopolization of the news media.

Rede vom Verlust, one of the bluntest in a series of speeches and statements in Grass's one-man war against German unification, is powerfully reworked in literary form in *Novemberland,* a slim cycle of poems first published in the weekly Hamburg newspaper *Die Woche* in February 1993 and in book form by Steidl the following month. Thirteen sonnets superimposed on 13 sepia drawings, the collection was immediately inspired by one more in an escalating series of right-wing outrages: in November 1992 in the northern German town of Mölln, just a few miles away from Grass's home in Behlendorf near Lübeck, a Turkish mother and her children were burned to death in a neo-Nazi firebombing incident. The poems have a common theme, namely, that the continued forgetting, repression, and denial of historical wrongs inevitably lead to their reappearance, even (or especially) in the brave new Germany of the 1990s.

"Novemberland" is *Deutschland,* Germany, a land of many Novembers: the abortive revolution of 1918, Hitler's Munich putsch of 1923, the Crystal Night of 1938, the unification of 1989, and, most recently, the Mölln murders of 1992. The 13 sonnets that constitute *Novemberland,* based stylistically on the sonnet form of the German seventeenth century, are very overtly about the present state—and, by implication, also the past and future—of the country. The reader familiar with German literature is immediately struck by the stylistic and tonal similarity of the first sonnet to Andreas Gryphius's famous sonnet of 1648, "Tränen des Vaterlandes" (Tears of the Fatherland), bemoaning the devastation of Germany after 30 years of war. In Grass's Germany the devastation is of a different order. Spread-eagled in all too proprietary fashion across the map of central Europe, the Germany of the present day, after two World Wars whose physical aftereffects were even more devastating than those of the Thirty Years' War, is the victim not of its double defeat but of its own flamboyantly successful recovery. As in *The Tin Drum* and *Dog Years,* however, the buried past refuses to stay buried, and present and future alike are held hostage by that undigested past in a land now more than ever divided as a result of its recent unification. There is little that literature and its civilized niceties can (or ever could) do against the savagery of such atrocities as the Mölln murders, but speaking out, however little effect it is likely to have, nonetheless remains just as much the writer's duty now as it was for the poets gathered at Telgte.

Novemberland, only 32 pages in print (no more than a single page in the original newspaper edition), is a poetic tour de force. It employs a controlled free verse imaginatively based on the traditional iambic hexameter of the same Baroque poets whose simulacra had provided the dramatis personae for *The Meeting at Telgte,* its best lines catching the incantatory and admonitory power of a Gryphius. The tone preserves a delicate balance between the carefully overblown style, imbued with religious and patriotic fervor, of the mid-seventeenth century and the carefully overcasual diction of the last decade of the twentieth century. The cycle is at once something entirely new in Grass's work in stylistic terms and a controlled recapitulation of thematic concerns dispersed throughout his work over the previous four decades: the (un)buried past from the Danzig trilogy, the desolation of the fatherland and the ambiguous role of the literary artist from *The Meeting at Telgte,* the scornfully pilloried xenophobia of *Headbirths,* and the autumnal (but by no means silent) resignation of *The Call of the Toad.*

Two years after the publication of *Novemberland,* Grass returned to the theme of postunification Germany in his longest (and perhaps most complicated) work to date, the almost 800-page novel *Ein weites Feld* (*Too Far Afield*).[1] The novel was a major media event well before it actually appeared in print. The story of its reception in Germany, indeed, tells a great deal both about the respective roles of literature and politics in that country in the final decade of the twentieth century and about Grass's public role as a writer by that time, almost four decades after the appearance of his phenomenal first novel, *The Tin Drum*. Grass's first public reading of extracts from the novel, in April 1995, drew an audience of 800 people, including an enthusiastically applauding Marcel Reich-Ranicki, the high priest of German literary reviewers and for many years Grass's most consistently negative public critic. Aggressively touted by publisher Gerhard Steidl as the "novel of the century," *Ein weites Feld* was originally scheduled to appear on 28 August 1995, Goethe's birthday. But Steidl, a master of the art of advertising, eventually "gave in" to public demand and released it more than a week earlier, letting it be known in passing that the novel was destined to do for the newly unified Germany of the 1990s what Thomas Mann's *Buddenbrooks* had done for the newly industrialized Germany of a century earlier. A first hardcover edition of 100,000, priced at just under DM 50 a copy, sold out immediately, and a first postpublication reading in the former East Berlin (where the novel is set) drew 1,400 people, 9 television crews, and 25 press photographers. Within two months of its publication, more than 200,000 hardcover copies had been sold, and 50,000 more were ready for the bookstores. Even allowing for the 4,500 free copies distributed to reviewers and booksellers as part of Steidl's huge production budget of DM 450,000, the cover price of the first five printings, totaling a quarter of a million hardcover copies, was well over 12 million marks.

Though critics reacted very positively when Grass gave the first public readings from *Ein weites Feld,* more than one ritually proclaiming that the old Grass of *The Tin Drum* was back at last, its actual appearance only four months later, despite the enormous number of copies sold, was greeted in the German press by a firestorm of withering criticism. Ruth Valentini, writing in the French newspaper *Le Nouvel Observateur,* spoke with considerable justification of a public "literary lynching."[2] Of roughly a hundred reviews published in the German media, barely a handful found anything at all to praise in the novel. The opening (and most devastating) salvo was fired, some days before the novel even officially appeared, by Reich-Ranicki, who proceeded to demolish Grass's work mercilessly both in a *Spiegel* cover story and on his own television talk show. The photomontage cover of *Der Spiegel* (a high-circulation German equivalent of *Time* magazine) depicted a grimacing Reich-Ranicki physically ripping a copy of the novel to shreds—a feat he then set out with great gusto to repeat as a reviewer, dismissing Grass, ostensibly more in sorrow than in anger, as simply not knowing what he was talking about as far as the politics of the former East Germany were concerned.[3]

A very large majority of German reviewers followed Reich-Ranicki's authoritative lead in completely panning the book—and, as in his case, their reaction was almost unanimously on the basis of its author's political opinions rather than because of any alleged literary or aesthetic failings.[4] As the British critic Anne McElvoy observed in the *Times Literary Supplement,* "the inordinate influence of Marcel Reich-Ranicki as a critic ensured that once he had produced a devastating attack, the discussion would shift from being centred on the merits of the book."[5] The sensationalistic tabloid *Bild-Zeitung* exclaimed with huge relish and in flaming headlines that Grass was a traitor to his country; the conservative weekly *Die Welt* portrayed the novel as a sustained 800-page attack on unification; *Die Zeit* dismissed it as a totally unreadable political tract. Only in the new states of eastern Germany was the reaction largely positive—though once again for political rather than literary reasons. Few reviews paid more than lip service to the possibility that Grass had written a text requiring a literary reading.

Too Far Afield is the first major narrative attempt to interpret the implications of German reunification. The novel's presentation of those implications is pervasively informed by a political skepticism that is nothing new to Grass: for 30 years he has remained faithful to his own vision of Germany as a federation of two states within a single cultural nation. Auschwitz, Grass had long argued, made the notion of a single powerful German state unthinkable. Five years after unification, Grass, if anything, intensifies his attack on what he continues to see as the arrogance of power and the unwillingness of an entrenched establishment to contemplate reforms allowing for a meaningful integration of the new federal states. So completely unswerving was Grass's stand against unification, and so completely counter to popular opinion, that it succeeded in alienating almost everyone, including most of his own left-wing friends and colleagues.

German reunification and its results for the former East Germany are at the center of *Too Far Afield.* In *The Call of the Toad,* which also cast a satirical eye on the new Germany, the emphasis is on the uninterrupted expansionism of what until very recently was West Germany; in *Too Far Afield* the emphasis shifts to what was formerly East Germany. The story plays mainly in Berlin and the formerly East German area between Berlin and the North Sea in the two-year period immediately following the fall of the Berlin Wall in 1989. The bitterness of Grass's opposition to German reunification, as we have seen, derives from his view that it was less a unification than a simple takeover of the weakened East by the dominant West, less a political marriage of two sovereign nations than a political rape. The most invidious emblem of this act of violence—and one that plays a central role in *Too Far Afield*—is, for Grass, the *Treuhandanstalt* (Trust Agency), the new federal agency (since dissolved) charged with organizing and overseeing the privatization of the almost 14,000 previously nationalized enterprises of the former East Germany. Some two-thirds of these enterprises were eventually more or less successfully privatized; the remaining third, however, involving some 3,500 businesses, had to be closed down, with much attendant unemployment and demoralization. A central theme of Grass's novel is the social depredation wrought by the Treuhand as an instrument of oppression employed by a colonizing power, a bureaucratic monster that destroyed the lives of thousands of people by putting them arbitrarily out of work in the service of a purely western view of how eastern affairs should best be conducted. The novel's originally planned title, indeed, was *Treuhand* (The Trust)—the change, as we may notice, shifting the primary emphasis from political exploitation to the role of the writer and intellectual in dealing with it.

Grass's novel is far from limiting itself to the immediate concerns of postunification Germany, however. The reunification of the 1990s is seen specifically against the backdrop of the first attempt at pan-German unity in the 1870s—a unity that eventually led to two disastrous world wars. By implication, the novel covers a century and a half of German history, from 1848 to 1989, the dates for Grass of two failed German revolutions, while dealing specifically with the two years from November 1989 to August 1991 (in which month Frederick the Great, King of Prussia, was formally reinterred in his onetime castle of Sanssouci in Potsdam). The symbolic focus of the action is the Kafka-esque Treuhand building on the Leipziger Strasse in Berlin, an apt symbol of oppression of the people by the state, as Gotthard Erler observes. Erected by the Nazis in the thirties as Göring's Air Ministry, it survived Allied bombing to become the central administration building of the increasingly repressive East German government and survived the collapse of East Germany to become the center of what Grass saw as the no less repressive Treuhand. The building is thus centrally connected with fascism and war, the division and reunification of Germany, and the misuse and redistribution of power (Erler, 157). Since Grass's central political point is the parallelism between the events of 1989–1990 and Bismarck's establishment of the German Empire in 1871, the paternoster elevator to be found in the Treuhand building further provides an irresistible (if parodic) symbol: German history of the last two centuries as a circular process with only apparent turning points, carrying Göring and Ulbricht, Honecker and Rohwedder (first president of the Treuhand) in turn up and around and down again. As always with Grass, however, such invitingly meaningful symbols need to be treated with considerable caution.

In order to tie the two historical periods of German unification together, Grass—in what Elsbeth Pulver calls a stroke of genius (Pulver, 49)—invents the figure of Theodor Wuttke, once an East German cultural functionary, now an elderly office messenger in the employ of the Treuhand (which inherited him with the building) and a skeptical observer of the events past and present of German history. Once a reluctant soldier in the *Wehrmacht,* and a war correspondent for the Nazis, Wuttke had supported the new East Germany after the war. He went on to become an increasingly disillusioned cultural lecturer in the *Kulturbund,* the East German government agency whose role was ostensibly to uphold the humanist and intellectual tradition in socialism, but which in practice was completely subject to the expediency-driven vagaries of its political masters. Wuttke's current central objective is severely limited and practical in scope: to save the building's rickety paternoster from the attentions of recently arrived Westerners who want to rip it out and replace it with neon and steel efficiency.

The most important single factor in Theodor Wuttke's life, however, is not politics but literature, more specifically the major German writer Theodor Fontane (1819–1898). Grass's title *Ein weites Feld,* for most German readers, immediately suggests the novelist Fontane, whose 1895 novel *Effi Briest,* written when Fontane was in his early seventies (and exactly a century before *Too Far Afield*), is one of the classics of nineteenth-century German realism. Effi Briest, like Flaubert's Emma Bovary, is a dreamer who comes to grief on the rocks of a harsh reality, and "Das ist ja ein weites Feld" ("That would take us too far afield") is the favorite (and conveniently evasive) expression of her good-natured but perennially preoccupied father, Herr von Briest—whose withdrawal from the assorted unpleasantnesses of life, for Grass, reflects Fontane's own attempts to withdraw from the unpalatable reality of the Prussian politics of his day. German history is likewise a long story, and in *Too Far Afield* Grass (who had been toying with the idea of a book on Fontane since as early as 1986) systematically interweaves elements from his celebrated predecessor's life and works and elements from that long and complicated story.

Wuttke, it emerges, was born on 30 December 1919 in Neuruppin in Brandenburg, on which day and in which town Fontane was also born exactly one hundred years earlier. Inspired by this coincidence of birth, Wuttke grows up to become a literary specialist—and a Fontane fanatic. Now, at the age of 70, he has spent more than half a century immersed in the details of the life and work of Fontane, to the point where (like Don Quixote—and Oskar in *The Tin Drum*) he is entirely unable or unwilling to distinguish between the actual life he has led and the alternative life he has read himself into. Not only does he know all 21 volumes of Fontane's collected works and letters by heart; not only does he have an appropriate Fontane quotation for every occasion. As Wuttke grows older he frequently seems to have difficulty in remembering that he is not Fontane himself, rather than just poor old "Fonty"—the nickname his obsession has universally earned him. Fonty's obsession provides Grass's narrative with a brilliantly economical means for the continual juxtaposition of German history of the nineteenth and twentieth centuries.

Wuttke's fascination with the writer he invariably refers to as "der Unsterbliche" ("the immortal one")—and who is never actually mentioned by name in the novel—is based on Grass's own growing fascination over the previous decade with Fontane, who had come to represent for him the archetypal figure of the German writer called upon (like himself) to balance the often conflicting demands of literature and politics. Fontane's sympathies as a young man, his biographers tell us, were with the revolutionaries of 1848; he went on, however, to become a political reactionary and allegedly even an informer on his onetime liberal colleagues. Later he moderated both of these extreme positions and developed into an enlightened conservative—only to show signs of becoming a revolutionary thinker all over again in his old age. Thus, for Grass, Fontane's brilliant literary oeuvre is written out of a highly problematic relationship with the repressive Prussian autocracy of his day and characterized by an uneasy mixture of skeptical detachment and political opportunism—a mixture that Grass unflatteringly portrays as typifying the role of the German intellectual.

The relationship between Wuttke and Fontane is not just a matter of a realistically portrayed obsession on Wuttke's part, however. Grass's text also parodically equips "Fonty" with a number of traits reflecting Fontane's own personality and family situation. Wuttke, for example, begins his career as a journalist, a war correspondent for Göring's Air Ministry, reporting primarily from France, but his reports tend to consist of admiring accounts of French cultural life rather than politically usable information, and there is even a suggestion that he may have been secretly working for the French Resistance. Fontane, who spent a dozen years reporting on Bismarck's wars against Denmark, Austria, and France in the late 1860s—wars that led to the first German unification—not only fulfilled his commission to write three official war books but likewise visited these enemy territories himself, and likewise wrote private accounts of his travels that were openly sympathetic toward the "enemy" (Erler, 158). Wuttke's disaffection from the petty bureaucracy of the East German state mirrors Fontane's disaffection from that of the Prussian state. Various figures from Fontane's biography reappear as parodic *Doppelgänger* in Wuttke's life. Wuttke's fiancée is called Emmi; Fontane's fiancée was called Emilie. Wuttke has four children, whose names are those of Fontane's four children and whose lives run teasingly parallel courses. Wuttke has an illegitimate daughter, just as Fontane did; Wuttke's rambling anecdotes are just as interminable as Fontane's are reported to have been; Wuttke, in short, as parodic reincarnation of Fontane, as *Doppelgänger,* repeats Fontane, just as the twentieth century, for Grass, repeats the nineteenth in their shared drive for German unification.

The relationship between Wuttke, Fontane, and Grass himself is one of the key structural devices underpinning the ironically reflexive presentational style of the novel. Fontane, in his writings, skeptically chronicled the rise of Prussia from defeated power to military giant and powerful unified state. Wuttke's skepticism concerning German unification thus mirrors not only Grass's skepticism but Fontane's as well. By the same token, however, Wuttke's views are not always just a copy of Fontane's: at one point, for example, Wuttke praises the writer Heinrich von Kleist's radical political views, while Fontane would have been most unlikely to do so (Pulver, 50). On the other hand, Fontane and Wuttke are alike in that both are by nature observers rather than actors and are praised at one point as not having wished to change the world—while Wuttke's creator Günter Grass, retaining and intensifying Fontane's political skepticism but far from mirroring his withdrawal from political affairs, has left no doubt as to his lifelong desire to change the world he lives in.

For Grass, literature and politics are inextricably linked, two sides of a single coin. The literary scholar Wuttke accordingly has an inseparable companion, an alter ego, a "day and night shadow," one Hoftaller, who is at once both an apparently harmless senior citizen like himself and a timeless embodiment of the professional spy and traitor throughout history, specifically German history. Treachery is an inescapable component of German history in the bleak summary of that history presented in *Too Far Afield,* and its latest manifestation is the unification that Grass has repeatedly characterized as a treacherous betrayal of the East by the West, as exemplified by the Treuhand. Hoftaller is ageless, immortal, and transtemporal (like the first-person narrator in *The Flounder*), and he has worked with equal conviction and diligence for the authorities in 1848, for the Prussian police apparatus in the 1870s, for the Gestapo during the Third Reich, and for the Stasi, the dreaded state secret service, throughout the 40-year history of the East German state. *Too Far Afield,* in short, returning to a theme that was central to both *Cat and Mouse* and *Dog Years,* is also a novel about the eternal predator and his eternal victims.

The Mephistophelian Hoftaller, professional informer, turncoat, and spy, is also an ostentatiously fictive creation. He is quite openly borrowed (with his creator's permission) from the East German writer Hans Joachim Schädlich's title character in the 1986 novel *Tallhover*—a postmodern piece of sleight of pen on Grass's part that left traditionalist critics spluttering indignantly.[6] Schädlich's novel likewise deals with German history, from pre-1848 Prussia to the East Germany of the 1950s, and Schädlich's Tallhover (like Grass's Hoftaller) is a perennial agent of the secret police, whatever the political party in power— implicitly suggesting that Germany, whatever the form of government, has always been a police state. Unlike his masters, who for the most part are constrained by political realities, Schädlich's Tallhover demands a utopian (or dystopian) state whose enemies would be ruthlessly exterminated. His perverted idealism eventually leads to his own destruction. Suspended from duty because of his excessive zeal following the East German workers' uprising of 17 June 1953, Tallhover is transferred to a historical archive. There, conscientiously working his way through a century of historical documents, he is able to right the wrongs of the past as he sees them by condemning their perpetrators to death, at least hypothetically and retrospectively. His final victim, this time real rather than hypothetical, is himself, also found wanting by his own exacting standards.

Grass, whose imaginative powers have never been questioned even by his most inveterate critics, obviously could have invented an entirely original shadow companion for Wuttke if he had wanted to. The textual point of recycling Schädlich's Tallhover is that while any individual Tallhover may die, the species lives on forever, coat discreetly turned as appropriate. If Fontane is "the immortal one" for Wuttke, Hoftaller is "the immortal one" for Grass. Hoftaller/Tallhover's main characteristic is his colorlessness, his inconspicuousness, and his eternal presence as "day and night shadow." Hoftaller is omniscient and omnipresent as far as Wuttke is concerned, knowing, as Gestapo agent, about his activities in France, as Stasi spy about his growing sympathy with dissident literary groups—just as Tallhover, as Prussian police agent, knew everything about Fontane's comings and goings and the revolutionary intentions of his literary associates. Hoftaller, however, Sancho to Wuttke's Quixote, Mephisto to his Faust, is personally no villain. He is even quite likable at times (and all the more dangerous for that), a civil servant just doing his job—and the implication is clearly that he continues to do so, whether for Prussia, East Germany, or the newly unified Germany.

Wuttke is the crucial link between Fontane and Hoftaller, between the world of literature and the world of politics. The two central themes of the novel, in which contemporary German politics and German history of the past two centuries are continually interwoven, are the allegedly disastrous effects of German unification (the second mirroring the first) and the alleged ineffectuality of the German intellectual throughout the past two centuries, continually kowtowing to the powers that be, continually spied upon and betrayed by the seedy likes of Hoftaller. The overall tone, however, is one of resignation rather than outrage: like the elderly lovers in *The Call of the Toad,* Wuttke and his shadow Hoftaller are already elderly men—as, of course, are the two writers Fontane and Grass. Wuttke eventually flees the new Germany, as he had previously (and unsuccessfully) attempted to flee the old East Germany. The reference to a final flight into death is patent in his political flight, as Elsbeth Pulver observes (Pulver, 52), reminding the reader that *Too Far Afield* can also be read as a book about growing old and dying, a theme that is presented (as it was in *The Call of the Toad*) with both compassion and humor.

Too Far Afield is thus certainly both a political and a historical novel; first and foremost, however, it is a *novel*—a point inadvertently or deliberately ignored by a very large majority of German-language critics. One of the central points of that novel is precisely that it allows Grass the literary artist (as opposed to Grass the politician) to relativize and question his own political views by a variety of formal means—spreading them, for example, across a number of characters; putting them in the mouths of characters we would not have expected to hold such views; having one character propagate them and another refute them; and so on. Grass himself has repeatedly observed that confusing the author's publicly stated personal opinions with the frequently contradictory opinions of his literary creations is an elementary interpretive fallacy. He has pointed out in interviews, for example, that while Wuttke's view of German reunification is as negative as his own, the novel also scrupulously advances the quite contradictory views of Fonty's granddaughter, Madeleine, thus serving to keep the discussion open—rather than attempting to bring it to a premature but tidy conclusion, as many of his critics were all too tempted to do.

The original conception of *Too Far Afield* (which Grass spent five years writing) was serendipitous: Grass had a prepublication copy of his friend Schädlich's *Tallhover* with him on his journey to India in 1986–1987, while his wife Ute had taken along Fontane's complete works. The confrontation of these two figures—the real and the fictional, the writer and the spy, the literary artist and the political functionary—found its appropriate historical context for Grass in the new German state after 1989, while their relationship is observed and presented by a nameless "authorial collective" that is parodically appropriate for the onetime collective endeavors of the workers' state of East Germany.

The central feature of *Too Far Afield* is neither the very limited development of its characters nor its very limited action, but rather the network of proliferating intertextual and intertemporal links it develops with German history (political, literary, and otherwise) over the past 150 years. The novel is thus a highly demanding one for the reader, and early reviewers made frequent use of the word *labyrinth*. *Too Far Afield,* a complexly structured and ironically reflexive text, is first of all a novel about the relationship of literature and politics in Germany, whether in the nineteenth or the twentieth century. Second, it is also a fictionalized quasi-biography of Theodor Fontane. Third, Grass's own political views on nineteenth- and twentieth-century Germany are diffused and refracted through the double prism of the invented twentieth-century "Fonty" and the reinvented nineteenth-century Fontane, and they are simultaneously filtered through the "scholarly" perspective of the collective narrative voice, identified only as "we in the archive." The reference here is to the real-life Theodor Fontane Archive in Potsdam, where the fictive members of the authorial collective work. It is typical of the novel's elusively suggestive style that the reader is implicitly invited to remember that Hoftaller, too, was an archivist, as were many in the land of the Stasi. Finally, adding still further to the complexity, while Wuttke quotes Fontane on every suitable (and many an unsuitable) occasion, those quotations are only sometimes authentic—on other occasions they are simply invented. The narrative voice likewise both imitates Fontane's comfortably rambling style and occasionally incorporates teasingly unacknowledged verbatim quotations from Fontane's works, especially his correspondence. The energetic views of the highly political citizen Günter Grass are certainly entirely undisguised in all of this, but their multiply fragmented and multiply self-interrogative presentation in *Too Far Afield,* a highly sophisticated literary artifact, belongs not to the realm of politics but to that of art, the art of the literary text.

It is very evident that objections to its author's politics simply prevented many critics from reading the literary text they were ostensibly reviewing. One of the most common alleged failings (other than political failings) identified by reviewers was that the novel's central characters are so blatantly artificial. Iris Radisch, for example, deplores the fact that both of the central characters are only "second-hand," with Wuttke aping Fontane and Hoftaller derivatively modeled on a character lifted bodily from the work of another writer.[7] In the light of such comments, Grass himself has observed in interviews that Wuttke and Hoftaller clearly demand to be read in the picaresque rather than the realist tradition, noting that if such narrowly realistic standards of characterization were applied to the great European picaresque novels from *Don Quixote* to *Bouvard and Pécuchet* (and we can certainly add *The Tin Drum* to the list), European literature would be very much the poorer for it. Grass's transmogrified borrowing of Schädlich's Tallhover is, of course, amply prefigured in his previous work in the similarly skewed borrowing of Grimmelshausen's Simplicissimus and Courage in *The Meeting at Telgte,* as also in the recycled version of his own Oskar Matzerath in *The Rat.* We may also remember the carefully anamorphic portraits of Brecht in *The Plebeians* and of a whole list of Baroque poets in *The Meeting at Telgte.* Reich-Ranicki, the most highly publicized attacker of *Too Far Afield,* is typical of the general reaction to it among German literary critics. He radically underestimates the textual artifice of Grass's novel, largely ignores the crucial distinction between authorial and fictional voice, deplores the lack of developed characters and a realistic story line, and has no time for such literary experiments as the attempt to echo Fontane's style. Such an approach, however, is entirely inadequate in the case of a novel whose intellectual allegiance is so much more clearly postmodernist than realist—and in which the lack of character development, for example, may be read precisely as parodically reflecting two centuries of German history in which, for Grass, there is likewise no development. The "history" purveyed in *Too Far Afield* is an inextricable, intertextual, intertemporal postmodernist weave of fact and fiction. Narrative irony and parody are pervasive in a novel replete with oblique allusions, biographical and literary games, and unacknowledged verbatim quotations from Fontane vying with passages that look as if they must be but are not. "Fonty" is a sophisticated literary joke; so is Hoftaller; so, certainly, among much else, is *Too Far Afield*. It has been observed, for example, that the name Wuttke is etymologically related to the Slavic *woda, wodka* (water), just as the name Fontane is related to the French *fontaine* (fountain). Wuttke/Fonty is also, of course, as we have seen, to some extent a humorous self-portrait of the Fontane-enthusiast Grass— just as Alexander Reschke, in *The Call of the Toad*, was a similarly ironic self-portrait of the artist as an old man.

Further intertextual links of various kinds also contribute to the richly allusive network of resonances set up by the text. Grass's ironic use of Fontane's biography as the central armature of his novel has been compared to Joyce's use of Homer in *Ulysses* and Mann's use of Nietzsche in *Doctor Faustus*. As an obliquely tilted historical summary of an epoch, *Too Far Afield* likewise suggests comparison with *Doctor Faustus*, complete with diabolical pact. Within Grass's own literary output it is comparable to *The Flounder* as a quasi-historical novel and to *The Meeting at Telgte* in its concern for the relationship between literature and politics. The fact that Tallhover becomes interested in Fontane's revolutionary involvement in the 1840s and is still, as Hoftaller, doggedly shadowing his *Doppelgänger* Wuttke 150 years later may well remind the reader of the fate of Victor Weluhn in *The Tin Drum*, still conscientiously pursued by the Gestapo in Adenauer's Germany of the 1950s. *Too Far Afield*, indeed, is suffused—as was *The Call of the Toad*—by this tone of melancholy reflection that the more things change, the more they remain the same. It is typical of the multileveled ironies of Grass's text that Wuttke's last journey (to France) can be read either as a return to the home of his idolized Fontane's Huguenot ancestors or as a journey to the land from which they, likewise caught up in historical currents beyond their individual control, were forced in their time to flee.

German history and German politics have always been entirely central to Grass's literary work. In *The Tin Drum*, now universally acknowledged as a self-evident classic of the German literary canon, he infuriated many German readers of the late 1950s by digging up memories of a recent past more tactfully left forgotten. In *Too Far Afield,* one of his most ambitious novels—and one that may well eventually achieve a similar status to *The Tin Drum* —he infuriated many readers of the mid-1990s by all too vigorously pouring cold water on the new and popularly acclaimed Federal Republic, while simultaneously appearing to defend the old and now publicly discredited Democratic Republic. In 1995 as in 1959 Grass demonstrated no talent at all for letting sleeping dogs lie. It is consequently entirely unsurprising that the sound and fury touched off by the appearance of *Too Far Afield* (as in the case of so many of his previous texts) had so little to do with his novel and so much to do with his politics.

Conclusion

Grass's new publisher, the Steidl Verlag in Göttingen, put together a 20-page congratulatory brochure with tributes from other writers on the occasion of his 65th birthday in October 1992. In it Nadine Gordimer wrote that no German author since Thomas Mann has had so great an influence on world literature as Grass, who is as important in his own generation as Joyce, Proust, or Musil were in theirs for expanding the frontiers of literature, for extending and complicating the relationship between the story told and the discourse that tells it, for demonstrating the liberating power of the narrative imagination, for concentrating, as great writers always have, not on the *what* but on the *how* of literature.[1] More than 12 million copies of Grass's works in some 20 languages—Chinese, Japanese, Turkish, and Finnish among them— including more than 4 million copies of *The Tin Drum,* have by now been sold worldwide. Steidl's marketing of the *Studienausgabe,* the collected edition of Grass's works, surprised no one in presenting Grass as incontestably the most important living German author, quoting John Irving's much publicized dictum that nobody could fail to read Grass and still count as well read.[2] Similar tributes were paid five years later, on the occasion of Grass's seventieth birthday, which saw the launch of a revised critical edition of his complete works.

Fame brings its attendant problems, however. Like Goethe and Thomas Mann before him, Grass had the great good—and bad—fortune to become famous with his very first novel. *The Tin Drum* not only accorded him celebrity status overnight, it was also held against him for close to the next 40 years, as even critics who had initially greeted it with major hostility increasingly bemoaned his perceived inability to repeat it. In his own country such critical judgments have been too often based far less on what Grass has actually written than on what he was remembered to have said in one political arena or another. Since the beginning of his career, as we have seen, reactions to Grass's work have polarized sharply, some readers applauding his artistic mastery while others react with outrage to his political opinions. In this book I have consciously chosen to focus on the former rather than the latter. That choice, however, should not obscure the fact that Grass has always very consciously adopted the role of the writer as public intellectual, à la

Sartre, ready to take a stand, invited or not (indeed especially if not invited), on any subject. His unflinchingly outspoken propagation of his political opinions has made him many enemies in Germany, including, most recently, those who consider him nothing less than a traitor to his country for his insistent denunciation of German reunification. Undeterred by bitter criticism of his opinions and intensely personal attacks on his presumption in setting himself up as moral watchdog of the western world, Grass has spoken out over the years—and continues to do so indefatigably—on an enormous range of subjects, national and international: the political situation in Poland, in Cuba, in Nicaragua, and, over and over again, in the Germany of which he is a highly active citizen; the desolation of the third world; in favor of European unity and against the overhasty reunification of the two Germanys; in defense of Salman Rushdie, of Christa Wolf, of foreigners in Germany, of gypsies and Sinti and Romanies, and against the rise of neofascist extremism; against the growth of environmental pollution, the increasingly inevitable destruction of the forests, and the final destruction of the planet. Most of his battles have been losing battles.

The sense of humane values and tolerance of the European Enlightenment have been unwaveringly central to Grass's thinking and work from their very beginnings. So have the sense of obligation as a citizen and an unswerving support for democratic socialism. There have also been, however, a sense of melancholy skepticism, which grew in intensity during the 1970s and 1980s, and a profound and similarly growing sense of the fragility of human existence. Nevertheless, there is no despair in Grass's pages, any more than there is in the work of his mentor Albert Camus; for both of them there is, instead, the tenacity of Sisyphus. As Michael Bullock finds, "Like Camus, Grass sees his task as one of rescuing and defending the imagination from the deadening, repetitive pressures of everyday reality. And it is this sense of human solidarity amid the increasingly menacing loneliness of modern society which attracts Grass to the Sisyphus metaphor and fuels his immense energy."[3]

The appeal to reason, moderation, common sense, and what should be common decency has also always been central to Grass's work. Good intentions, however, do not guarantee good art, and many a writer has come to artistic grief under the dead weight of entirely laudable intentions. Grass's style at its best brilliantly avoids that fate by means of what Bertolt Brecht called *Verfremdung* (distancing). It has always not merely invoked but exuberantly flaunted a fundamental and entirely characteristic discrepancy between content and form, between what Grass's texts seem to say and how they actually say it. (One of his earliest forays into literary theory, we may remember, is called "Content as Resistance.") He has an extraordinary ability to surprise his readers with completely unexpected juxtapositions of objects and ideas that force us into seeing what we are intended to see with completely new eyes. The effectiveness of his distancing technique, however, is very closely related to its shock value, its exhilarating inappropriateness—and its novelty. The very success of the Danzig trilogy, especially that of *The Tin Drum,* has thus made it all the more difficult for later works to enjoy anything like the same success.

Grass's work also consistently ignores the traditionally approved boundaries between literary (and extraliterary) genres. *The Tin Drum* contains a chapter written as a theater piece; *Dog Years* contains the scripts of both a radio play and a ballet; *From the Diary of a Snail* incorporates a scholarly essay on a Dürer etching; *The Flounder* includes an anthology of poems and a collection of recipes. More important than such embeddings or engulfings of one literary form within the fabric of another is the degree to which conventions traditionally deemed appropriate to one particular genre are evocatively expropriated for service in another. Grass constructs his earliest theater pieces, as critics have frequently observed, as theatrical extrapolations of the possibilities of lyric expression rather than as dramas in any received sense. Close to four decades later, his narratives from *Headbirths* to *The Call of the Toad* are to a large extent constructed as narrative interpretations of the possibilities of the essay as a literary form.

Indirection is at the heart of Grass's artistic technique, whether its immediate application is to narrative or poetry or graphic art or sculpture. Reduced to the banality of a formula, we might say that Grass's style, from its beginnings, has blended two entirely opposed moments. The minutely detailed naturalistic realism of his depictions of persons and behaviors and objects vies with what has been called the "fantastic realism" of overtly created worlds, poetic worlds whose flaunted fictionality undermines the so-called real worlds they obliquely reflect and refract. Grass is by no means the only modern writer or artist to attempt such a provocative juxtaposition, but few have done it with anything like his success. Flaunted inappropriateness has always been a central feature of Grass's style. It has been variously observed that the idiosyncratic bestiary that Grass has chosen to develop throughout his writing is composed without exception not of the noble beasts of traditional heraldry—eagles and lions, bulls and bears, stags and unicorns—but rather of commonplace and decidedly nonheroic creatures, such as snails and flounders, eels and seagulls, rats and toads. While we might be tempted as readers to accept the traditional literary bestiary as a presumptive carrier of some symbolic or allegorical meaning, we tend to be instinctively irritated by the sheer inappropriateness of Grass's choice. This inappropriateness thus very effectively demonstrates its function as a distancing device, whose purpose, however, is not so much a Brechtian attempt to prevent readers from being sucked into a comfortable narrative illusion as an ironic reminder that they are being sucked in anyway, in spite of themselves.

It is worth restating that what is of most importance throughout Grass's work as a writer is less the answers it appears to provide than the questions it invites us to continue exploring. From the beginning, Grass's texts are marked by a narrative complexity that we, as readers, ignore at our own risk. The gap between story and discourse, between the *what* and the *how* of narrative, is the single most characteristic and most crucial distinction in all of Grass's literary work. The richness and ambiguity of Grass's texts combine to ensure that the onus of decisions and answers comes to rest exactly where Brecht said it should be— squarely on the shoulders of the reader. Grass the artist, as opposed to Grass the citizen and politician, is not to be pinned down to single meanings. If he is still remembered as a major writer at the end of another century or two, as I firmly believe he should be, it will not be for the correctness or otherwise of his political opinions. As a writer he will be remembered for the revolutionary freshness of vision he brought to German writing after 1945—and for the unflagging vigor with which he continued to experiment with new modes of artistic expression, especially with new modes of narrative discourse, over the four decades following his first great success with *The Tin Drum*.

Notes and References

Preface

1. "The Dentist's Chair as an Allegory of Life," *Time,* 13 April 1970, 68–70.
2. John Irving, "Günter Grass: King of the Toy Merchants," *Saturday Review,* March 1982, 60.
3. *This Week in Germany,* 17 October 1997, 6.

Chapter One

1. Günter Grass, *Speak Out! Speeches, Open Letters, Commentaries,* trans. Ralph Manheim (New York: Harcourt, Brace, 1969), 89–90. An earlier version of some portions of this chapter appeared in my introduction to *Critical Essays on Günter Grass,* ed. Patrick O'Neill (Boston: G. K. Hall, 1987).
2. The listing here is indebted to two studies of the early North American reception of Grass: Sigrid Mayer, "Grüne Jahre für Grass: Die Rezeption in den Vereinigten Staaten," *Text + Kritik* (Munich) 1/1a (1978): 151–61; and R. L. White, *Günter Grass in America: The Early Years* (Hildesheim: Olms, 1981).
3. According to the systematic catalog of his artistic output in Günter Grass, *In Kupfer, auf Stein* (Göttingen: Steidl, 1986), Grass had single exhibitions of his graphic work in 1955, 1957, 1959, 1961, and, after a long pause, in 1969. He had 2 exhibitions in 1971; 3 in 1973 (including in the Goethe-Haus in New York); 10 in 1974 (including in New York and London); 12 in 1975 (including in Tokyo and Paris); 3 in 1976; 6 in 1977; and some 10 to 12 every year, all over the world, from 1978 to 1986. In 1994, Steidl Verlag published an expanded and updated version of *In Kupfer, auf Stein* that presents the complete graphic work from 1972 to 1993.
4. For a selection of Grass's arguments, see Günter Grass, *Two States— One Nation?,* trans. Krishna Winston with A. S. Wensinger (New York: Harcourt Brace, 1990).
5. Günter Grass, *From the Diary of a Snail,* trans. Ralph Manheim (New York: Harcourt Brace, 1973), 141.

Chapter Two

1. Martin Esslin, *The Theatre of the Absurd* (1961; Garden City, N.Y.: Anchor Books, 1969), 226–28.
2. Günter Grass, "Die Ballerina," *Akzente* 3 (1956): 531–39 (reprint, Berlin: Friedenauer Presse, 1963); Günter Grass, "Der Inhalt als Widerstand: Bausteine zur Poetik," *Akzente* 4 (1957): 229–35.

3. Ann L. Mason, *The Skeptical Muse: A Study of Günter Grass' Conception of the Artist* (Bern: Lang, 1974), 22; hereafter cited in the text.

4. Keith Miles, *Günter Grass* (London: Vision; New York: Barnes and Noble, 1975), 29.

5. Günter Grass, *Four Plays: Flood; Mister, Mister; Only Ten Minutes to Buffalo; The Wicked Cooks,* trans. Ralph Manheim and A. Leslie Willson. Introduction Martin Esslin. (New York: Harcourt, Brace, 1967; London: Secker and Warburg, 1968).

6. Günter Grass, *Onkel, Onkel* (Berlin: Wagenbach, 1965). The first act had already been published separately as a one-act play, *Die Grippe* (Influenza), in *Neue Deutsche Hefte* (1957–58): 35–44.

7. Translated as "Rocking Back and Forth" by Michael Benedikt and Joseph Goradza, in *Postwar German Drama,* ed. and trans. Michael Benedikt and George E. Wellwarth (New York: E. P. Dutton, 1967), 161–75.

8. *Modernes deutsches Theater,* ed. Paul Pörtner (Neuwied, Berlin: Luchterhand, 1961), 1: 7–72.

Chapter Three

1. The account of *The Tin Drum* given here draws substantially on previous essays of mine: "The Authority of Satire: Grass's *Die Blechtrommel,*" in my book *The Comedy of Entropy: Humour, Narrative, Reading* (Toronto: University of Toronto Press, 1990), 173–86; "Implications of Unreliability: The Semiotics of Discourse in Günter Grass's *Die Blechtrommel,*" in *Analogon Rationis: Festschrift für Gerwin Marahrens,* ed. Marianne Henn and Christoph Lorey (Edmonton: University of Alberta Press, 1994), 433–45; and "*The Tin Drum:* Implications of Unreliability in Günter Grass's *Die Blechtrommel,*" in my book *Acts of Narrative: Textual Strategies in Modern German Fiction* (Toronto: University of Toronto Press, 1996), 97–116.

2. John Reddick, *The "Danzig Trilogy" of Günter Grass: A Study of* The Tin Drum, Cat and Mouse *and* Dog Years (London: Secker & Warburg; New York: Harcourt, Brace, 1975), 3; hereafter cited in the text.

3. Günter Grass, *The Tin Drum,* trans. Ralph Manheim (New York: Vintage, 1964),17; hereafter cited in the text as *TD* and silently emended where necessary.

4. See Lester Caltvedt, "Oskar's Account of Himself: Narrative 'Guilt' and the Relationship of Fiction to History in *Die Blechtrommel,*" *Seminar* 14 (1978): 285–94.

5. On color symbolism in *The Tin Drum* see A. Leslie Willson, "The Grotesque Everyman in Günter Grass's *Die Blechtrommel,*" *Monatshefte* 58 (1966): 131–38.

6. See Gertrude Cepl-Kaufmann, *Günter Grass: Eine Analyse des Gesamtwerks unter dem Aspekt von Literatur und Politik* (Kronberg im Taunus: Scriptor Verlag), 299.

Chapter Four

1. Günter Grass, *Cat and Mouse*, trans. Ralph Manheim (1963; New York: Signet, 1964), 19; heareafter cited in the text as *CM*.

Chapter Five

1. Günter Grass, *Dog Years*, trans. Ralph Manheim (1965; New York: Fawcett Crest, 1966), 562; hereafter cited in the text as *DY*.
2. Michael Harscheidt, *Günter Grass. Wort—Zahl—Gott. Der 'phantastische Realismus' in den* Hundejahren (Bonn: Bouvier, 1976); hereafter cited in the text.

Chapter Six

1. The text of Grass's paper may be found in Günter Grass, *The Plebeians Rehearse the Uprising*, trans. Ralph Manheim (New York: Harcourt, Brace, 1966), vii–xxxvi. This edition, hereafter cited in the text as *P,* also contains a documentary report of the events of 15–17 June 1953 (113–22).
2. Volker Neuhaus, *Günter Grass* (Stuttgart: Metzler, 1992), 205; hereafter cited in the text.
3. Its reception in North America was lukewarm. In England, however, its production by the Royal Shakespeare Company in 1970 was a triumph. For a review of that performance by Ronald Bryden, who calls it "an immensely imposing play," see *Critical Essays on Günter Grass,* ed. Patrick O'Neill (Boston: G. K. Hall, 1987), 36–38.
4. W. Gordon Cunliffe, *Günter Grass* (New York: Twayne, 1969), 129.

Chapter Seven

1. Günter Grass, *Local Anaesthetic,* trans. Ralph Manheim (1969; New York: Fawcett Crest, 1971), 219; hereafter cited in the text as *LA*.

Chapter Eight

1. *Die 'Danziger Trilogie' von Günter Grass: Texte, Daten, Bilder,* ed. Volker Neuhaus and Daniela Hermes (Frankfurt am Main: Luchterhand, 1991), 17–18.
2. Günter Grass, *From the Diary of a Snail,* trans. Ralph Manheim (New York: Harcourt, Brace, 1973), 73; hereafter cited in the text as *DS*.

Chapter Nine

1. The treatment of *The Flounder* here incorporates material from my essay "The Scheherazade Syndrome: Günter Grass's Meganovel *Der Butt,*" in *Adventures of a Flounder: Critical Essays on Günter Grass'* Der Butt, ed. Gertrud Bauer Pickar (Munich: Fink, 1982), 1–15.

2. See Sigrid Mayer, "*Der Butt:* Lyrische und graphische Quellen," in *Adventures of a Flounder: Critical Essays on Günter Grass'* Der Butt, ed. Gertrud Bauer Pickar (Munich: Fink, 1982), 16–23.

3. Günter Grass, *The Flounder,* trans. Ralph Manheim (New York: Harcourt, Brace, 1978), 345,515; hereafter cited in the text as *F.*

4. Thus, for example, Silvia Tennenbaum, "A Baroque Fish Story," *Newsday,* November 1978.

5. An external indication of the centrality of this episode for Grass is provided by *The Meeting at Telgte,* in which he returns to the Thirty Years' War.

Chapter Ten

1. Günter Grass, *The Meeting at Telgte,* trans. Ralph Manheim (1981; Harmondsworth, U.K.: Penguin, 1983), 19, 23; hereafter cited in the text as *MT.* This edition also contains a helpful afterword by Leonard Forster.

2. S. S. Prawer, "Rising from the Rubble," *Times Literary Supplement* (London), 26 June 1981, 718.

Chapter Eleven

1. Gabriel Josipovici, "Making Holes in the Walls," *Times Literary Supplement,* 23 April 1982, 455; hereafter cited in the text.

2. Günter Grass, *Headbirths, or The Germans Are Dying Out,* trans. Ralph Manheim (1982; New York: Fawcett Crest, 1983), 135, 133; hereafter cited in the text as *H.*

3. F[ritz] J. R[addatz], "Der neue Grass: heitere Groteske ernster Nonsens," *Die Zeit,* 23 May 1980, 12.

4. John Leonard, "Consider a Billion Germans," *New York Times Book Review,* 14 March 1982, 11.

Chapter Twelve

1. Günter Grass, *On Writing and Politics, 1967–1983,* trans. Ralph Manheim (New York: Harcourt, Brace, 1985), 137. The present discussion of *The Rat* incorporates material from my essay "Grass's Doomsday Book: *Die Rättin,*" in *Critical Essays on Günter Grass,* ed. Patrick O'Neill (Boston: G. K. Hall, 1987), 213–24.

2. Günter Grass, *The Rat,* trans. Ralph Manheim (San Diego, Calif.: Harcourt Brace, 1987), 1; hereafter cited in the text as *R.*

3. Most German-language reviewers were respectful, but there were also flat assertions that the book was simply not worth reading. While received with substantial interest in North America, *The Rat* did not cause anything like the furor that had greeted *The Tin Drum* and *The Flounder.*

4. Grass's narrator refers to the real rat by the normal German word *Ratte;* the imaginary rat that appears in his nightmare visions is designated by

the likewise "imaginary" word *Rättin,* the English equivalent for which would be something like "ratess." Ralph Manheim uses the expression "She-rat."

5. The reference is to Gotthold Ephraim Lessing's *Die Erziehung des Menschengeschlechts* (The Education of the Human Race [1780]).

6. J. P. Stern, "Günter Grass's Uniqueness," *London Review of Books,* 5–18 February 1981, 14.

7. Günter Grass, *Zunge zeigen: Ein Tagebuch in Zeichnungen, Prosa und einem Gedicht,* trans. John E. Woods as *Show Your Tongue* (San Diego, Calif.: Harcourt Brace, 1989).

Chapter Thirteen

1. Günter Grass, *The Call of the Toad,* trans. Ralph Manheim (New York: Harcourt Brace, 1992), 18; hereafter cited in the text as *CT.*

Chapter Fourteen

1. Günter Grass, *Ein weites Feld* (Göttingen: Steidl, 1995). This novel has not yet appeared in English; translations are my own. A translation by Krishna Winston, *Too Far Afield,* is to be published in 2000 by Harcourt Brace.

2. Ruth Valentini, "L'affaire Günter Grass: Chronique allemande d'un lynchage littéraire," *Le Nouvel Observateur,* 21–27 September 1995, 52.

3. Marcel Reich-Ranicki, " . . . und es muß gesagt werden: Ein Brief von Marcel Reich-Ranicki an Günter Grass zu dessen Roman *Ein weites Feld,*" *Der Spiegel,* 21 August 1995, 162–69.

4. Among the notable exceptions who focused primarily on the text's literary qualities are Jürgen Busche, "Vom Glanz und Schmutz des deutschen Bürgertums," *Süddeutsche Zeitung,* 19/20 August 1995; Gotthard Erler, "Parallelbiographie: Günter Grass, *Ein weites Feld,*" *Neue deutsche Literatur* 43.6 (1995): 156–61; Jochen Hieber, " 'Ich will mich nicht auf die Bank der Sieger setzen': Ein Gespräch mit Günter Grass über den Roman *Ein weites Feld,*" *Frankfurter Allgemeine Zeitung,* 7 October 1995; Elsbeth Pulver, "*Ein weites Feld*—Fontane und die deutsche Gegenwart," *Schweizer Monatshefte* 75.12/76.1 (December 1995—January 1996): 49–52; and Wolfram Schütte, " 'Wie aus der Zeit gefallen: Zwei alte Männer': Günter Grass und sein *Weites Feld* oder Archivberichte aus der Gründerzeit der Berliner Republik," *Frankfurter Rundschau,* 26 August 1995. My account of *Too Far Afield* is indebted to Erler and Pulver (both hereafter cited in the text) for their reflections on the role of Fontane in the novel.

5. Anne McElvoy, "Traitors' State," *Times Literary Supplement,* 13 October 1995, 26.

6. Hans Joachim Schädlich, *Tallhover* (Reinbek bei Hamburg: Rowohlt, 1986).

7. Iris Radisch, "Die Bitterfelder Sackgasse," *Die Zeit,* 1 September 1995, 13.

Conclusion

    1. *Günter Grass zum 65.* (Göttingen: Steidl, 1992).

    2. John Irving, "Günter Grass: King of the Toy Merchants," *Saturday Review,* March 1982, 60.

    3. Michael Bullock, "Defending the Imagination," *Times Literary Supplement,* 23 December 1988, 1429.

Selected Bibliography

PRIMARY SOURCES

Narratives

Die Blechtrommel. Neuwied: Luchterhand, 1959. Trans. Ralph Manheim as *The Tin Drum.* London: Secker & Warburg, 1961; New York: Pantheon, 1962.

Katz und Maus. Neuwied: Luchterhand, 1961. Trans. Ralph Manheim as *Cat and Mouse.* New York: Harcourt, Brace; London: Secker & Warburg, 1963.

Hundejahre. Neuwied: Luchterhand, 1963. Trans. Ralph Manheim as *Dog Years.* New York: Harcourt, Brace; London: Secker & Warburg, 1965.

Örtlich betäubt. Neuwied: Luchterhand, 1969. Trans. Ralph Manheim as *Local Anaesthetic.* New York: Harcourt, Brace, 1969; London: Secker & Warburg, 1970.

Aus dem Tagebuch einer Schnecke. Neuwied: Luchterhand, 1972. Trans. Ralph Manheim as *From the Diary of a Snail.* New York: Harcourt, Brace, 1973; London: Secker & Warburg, 1974.

Der Butt. Neuwied: Luchterhand, 1977. Trans. Ralph Manheim as *The Flounder.* New York: Harcourt, Brace; London: Secker & Warburg, 1978.

Das Treffen in Telgte. Neuwied: Luchterhand, 1979. Trans. Ralph Manheim as *The Meeting at Telgte.* New York: Harcourt, Brace; London: Secker & Warburg, 1981.

Kopfgeburten, oder Die Deutschen sterben aus. Neuwied: Luchterhand, 1980. Trans. Ralph Manheim as *Headbirths, or The Germans Are Dying Out.* New York: Harcourt, Brace; London: Secker & Warburg, 1982.

Die Rättin. Neuwied: Luchterhand, 1986. Trans. Ralph Manheim as *The Rat.* San Diego, Calif.: Harcourt, Brace, 1987.

Unkenrufe. Göttingen: Steidl, 1992. Trans. Ralph Manheim as *The Call of the Toad.* New York: Harcourt, Brace; London: Secker & Warburg, 1992.

Ein weites Feld. Göttingen: Steidl, 1995. A translation by Krishna Winston, *Too Far Afield,* is to be published in 2000 by Harcourt Brace.

Plays

Hochwasser. Frankfurt: Suhrkamp, 1963. Translated as *Flood* in *Four Plays.*

Onkel, Onkel. Berlin: Wagenbach, 1965. Translated as *Mister, Mister* in *Four Plays.*

Die Plebejer proben den Aufstand. Neuwied: Luchterhand, 1966. Trans. Ralph Manheim as *The Plebeians Rehearse the Uprising.* New York: Harcourt, Brace, 1966; London: Secker & Warburg, 1967.

Four Plays: Flood, Mister, Mister, Only Ten Minutes to Buffalo, The Wicked Cooks. Trans. Ralph Manheim and A. Leslie Willson. Intro. Martin Esslin. New York: Harcourt, Brace, 1967; London: Secker & Warburg, 1968.

Theaterspiele (Collected Plays). Neuwied: Luchterhand, 1970. Contains *Hochwasser, Onkel, Onkel, Noch zehn Minuten bis Buffalo,* and *Die bösen Köche,* all translated in *Four Plays,* as well as *Die Plebejer proben den Aufstand* and *Davor.*

Max: A Play. Trans. A. Leslie Willson and Ralph Manheim. New York: Harcourt, Brace, 1972. Originally published as *Davor* (Beforehand), first in the journal *Theater heute* (1969) and later in *Theaterspiele.*

Poetry, Graphics, and Miscellaneous Texts

Die Vorzüge der Windhühner (The Merits of Windfowl). Neuwied: Luchterhand, 1956. Poems.

Gleisdreieck (Triangle of Tracks). Neuwied: Luchterhand, 1960. Poems.

Selected Poems. German text with trans. by Michael Hamburger and Ralph Manheim. New York: Harcourt, Brace; London: Secker & Warburg,1966. Selections from *Die Vorzüge der Windhühner* and *Gleisdreieck.*

Ausgefragt (Interrogated). Neuwied: Luchterhand, 1967. Poems.

New Poems. German text with trans. by Michael Hamburger. New York: Harcourt, Brace, 1968. Selections from *Ausgefragt.*

Gesammelte Gedichte (Collected Poems). Neuwied: Luchterhand, 1971.

Mariazuehren. Munich: Bruckmann, 1973. Trans. Christopher Middleton as *Inmarypraise.* New York: Harcourt, Brace, 1974. Poem with drawings and photographs.

Liebe geprüft. Bremen: Schünemann, 1974. Trans. Michael Hamburger as *Love Tested.* New York: Harcourt, Brace, 1975. Poems and etchings.

In the Egg and Other Poems. Trans. Michael Hamburger and Christopher Middleton. New York: Harcourt, Brace, 1977. Selections from *Die Vorzüge der Windhühner, Gleisdreieck,* and *Ausgefragt.*

Als vom Butt nur die Gräte geblieben war (When Only the Bones of the Flounder Were Left). Berlin: Galerie André, 1977. Etchings and poems.

Vatertag (Father's Day). Hamburg: Edition Monika Beck, 1982. Lithographs.

Zeichnungen und Texte 1954–1977. Ed. Anselm Dreher. Text selection and afterword by Sigrid Mayer. Neuwied: Luchterhand, 1982. Trans. Walter Arndt and Michael Hamburger as *Drawings and Words 1954–1977.* New York: Harcourt, Brace, 1982. Drawings in various media with poems and other texts.

Ach Butt, dein Märchen geht böse aus (Alas, Flounder, Your Tale Will Have a Bad Ending). Darmstadt, Neuwied: Luchterhand, 1983. Poems and etchings.

Radierungen und Texte 1972–1982. Ed. Anselm Dreher. Text selection and afterword by Sigrid Mayer. Neuwied: Luchterhand, 1984. Trans. Michael Hamburger, Ralph Manheim, Christopher Middleton, and others as *Etchings and Words 1972–1982*. San Diego, Calif.: Harcourt, Brace, 1985. Etchings and dry points with poems and other texts.

In Kupfer, auf Stein (In Copper, on Stone). Intro. Volker Neuhaus. Göttingen: Steidl, 1986; rev. ed. 1994. Photographic record of graphic work.

Mit Sophie in die Pilze gegangen (Gathering Mushrooms with Sophie). Göttingen: Steidl, 1987. Poems and lithographs.

Zunge zeigen: Ein Tagebuch in Zeichnungen, Prosa und einem Gedicht. Darmstadt: Luchterhand Literaturverlag, 1988. Trans. John E. Woods as *Show Your Tongue*. San Diego, Calif.: Harcourt, Brace, 1989. Texts and drawings.

Die Gedichte 1955–86 (Poems, 1955–86). Darmstadt: Luchterhand Literaturverlag, 1988.

Skizzenbuch (Sketchbook). Göttingen: Steidl, 1989. Sketches from Calcutta.

Totes Holz: Ein Nachruf (Dead Wood: An Epitaph). Göttingen: Steidl, 1990. Texts and drawings.

Kahlschlag in unseren Köpfen (The Clearcut Mind). Göttingen: Steidl, 1990. Lithographs.

Vier Jahrzehnte: Ein Werkstattbericht (Four Decades: An Account of Work in Progress). Ed. G. Fritze Margull. Göttingen: Steidl, 1991. Autobiographical account, with graphics and photographs.

Brief aus Altdöbern (A Letter from Altdöbern). Remagen: Rommerskirchen, 1991. Drawings and text.

Meine grüne Wiese: Geschichten und Zeichnungen (My Green Field: Stories and Drawings). Hamburg, Zurich: Luchterhand Literaturverlag, 1992. Collected early short prose studies and drawings.

Novemberland (Novemberland). Göttingen: Steidl, 1993. Poems and drawings.

Fundsachen für Nichtleser (Found Objects for Nonreaders). Göttingen: Steidl, 1997. Poems and watercolors.

Critical and Political Writings

Dich singe ich, Demokratie (Of Thee I Sing, Democracy). Neuwied: Luchterhand, 1965. Political pieces.

Der Fall Axel C. Springer (The Case of Axel C. Springer). Berlin: Voltaire, 1967. Political pieces.

Über meinen Lehrer Döblin (On Döblin, My Teacher). Berlin: Literarisches Colloquium, 1968. Literary essays.

Über das Selbstverständliche: Reden, Aufsätze, offene Briefe, Kommentare (On the Self-Evident: Speeches, Essays, Open Letters, Commentaries). Neuwied: Luchterhand, 1968. Political pieces.

Briefe über die Grenze: Versuch eines Ost-West Dialogs (Letters across the Border: An Attempt at an East-West Dialogue). With Pavel Kohout. Hamburg: Christian Wegner, 1968. Political pieces.

Speak Out! Speeches, Open Letters, Commentaries. Trans. Ralph Manheim. New York: Harcourt, Brace; London: Secker & Warburg, 1969. Selections from *Über das Selbstverständliche.*

Der Bürger und seine Stimme: Reden, Aufsätze, Kommentare (A Citizen and His Voice: Speeches, Essays, Commentaries). Neuwied: Luchterhand, 1974. Political pieces.

Denkzettel: Politische Reden und Aufsätze, 1965–1976 (Reminders: Political Speeches and Essays, 1965–1976). Neuwied: Luchterhand, 1978.

Aufsätze zur Literatur (Essays on Literature). Darmstadt: Luchterhand, 1980.

Widerstand lernen. Politische Gegenreden, 1980–1983 (Learning to Resist: Political Counterpositions, 1980–1983). Darmstadt, Neuwied: Luchterhand, 1984.

On Writing and Politics, 1967–1983. Trans. Ralph Manheim. New York: Harcourt, Brace, 1985. Selections from *Der Bürger und seine Stimme, Denkzettel, Aufsätze zur Literatur,* and *Widerstand lernen.*

Wenn wir von Europa sprechen: Ein Dialog mit Françoise Giroud (Speaking of Europe: A Dialogue with Françoise Giroud). Frankfurt am Main: Luchterhand Literaturverlag, 1989. Political discussion.

Ein Schnäppchen namens DDR: Letzte Reden vorm Glockengeläut (East Germany at Bargain Prices: Last Speeches Before the Sound of the Bell). Frankfurt am Main: Luchterhand Literaturverlag, 1990. Political pieces.

Deutschland, einig Vaterland?: Streitgespräch mit Rudolf Augstein (Germany, A Single Fatherland? A Debate with Rudolf Augstein). Göttingen: Steidl, 1990. Political pieces.

Schreiben nach Auschwitz: Frankfurter Poetik-Vorlesung (Writing after Auschwitz: The Frankfurt Poetics Prize Lecture). Frankfurt am Main: Luchterhand Literaturverlag, 1990. Political statement.

Deutscher Lastenausgleich: Wider das dumpfe Einheitsgebot. Reden und Gespräche (Sharing the German Burden: Against the Stultifying Compulsion to Unify. Speeches and Interviews). Frankfurt am Main: Luchterhand Literaturverlag, 1990. Political pieces.

Two States—One Nation? The Case Against German Reunification. Trans. Krishna Winston and A. S. Wensinger. New York: Harcourt, Brace; London: Secker and Warburg, 1990. Trans. of *Deutscher Lastenausgleich* and *Schreiben nach Auschwitz.*

Gegen die verstreichende Zeit: Reden, Aufsätze und Gespräche, 1989–1991 (Writing Against Time: Speeches, Essays, and Interviews, 1989–1991). Darmstadt, Neuwied: Luchterhand, 1991. Political pieces.

Rede vom Verlust: Über den Niedergang der politischen Kultur im geeinten Deutschland (On Loss: The Deterioration of the Political Climate in the United Germany). Göttingen: Steidl, 1992.

Schaden begrenzen (Damage Control). With Regine Hildebrandt. Berlin: Verlag Volk und Welt, 1993. Political discussion.

The Future of German Democracy, with An Essay on Loss. Ed. Robert Gerald Livingston and Volkmar Sander. New York: Continuum, 1993.

Angestiftet, Partei zu ergreifen (Forced to Take Sides). Munich: Deutscher Taschenbuch Verlag, 1994. Political pieces.

Die Deutschen und ihre Dichter (The Germans and Their Writers). Ed. Daniela Hermes. Munich: Deutscher Taschenbuch Verlag, 1995. Literary essays.

Gestern, vor 50 Jahren (Yesterday, 50 Years Ago). With Kenzaburo Oe. Göttingen: Steidl, 1995. Political correspondence.

Rede über den Standort (A Place to Stand). Göttingen: Steidl, 1997. Political statement.

Collected Works

Werkausgabe in zehn Bänden (Collected Works in Ten Volumes). Ed. Volker Neuhaus. Darmstadt, Neuwied: Luchterhand, 1987. 6,476 pp. Vol. 1 contains the poetry and early short prose studies; vols. 2–7 the narratives from *Die Blechtrommel* to *Die Rättin;* vol. 8 the plays; vol. 9 essays, speeches, open letters, and commentaries; vol. 10 interviews. Each volume has critical introductions and notes.

Studienausgabe (Study Edition). Göttingen: Steidl Verlag, 1993–94. 12 vols. 4,784 pp. Vols. 1–10 contain the narratives from *Die Blechtrommel* to *Unkenrufe;* vol. 11 the poetry and early short prose studies; vol. 12 the plays. A collected edition of individual texts in a uniform hardcover format; texts only, without critical apparatus; no editor named. In 1993, under license from the Steidl Verlag, the Deutscher Taschenbuch Verlag in Munich also began issuing what was intended to be a complete paperback edition in individual volumes.

Werkausgabe (Collected Works). Ed. Volker Neuhaus and Daniela Hermes. 16 vols. and 22 CDs. Göttingen: Steidl, 1997. 7,712 pp. Vol. 1 contains the poetry and early short prose studies; vol. 2 the plays; vols. 3–13 the narratives from *Die Blechtrommel* to *Ein weites Feld;* vols. 14–16 essays and speeches. Texts only, without critical apparatus; seven further paperback volumes of commentary and materials to follow in 1998; several further volumes containing correspondence, interviews, and graphic work to follow in subsequent years. The 22 CDs contain a 28-hour reading by Grass of the entire text of *Die Blechtrommel.*

SECONDARY SOURCES

Bibliographies

Hermes, Daniela. "Günter Grass: Auswahl-Bibliographie." *Kritisches Lexikon zur deutschsprachigen Gegenwartsliteratur.* Ed. Heinz Ludwig Arnold. Munich: Edition Text und Kritik, 1994. 26 pp. (loose-leaf format).

Neuhaus, Volker. *Günter Grass.* 2nd ed. Stuttgart: Metzler, 1992. Contains a concise and reliable bibliographical section (217–32).

O'Neill, Patrick. *Günter Grass: A Bibliography, 1955–75.* Toronto: University of Toronto Press, 1976. Still useful for the earlier work.

Books

Since this book is directed primarily at English-speaking readers, almost all the books listed here are in English. Only a few of the most useful of the many books in German are noted—all of which contain bibliographical references to further studies.

Brady, Philip, Timothy McFarland, and John J. White, eds. *Günter Grass's Der Butt: Sexual Politics and the Male Myth of History.* Oxford: Clarendon Press, 1990. A collection of essays on *The Flounder.*

Brode, Hanspeter. *Günter Grass.* Munich: Beck, 1979. A good short introduction in German to the earlier work.

Cunliffe, W. Gordon. *Günter Grass.* New York: Twayne, 1969. Still a useful introduction to Grass's work up to *The Plebeians Rehearse the Uprising.*

Hayman, Ronald. *Günter Grass.* London, New York: Methuen, 1985. A brief but suggestive survey of Grass's work up to *Headbirths,* with particular attention to his style.

Hollington, Michael. *Günter Grass: The Writer in a Pluralist Society.* London: Marion Boyars, 1980. Good on the political contexts of Grass's work.

Keele, Alan Frank. *Understanding Günter Grass.* Columbia, S.C.: University of South Carolina Press, 1988. A general introduction to Grass's work up to *The Rat.*

Lawson, Richard H. *Günter Grass.* New York: Ungar, 1985. A general introduction for the reader new to Grass.

Leonard, Irène. *Günter Grass.* Edinburgh: Oliver & Boyd, 1974. On the relationship between Grass's literary and political activities and its effect on the reception of his work.

Mason, Ann L. *The Skeptical Muse: A Study of Günter Grass' Conception of the Artist.* Bern: Lang, 1974. An excellent introduction to Grass's work up to *Local Anaesthetic;* particularly good on matters of style.

Mews, Siegfried, ed. *"The Fisherman and His Wife": Günter Grass's The Flounder in Critical Perspective.* New York: AMS Press, 1983. A collection of essays on *The Flounder.*

Miles, Keith. *Günter Grass.* London: Vision; New York: Barnes and Noble, 1975. A somewhat idiosyncratic introduction to Grass's work up to *From the Diary of a Snail;* good on the wider literary contexts.

Neuhaus, Volker. *Günter Grass.* 2nd ed. Stuttgart: Metzler, 1992. The best introduction in German to every aspect of Grass's work, with many bibliographical references.

O'Neill, Patrick, ed. *Critical Essays on Günter Grass.* Boston: G. K. Hall, 1987. Twenty-one reviews and articles on Grass's work up to *The Rat,* with a general introduction.

Pickar, Gertrud Bauer, ed. *Adventures of a Flounder: Critical Essays on Günter Grass'* Der Butt. Munich: Fink, 1982. A collection of essays on *The Flounder.*

Reddick, John. *The "Danzig Trilogy" of Günter Grass: A Study of* The Tin Drum, Cat and Mouse, *and* Dog Years. London: Secker & Warburg; New York: Harcourt, Brace, 1975. Excellent introduction to *The Tin Drum* and *Cat and Mouse;* somewhat less so for *Dog Years.*

Thomas, Noel. *The Narrative Works of Günter Grass: A Critical Interpretation.* Amsterdam, Philadelphia: John Benjamins, 1982. A careful and detailed study.

Vormweg, Heinrich. *Günter Grass.* Rowohlts Monographien. 2nd rev. ed. Reinbek bei Hamburg: Rowohlt, 1993. A biographical study (in German) of Grass's development as a writer.

Willson, A. Leslie, ed. *A Günter Grass Symposium.* Austin: University of Texas Press, 1971. Six excellent essays on the early work.

Articles

In addition to the articles contained in the collections by Brady et al., Mews, O'Neill, Pickar, and Willson mentioned in the selected bibliography, and those referred to in the notes to individual chapters, several hundred articles in various languages are systematically listed in the bibliographies by Hermes, O'Neill, and Neuhaus, which the interested reader is advised to consult.

Archive

The Deutsches Literaturarchiv in Marbach am Neckar (postal address: Deutsches Literaturarchiv, Postfach 1162, D-71666 Marbach am Neckar, Germany) houses a Günter Grass archive whose original contents were donated in 1977 by Grass and his then publisher, the Luchterhand Verlag. Continually expanding, the Grass archive now consists of some 120 large binders and some 30 filing boxes containing several thousand newspaper clippings, reviews, journal offprints, and miscellaneous materials in a variety of languages.

Index

The Author

Patrick O'Neill taught at University College Dublin in Ireland and at the University of British Columbia in Vancouver before moving to Queen's University in Kingston, Ontario, where he is currently a member of the Department of German Language and Literature, specializing in modern narrative and narrative theory. His recent books include *The Comedy of Entropy: Humour, Narrative, Reading* (1990), *Fictions of Discourse: Reading Narrative Theory* (1994), and *Acts of Narrative: Textual Strategies in Modern German Fiction* (1996), all published by the University of Toronto Press. He has been writing on the works of Günter Grass for many years and is also the compiler of *Günter Grass: A Bibliography, 1955–1975* (Toronto, 1976) and the editor of a volume of *Critical Essays on Günter Grass* (Boston, 1987).

The Editor

David O'Connell is professor of French at Georgia State University. He received his Ph.D. in 1966 from Princeton University, where he was a National Woodrow Wilson Fellow, the Bergen Fellow in Romance Languages, and a National Woodrow Wilson Dissertation Fellow. He is the author of *The Teachings of Saint Louis: A Critical Text* (1972), *Les Propos de Saint Louis* (1974), *Louis-Ferdinand Céline* (1976), *The Instructions of Saint Louis: A Critical Text* (1979), and *Michel de Saint Pierre: A Catholic Novelist at the Crossroads* (1990). He has edited more than 60 books in the Twayne World Authors Series.